THE ADMINISTRATIVE STATE

THE CHICAGO LIBRARY OF COMPARATIVE POLITICS

ROY C. MACRIDIS, EDITOR

The Soviet System of Government

JOHN N. HAZARD

The Administrative State

FRITZ MORSTEIN MARX

THE ADMINISTRATIVE STATE

An Introduction to Bureaucracy

By Fritz Morstein Marx

THE UNIVERSITY OF CHICAGO PRESS

Library of Congress Catalog Number: 57-6987

THE UNIVERSITY OF CHICAGO PRESS, CHICAGO 37
The University of Toronto Press, Toronto 5, Canada

FOREWORD

Bureaucracy—growing in democratic and totalitarian systems alike—has been the object of many studies in recent decades. But even though sociologists and political scientists join hands to identify and compare the basic types and forms of bureaucracy, their co-operation is not always fruitful. Sociologists, for their part, like to seek generalities that emphasize "structure" and "role" at a very high (and sometimes vague) level of abstraction. Political scientists, in turn, tend either to indulge in exhaustive descriptions of institutional forms or to deal with broad value judgments, notably the relationship of bureaucracy to democratic principles. The dryness of sociological abstraction, therefore, has often been matched by the political scientist's concern with institutional trivialities or, conversely, his wide judgments of "good" and "bad."

Professor Morstein Marx, in this second volume of the "Chicago Library of Comparative Politics," combines the best traits of sociology and political science while avoiding their characteristic faults. In place of vague abstractions he utilizes more modest concepts, and he introduces evaluative remarks only after his observations make such remarks necessary and desirable. In presenting a number of analytical tools, he examines the main forms of bureaucracy, relates bureaucracy to the industrial revolution, and points to the most significant functions of the bureaucrat and the bureaucracy in a political system. At the same time he boldly faces value problems posed by the growth of bureaucracy—notably the problem of individual freedom and responsibility.

The author never loses sight of the often-forgotten truth that comparative analysis should make facts more understandable. In every case he complements his conceptual analysis with a study of specific institutional forms. Thus the reader is led to think in terms of concrete governmental practices as well as illuminating generalizations. Furthermore, he is led to study bureaucracy in the context of given political systems under different historical and ideological conditions. The Prussian bureaucracy, the Swiss civil service, and the British, American, and French administrative systems pass in review to highlight generalizations and to exemplify current trends.

v

Perhaps the broadest underlying thesis of this book is the increasing participation of modern bureaucracies in the decision-making process of governments. This thesis should be examined in the light of traditional theory, according to which the "bureaucrat" simply executes decisions and policies made elsewhere. Mr. Morstein Marx argues that the present trend in no way constitutes a threat to democratic government. Indeed, the complexity of modern bureaucratic apparatus, the need for division of labor within it, and its internal rational organization breed a complex of attitudes that are incompatible with discretionary rule and arbitrary control and provide internal limits even to totalitarian governments. The reader would benefit greatly by contrasting the author's dispassionate analysis with some recent works in which the civil servant is said to be a "despot," or to man the parapets of the new "garrison state," or to plot the overthrow of democratic institutions in complicity with the managers of the great industrial corporations.

A number of issues raised by the author will be complemented in forthcoming volumes in this series, especially a volume on the executive branch of government and one on legislative assemblies. The present book fits well into a series meant to challenge the reader to independent thought, and it stands as a solid, self-contained introduction to the study of public administration and bureaucracy.

Roy C. Macridis

ACKNOWLEDGMENTS

A book like this, dealing with modern government in its administrative characteristics, as a source of a myriad of decisions touching the public, requires a basis in experience as well as in knowledge. It could not present the subject with sufficient intimacy if it were a mere distillate of other books. It must be in good part a scout's report: "I saw it."

For such intimacy the author has certain qualifications. He has lived much of his occupational life as part of the bureaucracy, civilian and military. And fate has furnished him this experience successively under different national auspices.

In addition, a very considerable broadening of the base of observation has resulted from the large though inconspicuous contributions of others—public servants and scholars from many lands with whom the author has had the good fortune of becoming acquainted over the years. Through these personal relations and the frank conversations they engendered the author has had vast benefit, which he is glad to acknowledge.

Still others have proved their friendship by devoting the necessary time to reading the whole or parts of the manuscript. Their constructive criticism has done much to improve the book. Grateful recognition is therefore due to Helen L. Chatfield, Taylor Cole, James L. Kunen, Milton M. Mandell, Peter Morstein Marx, C. Herman Pritchett, Richard L. Sharp, and Kurt Wilk.

F. M. M.

TABLE OF CONTENTS

CHAPTER 1

THE NATURE OF THE "ADMINISTRATIVE STATE"

How well the administrative machinery of modern government performs, how well it can be expected to perform under present circumstances, and along what lines its performance might be improved—these are hotly debated questions today. Although shrouded in partisan propaganda, they deserve answers on the basis of dispassionate analysis and informed judgment. But that does not mean that the answers may be left to the specialist. As modern government has made administrative action the prime instrument of its day-by-day operation, so public administration has moved more and more toward the center of governing. The working of the administrative machinery is therefore a matter of vast significance to the success of government itself and thus to the well-being of every citizen. It is one of the great political issues of our time.

To begin our examination of this issue, we need to come to grips with the administrative machinery of modern government in its order of magnitude as well as its structural form. "Big government" requires a large apparatus to carry out its many functions. How did the large-scale apparatus develop? In particular, how can we explain the extraordinary growth of the civil service? But we must also examine the organizational pattern of public administration, especially the place occupied by the higher career group. Finally, we should ask ourselves whether or not popular rule provides adequate control over the administrative system. The opening chapter of this book is meant to be a brief but useful orientation to those questions.

THE NEW MACHINERY

Impact of the Industrial Order

One of the conspicuous characteristics of modern government is the large and still increasing number of its functions. The performance of these functions requires elaborate administrative machinery.

1

As a result, the bulk of what government does today is of an administrative nature. Without minimizing the significance of legislation and the role of courts of law, public administration has become more important for the general effectiveness of government.

The development of the administrative machinery of government to its contemporary size corresponds broadly to the evolution of the industrial order. Industrialized, urbanized societies depend on government in various capacities—as regulator, as mediator, as underwriter, as provider of services, as source of subsidies and loans, as promoter of national standards of "decent living," and as economic and social diagnostician and repairman. To critics, much of this may spell the "welfare state," by which they mean the opposite of what the term seems to suggest—that is, a condition of self-induced stagnation and eventual decay. Some even see man on the "road to serfdom" or at least unwittingly abetting the return of the "police state," with its paternalistic snooping and its stifling grip. True enough, the new liberal's faith in "positive government" is a far cry from the earlier liberal ideal of government restricted to the role of "night watchman." But if the new liberal cannot be expected to take kindly to a loaded phrase such as "welfare state," he has come to make his peace with the more neutral concept of the "administrative state," especially with its practical realities.[1]

One of the practical realities of the "administrative state" is the participation of a considerable body of full-time officials in the day-to-day conduct of public affairs. This nearly permanent body is often called the bureaucracy. Although it is meant to function as an instrument of government controlled by those who hold political power in the name of the people, the bureaucracy is itself a source of power, if only by giving government the apparatus for accomplishing its aims. Depending upon its character, the bureaucracy can be both an active force and a passive weight in the life of the nation.

1. In phrases such as "welfare state," "police state," and "administrative state" the word "state" is used as political theorists have generally used it—that is, in the sense of the embodiment or the organization of the nation or in the sense of the political system as a whole. But it must be borne in mind that there has never been a state devoted exclusively to "welfare" or "police" or "administration." When there is talk of the "welfare state," for instance, what is usually meant is a political system or a continuing policy with a *predisposition* toward "welfare" in an undesirable excess, cuddling man to the point where he is glad to "let George do it"—"George" being the state, or government. Of course, throughout the ages the state has been justified in terms of its capacity for fostering the general welfare, and the American Constitution specifically declares that it is one of its basic purposes to "promote the general welfare." Similarly, the "administrative state" should be thought of not as a state devoid of legislative and judicial organs but as a state in which administrative organization and operations are particularly prominent, at least in their quantitative aspects.

Functions and Personnel

In the United States an example of the broad correlation between the emergence of industrial society and the growth of administrative machinery is the history of the departmental system in the federal government since 1850. Not counting the recent regroupings in the military establishment, especially the formation of a combined Department of Defense (1949), the four executive departments created during the last hundred years, together with a host of other governmental agencies, have all been geared to the interest structure typical of an increasingly industrial country. These four departments are Agriculture (1862), Commerce (1903), Labor (1913, previously combined with Commerce), and Health, Education, and Welfare (1953). Moreover, although the Department of Labor is the smallest of the ten executive departments, these four together have as many employees as the total of the other departments, omitting the Department of Defense and the Post Office Department, which as the two largest federal employers are in a class by themselves.

Looking at the federal government as a whole, we find that the number of civil servants has grown twenty times during the first half of our century, from less than 100,000 in 1900 to more than 2,000,000 in 1955. This is a remarkable thing, even when allowance is made for the fact that in 1900 the civil service represented considerably less than half the total of all federal employees, whereas in 1955 it was close to nine-tenths. What is no less interesting is that the rate of growth has gone up steeply in the last fifteen years. For example, before the outbreak of World War II (1939) the number of civil servants was still little more than six times what it had been in 1900. The sharpest upturn was brought about by the war and its aftermath, with unparalleled international tensions and the enlarged responsibilities of the federal government.

By comparison, although in republican Italy the swelling rolls of the bureaucracy have led to bitter denunciations of the government, the actual increase in recent years has been much less than in the United States—from 784,000 in 1937 to 1,133,000 in 1954. For France the roughly corresponding spread was from about 700,000 in 1933 to 970,000 in 1950. This indicates a slower rate of growth than the doubling of the total which France experienced from 1911 (350,000) to 1933, but it comes to about the same as the rate shown in the French statistics for the middle decades of the past century (1839: 130,000; 1871: 220,000). In England a parallel doubling of the number of civil servants occurred between 1911 (172,000) and 1938

(348,000). However, since then the figure has risen to almost 725,000 (1955), which represents a doubling again—a much faster rate of relative growth than the Italian and the French rates for the same period. But even comparatively less strained countries show steady increases in the number of civil servants. In Switzerland, for example, the total went up from 63,000 in 1938 to 94,000 in 1953. In Denmark the figures are 37,000 in 1938 and 48,000 in 1949. Canada has witnessed a growth which considerably exceeds the doubling demonstrated in England—from 46,000 in 1939 to 132,000 in 1952.

It is easy to see that, when a nation adopts a social security system, it will need additional government employees to administer it. As a matter of fact, however, rising civil service figures are not readily explained in terms of personnel requirements for particular new functions alone. In addition, established agencies usually get bigger. The actual growth of the civil service is thus the product of various factors. The interaction of these factors is both more complex and more obscure than a simple listing of new governmental activities. To turn once more to Canada, the increase of 86,000 public employees from 1939 to 1952 did not result simply from a rash of new dominion functions. On the contrary, the increase was distributed quite widely among existing functions, with no less than five departments getting a substantial share. More than one-fourth of the increase went to National Defense. Almost one-seventh fell to Veterans Affairs. Then came Post Office, National Revenue, and Labor (Unemployment Insurance Commission), each picking up about 8 per cent.

WHY MORE AND MORE?

Rate of Civil Service Growth

Important as the matter is for sound public management and budgetary control over governmental expenditures, if we were to ask what the appropriate rate of growth for the civil service based upon workload is, the answer would have to be an admission of ignorance. The same would be true if we asked more modestly about the normal rate of growth, considering the record of experience at home and abroad. It follows that excessive growth is not something that can be spotted with the naked eye unless the development seems completely out of hand. Here is a field of research that still awaits cultivation despite the promise of great practical returns.

In order to arrive at a working formula by which to appraise civil service growth, it may first be necessary to achieve reasonable comparability of the statistical information built up in the different countries. To hack our way into this thicket would be a heroic undertaking. An attempt to use the currently available statistics on a comparative basis is bound to trip up the unwary, for "civil service" may mean different things in different countries. It may include or exclude such categories as contract employees, temporary appointees ("unestablished" civil servants, in British parlance), "industrial" employees (for instance, those on the payroll of nationalized industries), and teachers.

Of the total number of government employees for Italy (1,133,000 in 1954), more than 300,000 came under the Department of Public Instruction, which has charge of the educational system. Most of these were public school teachers. Similarly, the teachers are counted as part of the civil service in France. On the other hand, public teaching, being outside the range of national responsibility, is not included in the national civil service figures either in England or in the United States. To take another example, the employees of the postal administration, the national railways, and the government-owned telephone and telegraph system are usually listed separately in Italy, whereas they constitute the bulk of the civil service in Switzerland. What makes the matter still more confusing is that one and the same country may employ simultaneously various concepts of "civil service" in its statistical compilations or change these concepts from time to time for reasons good or bad.

But civil service statistics are tricky also because there is no standard set of functions exercised by all governments. In a federal system like the United States, Canada, and Switzerland, for instance, the national government is not burdened with the same responsibilities carried by a unitary state like France or Italy, which lacks the intermediate level exemplified by American state government. Again, even in a political system lacking federal features, strong institutions of local government relieve the national government of certain responsibilities. This is well demonstrated by the example of England, where local government has long played a vital role, in contrast with Italy, where local autonomy has been overshadowed by central control. On the other hand, both within federal systems and in the relationship between the national government of a unitary state and its local governments, transfers of functions continue to occur, mostly upon the broadest shoulders. Hence much of the increase in functions on the national level, and the related rise in civil service figures, may merely reflect a placement of functions where they can best be carried out.

A considerable part of the growth of the federal civil service in the

United States can be traced to such functional adjustments within the federal system. These adjustments have usually been made by decision of Congress—that is, to satisfy public preferences. In addition, however, there is no question that during the twentieth century a quiet revolution has taken place in American attitudes toward the proper role of government in the life of the people.

The extraordinary rate of civil service expansion is therefore far from surprising. In 1900 it was still possible to think of the United States as an uncrowded nation living off the bounty of a continent. The federal government was still at the threshold of the "administrative state," compared with the scope of administrative organization that most European countries had found necessary to establish much earlier. Thus the upswing in civil service figures during the last fifty years is accounted for in part also by the pace with which American government, before the great economic depression of the thirties as well as in its wake, caught up with the remainder of the Western world. In relatively little time the nation developed an administrative system that in its range of activities and its organizational structure has come to resemble rather closely the pattern familiar in Europe. These considerations introduce obvious qualifications into any sweeping conclusions we might draw from the fact that for each federal civil servant on the rolls in 1900 there are twenty now.

It is also true that we can make too much of varying rates of relative growth, such as a doubling of the total compared with an increase of 10 per cent. Although these rates are far apart, they do not necessarily indicate a significant difference in actual numbers added. For example, we saw earlier that the British civil service had doubled between 1938 and 1955, whereas the comparable increase in the Italian civil service was less than half the total number for 1937. But in actual figures the increases for the two countries were quite close—377,000 in England and 349,000 in Italy, compared with 270,000 for France. Indeed, the Italian figure is proportionately more arresting when we remember that this increase was piled upon a total (for 1937) which showed the bloated condition of the totalitarian system of fascism.

Thus we go from one thing to another, and the end in this unraveling of civil service statistics is not yet in sight. For it is clear that there is still a whole battery of general factors requiring detailed attention. These include density of population, economic structure, social stratification, technological development, political traditions, and even cultural characteristics. Exactly how each of these factors affects the expansion of the civil service has thus far remained a matter of brave conjecture.

"Parkinson's Law"

Fortunately, we are no longer without a brilliantly conceived theory on the subject of civil service expansion. In its issue of November 19, 1955, the London *Economist* told its readers of a "startling discovery"—the discovery of the law that governs the growth of the civil service. A merry exercise in tongue-in-cheek statistics, the anonymous article spoke of this law as "Parkinson's Law" ("Why? Why Not?" asked the editor in a footnote). According to the article, the size of the officialdom and the volume of work "are not related to each other at all." On the selectively examined evidence the annual increase in personnel was estimated, irrespective of workload, to be on the average about 5¾ per cent.

This rate of growth was laid to two factors. The first was found in the tendency of overworked civil servants to seek relief by bringing in assistants in pairs so that each would be "kept in order by fear of the other's promotion," whereas neither could become a competitor to his superior. This "law of multiplication of subordinates" was shown to bring in motion the second factor, expressed as the "law of multiplication of work." For in every instance that there are three civil servants instead of one—or seven, after each assistant in due course has got himself two assistants of his own—they will "make so much work for each other that they are fully occupied."

We may be misled by the whimsey of this article to overlook the hard core of sense in it. For it can hardly be denied that we encounter in the physical expansion of public administration the evidence of irrational as well as rational influences, meeting in queer cross-currents. These cross-currents may produce quite different results from nation to nation. "Parkinson's Law" allows for variation in its effects. During World War II, for instance, in operations requiring the teaming-up of American and British administrative personnel, humorous acknowledgment was made many times of the oddly disproportionate ratio of participants from either side. For each civil servant the British contributed, the American counterpart seemed to run to three, five, ten, or even twenty, not because it took that many, but because each attended to only part of the business as a specialist for this or that aspect. Allowing for intentional exaggeration in such calculations, there remains nevertheless the suggestion of a basically different staffing concept or staffing habit. Such concepts and habits may have their roots in the cultural setting rather than in anything else.

But "Parkinson's Law" does need amplification. It deals very illuminatingly with the fact that the civil service never stays put—

indeed, that it *must* grow bit by bit. What "Parkinson's Law" leaves out is the equally important fact that national emergencies such as wars and economic depressions provide a multiplier effect. They boost civil service totals and annual budgets in steeply ascending order to new plateaus from which there is only a partial descent to subsequent levels of "normalcy." Again, why that is so has not yet been satisfactorily explained.

Zestful Advance

It should not be concluded, however, that the rise of administrative machinery is being viewed everywhere as something that ought to be watched but cannot be prevented. When a nation is rushing forward to save itself from calamity, as in the case of Franklin D. Roosevelt's New Deal, the building of administrative organization and the manning of new agencies may be an exhilarating experience and a cause of common rejoicing. Something of the same spirit can be observed today in newly independent nations or in other countries which see their welfare bound up with the adoption of modern ways. As an illustration, India's Prime Minister Nehru said in 1955 at a mass meeting of officials away from the capital:

Our scientific departments have grown tremendously. Our Ministry of Commerce and Industry has grown very greatly. There is a new Ministry of Production, there is a new Ministry of Planning and so on. Our Ministry of Health functions in a bigger way, our Ministry of Education functions in a much bigger way, every ministry functions in a very much bigger way and many new ministries have come into being. Take Defense. Previously Defense was really an organization here to carry out the basic policies laid down in London—just to give effect to them. Now we grow. We have to lay down our policies. We have to develop not only the outer structure of defense but the industrial apparatus behind defense. The Defense Ministry today owns great industries all over, just like a number of other ministries. The Communications Ministry owns great factories making telephones and what not. The Railway Ministry owns Chittaranjan Locomotive Works and the Integral Coach Building Factory near Madras. You see how all this goes on growing. It is an enormous growth.[2]

A statement like this conveys eloquently the promise of active government. It is a profession of unflagging faith in the potentialities of the "administrative state." It is an almost poetic evocation of the creative spirit, committed to a crusade for the betterment of man's lot. It has nothing in common with that somber note of resignation or despair so frequently sounded in the Western world, suggesting man's helplessness as he faces the massive structure of the contem-

2. "A Word to the Services," *Indian Journal of Public Administration*, I (1955), 292.

porary administrative system. The contrast comes alive with dramatic effect when we simultaneously hear the state called a "monster," object of man's "tangled hate-love" which "at once chains him to public administration and makes him shrink from it," a monster against whose "octopus arms" man "struggles continuously in panic," but which he strengthens at the same time by "a thousand demands upon government," thus "himself furnishing the provocation to a totalitarian drive for putting everything under administrative authority."[3] These words gain an ironical resonance when we discover that they were written for Germans, whose high regard for a well-ordered "administrative state" has long been proverbial.

OUTLINE OF ADMINISTRATIVE STRUCTURE

Political Direction

The metaphor of the administrative "octopus" implies that the bureaucracy is a phenomenon of nature, untamed and untamable. In actual fact no administrative system is legally autonomous, a corporate body governed solely by itself. Each administrative system is made subordinate to political direction exercised on behalf of the citizenry, under totalitarian as well as democratic government. Thus the bureaucracy is bossed by a political control group made up of each department's top command supported by hand-picked aides. Generally, this control group is held together by a chief executive, who is installed directly or indirectly by the will of the political majority, whether in fact or in fiction. Hence it is well to bear in mind at the start that all administrative structure is linked to political structure as a door is held to a wall. The door can get away only when the wall falls in. If the door gets stuck in the frame, a bounce is all that is needed to push it open.

To put it differently, the bureaucracy is the organization of personnel that government needs for the exercise of its continuing functions to get and keep things going, under the constant supervision of political superiors. What is the general character of this personnel? Unsophisticated administrative systems gather their manpower among the supporters of the regime in power. But when there is public pressure for efficiency of performance in government agencies, the bureaucracy is bound to reflect acceptable standards of competence. Under such circumstances the desirable product is administrative effectiveness, under conditions of political control. In other words, the attainment of administrative effectiveness is not to

3. Karl Streithaupt, "Untier Staat," *Frankfurter Allgemeine Zeitung,* August 13, 1955.

run free of political responsibility to the people as the consumers of the product.

To serve the consumers, the agents of political direction require expert advice on what to do to get administrative results—whether these agents be boards or commissions, as they are in some instances, or whether control be concentrated in a single official, as is the predominant pattern. If political direction is to be translated into responsive administrative operations, reliance must be placed upon a top cadre of career men to serve as the conveyer belt. Their skill is needed to make the department do what its political head, acting for the chief executive, wants it to do.

The Higher Civil Service

Great differences arise among administrative systems from differences in the composition of this top cadre of career men. Suppose they came up to the highest positions simply on the strength of having proved to be good hands at practical things over a considerable number of years. Then they might fall woefully short of the breadth of vision, the intellectual resources, and the physical stamina necessary to cope with large-scale administration as well as to give discerning advice to their political superiors. Now suppose they were recruited into the junior level of the higher career group directly upon completion of their college or university studies. Then they would be unlikely to show the same inadequacies, although they might cultivate a class point of view and perhaps be more loyal to one government than to another. But even where the higher civil service draws its candidates from the colleges and universities, significant differences in outlook and action may become evident, depending on the educational emphasis. It is obviously not the same whether the "university man" is primarily trained in analytical discipline or whether he has tilled a particular field such as public administration or business management without enriching his mind from a more diversified intellectual diet.

On this score the British preference, for instance, has been consistently for a general type of education, coupled with evidence of high academic achievement in any subject of the candidate's choosing, whether Sanskrit, philosophy, or Elizabethan literature. This is in sharp contrast to picking one's course of study to learn all about such things as budgeting or personnel administration. The British formula goes back to the views set forth a hundred years ago by the historian Macaulay, a man of equally extraordinary success as member of Parliament, as administrative reformer, and as author of the

History of England. In the light of his own observation, Macaulay insisted that Britain's need in governing India was for young men who, instead of being specially trained for such service, entered it with a record of academic distinction earned in pursuit of a gentleman's education. Today's Administrative Class, the top group in the British civil service, numbers only about 2,800, or less than half of 1 per cent of the total (1955). But this small body has gone far to impress the characteristics of an institution upon the conduct of public administration, in integrity and impartiality as well as in devotion and *esprit de corps.*

For an understanding of the basic structure of public administration we must appreciate the pivotal role of the top cadre in the civil service. Although under political direction, this group represents the head in the anatomy of the departmental body, in planning as well as in execution. As the head in relation to the other parts of the body, it decides priorities for administrative operations, defines the general pattern of assignments, provides timetables for performance, supervises the conduct of activities, looks out for trouble spots, and evaluates results. Hence the higher civil servants have much to say about what the remainder of the department is busy with. That is true not only with respect to the clerical force, with its diversified tasks, but also with respect to the professional specialists. Of these, there are today many categories. We may think, on the one hand, of legal and accounting staffs and, on the other, of economists, engineers, statisticians, meteorologists, chemists, physicians, and the like, depending upon the particular functions exercised by the department.

In turn, the flavor as well as the vigor of the influence exerted by the top cadre in the civil service are determined both by the rules of access to the higher positions and by the kind of men moving into these positions. An illustration is furnished in Italy, where it has become a matter of concern that for a considerable time the poorer south has sent a disproportionate share of aspirants into the civil service. The thing regarded as most serious in this development has been the gradual packing of the bureaucracy with individuals showing "southern attitudes," both in a preoccupation with their economic security and in a display of authoritarian thinking.

The Departmental System

We may also talk about administrative structure as another kind of division of labor—not by service groups but as an allocation of functions and responsibilities either among governmental agencies or in terms of bureaus, divisions, and offices within a given department. Thus, in the United States the various functions of the federal government are distributed among ten executive departments and more than fifty other agencies, ranging in size from the bulky Veterans Administration to the tiny Smithsonian Institution, and including the Tennessee Valley Authority, a government corporation. All in all, these sixty-odd members of the executive family have some two thousand operating components (1956), as counted by the Senate Committee on Government Operations. Finally, various types of surveillance are extended over the whole edifice, usually in the name of the chief executive, by central management and control agencies such as the Bureau of the Budget.

As an example of departmental organization, and the stresses and strains that may arise inside it, we may look briefly at the Department of Health, Education, and Welfare. At its helm is the secretary, aided by an undersecretary, two assistant secretaries for federal-state relations and for program analysis, respectively, and such additional officers as the director of administration. The department's regional directors represent the secretary in their particular areas. This, then, is the directing mechanism of the department. It includes the secretary's "staff" personnel—that is, those who render him planning, reviewing, reporting, and other management services without exercising authority of their own.

The departmental "line" establishments, proceeding under delegated operating authority, look like overgrown extremities when compared with the "overhead." There is the Public Health Service, with its Bureau of Medical Services, its Bureau of State Services (for joint federal-state programs), and the National Institutes of Health (for medical research). There is the Office of Education, a service supplying technical information and advice. There is the Social Security Administration, another large component, divided into the Bureau of Old-Age and Survivors Insurance, the Bureau of Public Assistance, the Children's Bureau, and the Bureau of Federal Credit Unions. The Office of Vocational Rehabilitation gives attention to the vocational interests of the mentally as well as the physically handicapped. Still another element in the department is the Food and Drug Administration. Finally, the department is in charge of Saint Elizabeths Hospital, an institution for the mentally ill, and supervises three government-aided corporations: the American Printing House for the Blind, Gallaudet College for deaf students, and Howard University, founded in 1867 to mitigate the lack of higher educational facilities for Negroes.

Authority, Advice, and Accountability

This sketch of administrative structure should make it clear that the organizational setting is the scene of both unifying drives and clashes of motivations. But it is also a mechanism for bringing together divergent forces. That becomes evident when we look at the structure in still another way, in the sense of three principles that inevitably collide time and again. The first of these principles is that of authority, or of hierarchy, as authority puts one will under another. The sign of hierarchy is the succession of levels of decision, with each giving orders to the lower levels. Thus the impact of hierarchy is vertical, downward. The principle of authority meets a counterforce in the principle of advice. Authority cannot stand on its own for any length of time without being exercised in pursuit of purposes that somehow make sense. Indeed, authority benefits from the support of reason. That is why it needs advice, why good advice usually cannot be ignored. A continuous flow of advice requires a process of consultation. With the sweeping advance of specialization in our day and with the corresponding proliferation of points of advice, the consultative principle has gained increasing scope. Thus the vertical drive of authority is blocked at many places by the lateral relationships of an advisory character, with the result that the original direction is changed frequently. The third principle that operates in the administrative setting is the principle of accountability for actions taken. Accountability calls for the least exertion when the action taken rests on authority sustained by advice—when there is neither arbitrary authority, unsupported by consultation, nor forsaken counsel, reduced to obstructing authority.

The principle of accountability generates a quest for cover. He who is answerable likes to have ready answers. Thus the principle of accountability has a corollary in the principle of safety. To be safe in terms of accountability is worth more than to be right.

Many day-by-day activities can be explained as the interaction of these three principles, and one of the most conspicuous consequences is the pressure for putting things in writing. That is why so much administrative action takes the form of drafting, redrafting, reviewing, amending, and approving papers. The need for having almost everything in black and white springs from the basic interests affected. Authorities want to foreclose misunderstanding about actions ordered; advisers want their recommendations on record; and those accountable want to be able to justify their action or lack of action at a later date. Even the nine carbons of the record copy may pay off handsomely as a way of showing all concerned what was done and of reminding some of them of what they have subsequently to do.

PUBLIC ADMINISTRATION AND POPULAR RULE

Diffusion of Authority

Considering the interaction of what has here been called the principles of authority, advice, and accountability, it is not difficult to identify one of the biggest problems in the operation of the administrative system under popular rule. The representative aspirations of popular rule make it hard to tell who in government has the last word. Authority is highly diffused, compared with the much simpler master-servant relationship under absolutism.

In the historic beginnings of the modern "administrative state," in Brandenburg-Prussia from the second half of the seventeenth century into the first half of the eighteenth, the authority of the king was supreme. If he recognized the need for surrounding himself with the "best heads" wherever they could be found, in the words of Frederick William I of Prussia, advice could be translated into the most far-reaching order by the royal hand signing a piece of paper. As an example, the ruler's assent was all it took for the progressive mind of Count Mikhail Speranski to initiate, in the name of Tsar Alexander I, the great reform project by which in 1822 Siberia was raised from the condition of an exploited colony to full standing as a vital region of the Russian Empire.

Compared with this direct channel connecting advice and authority, the interaction of both has become pluralized to an extraordinary degree in the working of public administration under popular rule. Instead of the decision of a monarch able to settle a matter in his own mind, the changing preferences and abiding uncertainties of the electorate are projected upon the factional specter of the party system and eventually upon the divided concerns of the legislative and the executive branches. In turn, the legislature is usually divided into two bodies. With authority so hard to find for protection and so hard to come by for self-defense, governmental agencies try to build up and maintain close relations with various interest organizations, which they come to regard as their clientele. These organizations are likely to impress their point of view upon departmental policy, thus shredding authority further.

Effects of Constitutional Structure

In a fully developed parliamentary system the dispersal of authority that flows from popular rule is offset to a considerable extent by the constitutional link between the legislative majority and the cabinet as its executive committee. The leadership of the majority party and the government are made into essentially one and the same thing by the bond of political responsibility. By contrast, congressional-presidential government on the model of the United States has greatly increased the pluralization of relationships in the interplay of authority and advice. Indeed, it has produced a tendency for either branch of government to avoid the other as far as possible. Both Congress and the President are best satisfied to accomplish their aims on their own. As a result, the concept of national authority is very blurred. It lacks the clarification that a stronger two-party system would supply.

In parliamentary government, moreover, the legislative leaders are either active ministers of the government or would-be ministers on the opposition bench. Both groups of leaders therefore automatically appraise legislative proposals with their eyes upon the resulting administrative responsibilities. In the United States the legislative branch has no similar reason to be seriously concerned with the impact of statutory enactments upon the administrative system. Rarely have the managers of Congress seen service as managers on the executive side of the federal government, and seldom do they look forward to such service.

Under such circumstances the civil servant is hard put to know his master. It follows that the behavior of the bureaucracy will show strong temporizing tendencies, an uneasy groping for policy that is both free of equivocation and likely to stand up, a deep-seated fear of stepping on the toes of the large body of voters as well as the considerable number of lawmakers who recoil from committing themselves in terms of general policy. With a greatly enlarged political no man's land and with the nebulous state of ultimate authority, it is an exasperating task to try to join political direction and the technical advice of the career element in a productive synthesis.

CHAPTER 2

ASPECTS OF BUREAUCRACY

The first chapter gave some idea of the nature of the administrative state and of the role played by the modern bureaucracy in the conduct of a government's functions. But "bureaucracy" is a word often used without exact indication of the meaning ascribed to it. This second chapter seeks to make clear the principal meanings of the word and, in doing so, to show the several aspects or dimensions of bureaucracy.

The ambiguity of the word "bureaucracy" is often exploited for deliberate befuddlement. We must distinguish (1) bureaucracy as a particular form of organization, more specifically as a general design for the conduct of public administration, and (2) bureaucracy as an ailment of organization, an ailment obstructing good management. We must also distinguish (3) bureaucracy in the sense of "big government," an establishment of vast proportions which is joined in countless ways to the social and economic order, for better or worse, and (4) bureaucracy thought of as a blight, always for the worse, falling on liberty. Bureaucracy is considered a blight by those who are ready to indict modern government for the responsibilities it has assumed.

BUREAUCRACY—AN AMBIGUOUS TERM

A Case of Highbrow Talk

Judging by the way it looks and sounds, "bureaucracy" is not the sort of word that grows out of the talk of ordinary people. For that matter, it is not likely to take hold in the common man's vocabulary. There must be millions who have never heard of "bureaucracy." But everybody who has heard of it either suspects or knows that "bureaucracy" is a bad word or a word for a bad thing. That much is clear to him even though he may hesitate when asked to tell exactly what the word means.

Perhaps, while forming his answer, he will think first of a similar word—"democracy." Possibly he knows the roots of that word as well as its meaning—that is, government by the people, or popular rule. Putting two and two together, he may come up with the answer that bureaucracy means government by bureaus, or public agencies. With that he would be right in a way. He may add that bureaucracy is bad because government by public agencies would make these agencies the masters of the people.

In not a few countries, however, particularly those of continental Europe, statesmen and editorial writers as well as scholars speak of bureaucracy as one may speak of the weather. There the word means simply the body of regular government employees mostly in the specific sense of the civil service, especially the higher service. In this bland meaning the word is also applied to the administrative system as a whole. Nevertheless, even in these countries it is not flattering to be called a bureaucrat, in the sense of acting in a bureaucratic manner. For, as with Americans, a bureaucratic manner means such things as doing everything by regulation, ignoring better reasons, and being coldly aloof from the outside world. In contrast with the United States, however, European references to bureaucracy—in particular *the* bureaucracy—are ordinarily free from derogatory intent or implication. On the whole, unlike American usage, the term has come to be emotionally neutral in Europe.

French Pedigree

Although "bureaucracy" may be counted among the notorious words of our age, its origin is not entirely clear beyond the hint of French ancestry. The first half of the word has been traced to the Latin *burrus,* meaning a dark and somber color—a color suitable for solemnity and possibly also to cloak evil deeds. In Old French a related word (*la bure*) meant a certain kind of cloth used on tables, especially in places where public authorities were holding forth. In other words, even the officials of distant times apparently did not deem an honest table good enough to support their elbows. From the tablecloth, the table covered with it got the name *bureau,* and next this word was applied to the office room itself. It has been claimed that the creative mind first to envisage the public offices as the operating government by speaking of it as *bureaucratie* was Vincent de Gournay, an eighteenth-century French minister of commerce. In all probability he intended to express the critical point of view of private enterprise.

Although a hideous example of teaming French with Greek, and obviously not meant to win friends for officialdom, the new word gained a footing because of its nice argumentative edge. It soon spread to other countries. Not surprisingly, it came into considerable vogue in nineteenth-century Germany, where a highly developed civil service, steeped in the spirit of authority, encountered the liberal surge. As a matter of fact, the Germans were so taken with the French term that before long they gave it Teutonic braids by spelling it *Bürokratie*. But the real flowering of the word in many languages is a recent development. Equally recent is the systematic description and analysis of bureaucracy both as an arm and as part of the mind of modern government, public administration in the context of the industrial society. This is a field of study which in its origins is largely identified with the work of the German historian and sociologist Max Weber.[1]

Government of Bureaus versus Government by Bureaus

In speaking against administrative tyranny in the alleged defense of the people, a versatile politician knows how to clinch his case by thundering about bureaucracy. All that may have happened is that

1. Max Weber (1864–1920) has gained a growing following in the United States as well as in other countries, although some of his concepts and conclusions have caused critical comment, in part on the basis of assumptions about his purposes and intent; a considerable body of his writings is now available in English. One should add, however, that the line of prophets of the "administrative state" includes other great names, such as Italy's Gaetano Mosca, whose work has not yet found the recognition it merits, perhaps because he is often placed in the company of the "elitarians"—the school of thought which, like "honest" John Adams, Jefferson's most profound antagonist, sees nature or the "facts of life" in alliance with government by the few, by an elite. For a brief appraisal of Mosca's theories see Fritz Morstein Marx, "The Bureaucratic State," *Review of Politics*, I (1939), 457 ff.

In the United States one of the foremost pioneers to focus attention upon the administrative structure of modern government was Frank J. Goodnow (1859–1939). Turning to the next generation of American scholarship, we must name Leonard D. White, who has further added to the esteem earned by his research in his recent studies devoted to the history of federal administration. In the sphere of comparative government a landmark was set by Herman Finer with the publication in 1932 of his *Theory and Practice of Modern Government*, including an admirable treatment of the background as well as the significance of public administration. Carl J. Friedrich's contribution in this area has been equally outstanding and influential, as has Arnold Brecht's. In the sphere of the sociological theory of bureaucracy Robert K. Merton has done distinguished work, and the number of those worthy of mention has considerably increased during the last few decades. For a bibliographical listing see the Selected References at the end of this book.

one of his constituents failed to get what the particular governmental agency was not authorized to let him have under law. But the cry of bureaucracy rings loud and true irrespective of the merits of the case. Yet, if popular rule employs administrative machinery to make itself effective over the wide range of present-day governmental activities, the citizen has no good reason to act as if this machinery were the product of diabolical cunning. Measured by quantity, modern government—whatever the degree of popular rule reflected in it —consists of the performance of continuing functions by public agencies to a much greater extent than at any time in the past.

In the practical experience of the citizen, government has become indeed largely one of public agencies, one of bureaus. He deals with these agencies, for the most part, when he has any dealings with government. Government *of* bureaus, in this sense, is different from government *by* bureaus. There is no government *by* bureaus when the administrative system acts in accordance with the decisions of the representatives of the people and accounts to them for what is being done. Obviously, government of bureaus is much more appealing than a government operated by commissars, investigators, bosses, or crooks. Moreover, if we think of *bureau* in the sense of an office table, especially a desk, bureaucracy appears to be the equivalent of government from behind desks, or "desk government." Who would not rather be governed from behind desks than from the back room of the corner saloon or the boudoir favored by the chief of a junta?

"Desk Government"

Certainly, to modern man the desk is not a symbol of either elevation or authority. On the contrary, it is as common as the income tax, which touches high and low. Today uncounted millions spend their working hours seated behind desks. With but slight exaggeration it can be said that this has become the productive posture of the white-collar breadwinner everywhere. In addition, with the advance of automation, the chair, if not the desk, increasingly becomes also the companion of the man who watches the machines. Modern society is turning into a "sedentary society" in which the chair serves as both the means and the symbol of production. In social ranking, then, the man at the desk is a reasonable facsimile of everybody, and he is likely to do something useful.

"Desk government," obviously, is a phrase without terror. It suggests forethought and planning, analysis of the facts, considered decisions, direction and co-ordination on a rational basis, predictability of performance, and assurance of results. It alludes to the contribution of the mind, highly esteemed in the era of science and technology. It carries a connotation of knowledge and even of insight. No doubt, twentieth-century government with its great burden of responsibilities should be informed as well as imaginative, capable of assembling and interpreting the data essential for policy-making, and sophisticated in designing longer-term programs. In short, modern government cannot afford to be less than intellectually resourceful. If this is the mark of bureaucracy, we should clamor for more rather than less bureaucracy.

Despite its possible merit, however, bureaucracy is seldom praised; and it is often slighted by those who, openly or secretly, plead a special cause. Specifically, even before the time of De Gournay two camps had existed, separated by one of the enduring dividing lines of politics. On the one side were those who regarded government as basically allied with their interests. On the other side stood those who looked upon government as an impediment to the pursuit of their interests. Denunciation of bureaucracy, naturally, was a promising tactic for this second group—most frequently the spokesmen of private enterprise when they were anxious to stay the arm of government regulation. To them, bureaucracy essentially meant government and all its works. In fact, the more efficient government showed itself, especially in the discharge of its administrative functions, the less could leaders of private enterprise say in its favor, because it was then that much more dangerous.

The same hostile predisposition shows up when the folklore of the contemporary business civilization presents large-scale private organizations as wholesome and productive and corresponding structures of public administration as heavy-handed and wasteful. For instance, many Americans are inclined to view as national assets such giant corporations as General Motors, Standard Oil of New Jersey, and United States Steel, without including formations of this kind under the heading of bureaucracy. Conversely, as Harold D. Lasswell has pointed out, there is no general cartoon figure presenting government as a constructive or beneficial factor. In most of the invective directed at bureaucracy we may therefore find upon close examination a bias based upon narrow self-interest.

It is clear, then, that "bureaucracy" is an ambiguous term. We saw that it could mean quite different things. It might mean, *first,* the type of organization used by modern government for the conduct of its various specialized functions, embodied in the administrative system and personified more specifically by the civil service. Bureaucracy might mean, *second,* a mechanistic and formal approach in carrying out such functions, literal and "inhuman" to the point of indifference toward the effects achieved. This is a common failing of large-scale organization, whether public or private. *Third,* bureaucracy might mean one or two other things or both at the same time. On the one hand, it might mean the kind of government that shoulders a large burden of responsibilities in support of the economic and social order. On the other hand, it might mean a political condition in which the executive branch plays a role increasingly more important in relation to the role of the legislative and judicial branches. This is decried, we recall, as the "welfare state," but it is also spoken of sympathetically as the "service state." And, *fourth,* bureaucracy might mean government subject to control, not by the electorate, but rather by a group of power-hungry, visionary functionaries. Each of these meanings calls for closer examination.

BUREAUCRACY AS STRUCTURE OF ORGANIZATION

Concentration of Responsibility

To speak of bureaucracy as designating a particular structure of organization suggests technical rather than ordinary man's language. For it is not likely that the proverbial man in the street would be fascinated with anything as abstruse as structures of organization. This is a subject closer to the heart of the specialist, who must know which organizational structure is best suited for particular purposes. A subject about which specialists must know is of equal interest to the scholar, who feels he should know first, or more about it, so as to teach the specialists.

One concept of the bureaucratic type of organization gained considerable currency during the second half of the nineteenth century in the German terminology of public administration. That concept came to mean about the same thing Americans have in mind when they talk of single-headed departments, in contrast with organizations headed by collegial bodies, such as boards and commissions, with each member essentially the equal of every other, including the chairman. More specifically, in accordance with this terminology, a bureaucratically organized agency was one directed by a civil servant who alone was responsible for the actions of his subordinates; these simply exercised the authority of the man at the top. In the same way, a departmental system organized on such principles was referred to as "bureaucratic" in character. Implicit in the term was a strong suggestion to the effect that this structure imparted efficiency. If the French were torn between indignation and amusement over *bureaucratie,* the Germans managed to drain the word of all satire and to make it the label of a system of superior accomplishment.

Another meaning of bureaucracy is more familiar and more recent as applied to organizational structure. It refers to a type of structure manned by trained personnel who are grouped in specific command relationships. Bureaucratic organization in this sense is equally and conspicuously serviceable for a large variety of public and private purposes in industrial societies.

Hierarchy and Control

The type of organization called bureaucratic in this now widely used sense has several unmistakable characteristics. They include—as principal factors—hierarchy, jurisdiction, specialization, professional training, fixed compensation, and permanence. Hierarchy is perhaps the most important. As a concept applied to the doing of things, hierarchy signifies a scheme of interlocking superior-subordinate relationships. In such a scheme John Doe may be the boss of a number of underlings who—short of exceptional circumstances—defer to his authority as if he were king. Each of these underlings, again, may command still others, and so the scheme goes down to the very base. But John Doe is far from being king, for normally he gets his orders from somebody higher up; and, even if he were at the very top, the presence of restrictive considerations will usually prevent him from issuing the sort of orders closest to his heart. But if John Doe is at the top and issues a particular order to be implemented throughout the organization, he can be reasonably sure that everybody, from one level of internal control to the other, will get busy doing what the order demands.

The advantage of hierarchy as an organizational device is obvious from this bare outline. Through the scheme of interlocking superior-subordinate relationships even the largest organization can be held together and be made to act as a single, cohesive body. Yet the responsibility for direction from the top is not overextended, because every order, traveling down, is reinforced by the way it secures attention on successively lower levels of control. In turn, confusion is reduced, because each human being within the organization ordinarily knows precisely from whom he gets orders and to whom he is to pass them on.

The performance of superiors in transmitting orders received by them to their subordinates can be observed and controlled with relative ease. It can be stimulated by prospects for advancement and threats of disciplinary action. As a result, instead of losing force because of the distance it has to cover in moving throughout the organization, each order from above gains new force as it proceeds from one superior-subordinate relationship to the next lower one. In the chain of superiors each puts his own authority behind the order. Equally important, not only does hierarchy make it easy to transmit orders which set in motion specific actions but it is as effective in conveying to all parts of the organization a general sense of direction, a common approach, a basic point of view, and even an operating doctrine. Hierarchy, then, enables an organization—even one in which large numbers of human beings have been brought together—to move toward specified goals with the least amount of floundering and friction.

Jurisdiction and Specialization

As a characteristic of the bureaucratic type of organization, the concept of hierarchy is linked with that of jurisdiction. This term, in the organizational context, refers principally to two things. First, it indicates a formal recognition that the individual organization is committed to discharging particular functions and these alone, usually in relation to a defined geographic area. Second, jurisdiction is made part of the internal division of labor within the organization.

For example, a municipal department of welfare as a matter of jurisdiction will indicate that it is available for the handling of applications for public assistance; but it will not undertake to furnish supervisors for playgrounds, playground supervision being outside its jurisdiction. The welfare department would also make a distinction between an application coming from a resident of the town and one being mailed in by a resident of a neighboring town. The bureaucratic type of organization will thus gain increased efficiency by sticking to what it is equipped to do in terms of its jurisdiction, without trying to do other things. In addition, the external jurisdiction—that is, what an organization is to do—will be translated into internal jurisdiction in the sense of detailed assignments for all components of the organization, down to what each individual at his working place is meant to do, such as the filing clerk in the receiving branch of the day-care division, for instance.

Jurisdiction amounts to an acknowledgment of readiness to do certain things and not to attempt others. Thus a basis is established for identifying the particular specializations that the organization requires for the accomplishment of its ends. The chain of superior-

subordinate relationships provides a convenient pattern for so grouping employees possessed of a specialized competence as to make
best use of them. Different kinds of specialists are needed for different kinds of agencies—for example, social workers, cartographers,
bacteriologists—but most agencies cannot be without specialists
having to do with effective conduct of administration. For this
reason the bureaucratic type of organization must value professional
or technical training. An ordinary man of good will, lacking such
training, will simply not get in—unless he has "pull."

Fixed Compensation and Permanence

Even more significant for the nature of bureaucratic organization
is the fact that ordinarily no one active in it is at the same time the
owner. Typically, everybody is an employee working for a fixed
compensation, which in nearly all instances is unrelated to the
measured or assumed success of the organization and the actual
pressure of business. The compensation, as a rule, is paid on the
basis of a set schedule from a general treasury. It is not paid by
individual superiors at their discretion, nor is it raised in the form
of fees collected from applicants or customers, in the sense that the
pay depends on how much money has been taken in. Those making
up the organization do not view it as a tangible asset at their disposal, for they lack control over it, especially over the physical
means by which the product of the organization is turned out.

Finally, the bureaucratic type of organization reflects considerable
long-run continuity. The survival of a private business firm is ultimately subject to the selective test of the market. This test, however,
is usually less strenuous to a large economic organization that supplies a sizable share of the total demand. Public agencies exercising
functions deemed to be in the common interest enjoy still greater
tenure. This is true even though antagonistic public sentiment, retrenchment, or changing circumstances may have sharply contractive effects, leading to the liquidation of entire departments in extreme cases.

Professional Point of View

As a type, bureaucratic organization indicates sophistication in
both design and operating method. Calculated to increase efficiency of performance, it is the product of applied reason, an expression of rationality. It is on these grounds that both the structural
perfection of the bureaucratic type of organization and the increasing

use of machine processes as a manpower substitute are often referred to as *rationalization* in other countries.

But the characteristic of rationality comes in view from still another angle. With the evolution of the bureaucratic type of organization in modern public administration, a foundation was laid for the formation of a body of civil servants who worked for the government as a lifetime career. The very presence of this professionally trained body exerted a rational influence upon the way in which government reached decisions. It is thus understandable why the factor of rationality has been emphasized as both the characteristic working approach and the outstanding contribution of the modern bureaucracy. In the unrestrained interaction of political forces the strongest pressure would usually win out. But in a technological civilization as complex and sensitive as ours, a crude test of political strength is not a satisfactory source of public policy. A moderating influence is needed, which gains its persuasiveness from the knowledge of pertinent facts. Hence the existence of a screening operation, singling out for proper attention the pros and cons of competing alternatives of action, is a highly welcome thing. Governed to a considerable degree by professional standards and likely to value a reasoned approach, the modern career service, under favorable conditions, can function as a significant support of rational consideration in politics.

BUREAUCRACY AS AILMENT OF ORGANIZATION

Loss of Mental Flexibility

It seems hardly plausible that bureaucracy could be an ailment of organization if—as we saw—the word also connotes a specific type of organizational structure that commends itself for its strength. The explanation must be found principally in the fact that the bureaucratic type of organization gives rise to certain tendencies that pervert its purpose. Some of its strength—and in extreme cases all of it —is drained off constantly by vices that paradoxically spring from virtues.

In trying to spot the symptoms of the organizational ailment widely called bureaucracy, it may be best to go back to the main characteristics of the bureaucratic type of organization as outlined in the preceding section. Let us begin again with hierarchy, in the sense of a scheme of interlocking superior-subordinate relationships. It was said earlier that such a scheme is singularly well suited to make all those within even a large organization move as one body.

Things go in channels, as the insider expresses it—that is, in channels of command or control. The things that flow down in these channels are orders, and the things that flow up are either responses to orders or raw materials for still further orders, such as reports on conditions which may call for guidance or proposals for action to be taken higher up. But the very efficacy of control, including the way in which it shapes the attitudes of all participants, inevitably carries with it a loss of mental flexibility. A conveyer-belt psychology spreads throughout the organization like a curse.

Hierarchy as Deadening Influence

This loss of mental flexibility takes many different forms. For one thing, those within the organization may be so overawed by orders that they do not move unless explicitly directed. Adoption of this point of view, moreover, adds to the convenience of the participants, especially if a special effort is needed to explain to the superior each instance in which action was taken without direction. In such a setting, personal initiative is not encouraged. Doing things on his own may in fact expose the "eager beaver" to sharply critical reaction. As a counterpart, orders may not be questioned by those meant to carry them out even though it is clear to them that the situation under their eyes requires a different solution. In addition, hierarchy can stimulate a division of those within the organization into strata or layers which come to function as particular interest groupings, each with its own work outlook and its different degree of allegiance to the organizational purpose. As a result, when there is no bond between them, it becomes perfectly all right for the subordinate to let the superior make a fool of himself.

Hierarchy can therefore turn into a deadening influence, prone to reinforce set ways and traditional arrangements. The best justification for doing a thing in a particular fashion is that "it is done that way." The traditionalism fostered by hierarchy induces a transfer of personal responsibility to authoritative images. "I was told to do that" is the best of reasons. But the next best is that the boss likes it this way and would so do it himself. There is a civilian counterpart of the tragicomic figure of the British commander-in-chief who on the eve of the charge of the Light Brigade at Balaklava, as with every other strategic or tactical decision, first asked himself how the great Wellington would have done it.

The symptoms of the bureaucratic malady show up also in the assertion or denial of jurisdiction. Assurance of being well prepared to perform certain functions may induce an organization to advance extravagant claims in support of its presumed monopoly of satisfactory service. In public administration this attitude accounts for the familiar spectacle of bitter wrangles between different departments over which has actual jurisdiction in the matter. Conversely, when the subject is "hot" because of public controversy, each department may fight with equal determination to have another department accept jurisdiction.

Quite the same thing can be observed in the way individuals within an organization seek to build up their jurisdiction from motives entirely unrelated to the goals of the organization. Expansion of one's recognized sphere of action brings with it an enlargement of his personal importance within the organization. Greater personal importance is prized for psychological reasons quite apart from the prospect of gains in formal status or economic benefit such as promotion or a raise in pay. But unless it helps in "empire-building," everyone may find it best to "stick to his assignments." The bureaucratic fires that shoot up elsewhere need not be noticed, much less attended to, for they singe somebody else.

As a characteristic of the bureaucratic type of organization, specialization has a multiplying effect upon institutional competence. Each needed specialization available in the organization increases its resourcefulness. But one must not overlook the spirit of self-isolation that so often grows spontaneously in the occupational attitude of the specialist. In the sheltered precinct of his specialization he alone knows best; he is therefore best satisfied if he can keep out of the way of the formal authority higher up in the organizational structure. Authorities are all too likely, as he sees it, to impose their uneducated will upon him, which he regards as downright interference.

Yet, on his own, the specialist often makes recommendations inadequately related to the particular policies of the organization of which he is a part. Typically, the specialist strains against having his occupational contribution trimmed to the operating decisions made at the top of the organization. This explains why in the activities of an organization the specialist is often happiest when he can concentrate on his "own business," determined not to worry about other things. As far as he can, he will try to get around the demands of the policy-makers in the organization who press him to come forward with a result to their liking. The same situation arises in the relationships among representatives of different specializations. The economist, for example, concerned with better forecasts of trends, may be anxious to keep the tight-fisted fiscal officer out of his hair, while the fiscal officer tries his best to avoid the personnel director, who wants to talk with him about the agency's need for additional staff.

Disengagement from the Public Interest

Making a living on fixed pay, based upon a schedule largely indifferent to individual performance, can inspire both a desirable determination to do an honest day's work, without demoralizing servility, and an undesirable withdrawal into personal interests at variance with the aims of the organization. Those within a large bureaucratic organization are not, as a rule, personally affected by the fluctuating fortunes of the organization, especially when it enjoys a reputation for institutional immortality. The working force may feel about its part in the organization as one feels about having a part in the morning and evening ride in a crowded bus. There is no common spirit. One day is like the other. As far as personal exertion is concerned, all one needs to do is to get by.

Despite the superiority that it imparts to the bureaucratic type of organization, the drive for rationality which is generated by it may have a negative effect when it stimulates self-sufficiency. Rationality is linked not only to a tested methodology of analysis but also to an objective point of view. Objectivity in examining issues, as an occupational habit, puts value on a retreat from active partisanship. Indeed, in the realm of public administration the career bureaucracy can serve as a permanent instrument of government under conditions of changing party control only by acknowledging and practicing the virtue of neutrality. Such neutrality is the premise for loyal support of any lawful government. On the other hand, neutrality may foster a personal disengagement from any kind of political choice, including even the difference between constitutional and unconstitutional means or ends in the actions of the government of the day.

Thus the career bureaucracy, presuming to be rational instead of partisan, may come to show callousness in matters of constitutional principle, disdain for party contest, unresponsiveness to changing political leadership, arrogance in trusting its own judgment, and, ultimately, even a yen for trying its own hand at governing when there is political stalemate. The principle of institutional neutrality can be perverted into a neutralization that commits the civil servant to nothing but astute defense of his public status.

BUREAUCRACY AS CHARACTERISTIC OF MODERN GOVERNMENT

Rise of "Big Government"

Much of this book deals with bureaucracy in the sense of a type of organization utilized in the conduct of public administration and with the mode of operation of the bureaucratic type as well. As shown in the preceding section, however, the bureaucratic type of organization is not easily separated from its pathology. For this reason more will have to be said about bureaucracy as an ailment of organization. The two interrelated aspects, in turn, cannot be fully understood unless they are placed in the context of modern government, the kind of government characteristic of predominantly industrial societies. The conspicuous thing about this kind of government is that within less than a century it has developed into "big government," pushed into a role supporting the machine economy and heavily concentrated populations. True enough, the pace of development, affected by political traditions and economic necessity, was not the same in different nations; but ultimately government everywhere had to lend an organizing hand to stabilize the emerging industrial order.

Pressure and Counterpressure

"Big government" is the result of many things associated with industrialization and urbanization. Something had to be done to reduce the inequities as well as the instabilities of the industrial drive in the raw. Something had to be done to make it possible for massed populations to exist in the congested city. Something had to be done to sustain social security as a protection of breadwinners and as an economic defense of purchasing power. Government was therefore induced to undertake numerous activities that an agrarian order and rural living had been able to do without. In fact, the urban structure of today's industrial society costs the general taxpayer many times the amount he contributes in support of the rural way of living. But the expansion of public functions, though prompted by the push toward industrialization, has also carried into rural life many new services as well as many improvements in old ones.

Considering the nature of the development, it is ironic that the most clamorous opposition to the expansion of governmental functions has come from the spokesmen of free enterprise, mainly the new industrial leadership. Both regulatory and service activities initiated by government have been denounced as "creeping socialism" and the like, with little regard for the fact that these functions, by and large, have been assumed reluctantly to mend the holes torn in the social fabric by the industrial revolution.

Whose Government?

As we saw earlier, statistical evidence tends to demonstrate that one of the strongest periodic prompters in the growth of "big government" has been calamity. Adversity apparently not only drags government to the center of the stage but also keeps it there after the emergency has ended. Is it to be assumed that public preference and the aims of statesmen, even under popular rule, may not challenge prevailing views about what is proper for government until the country is in the grip of an emergency? Or is it to be assumed that electorates acquiesce in "bigger government" once it has got bigger and that nothing much can be done about it? Each question is disturbing in its implications. The growth of governmental functions appears to have much to do with concepts of what the industrial order requires for its own continued health. It evidently has less to do with ideas about distributive justice and the happiness of men.

If big government were to be rejected categorically, the rejection would extend equally to the whole of the industrial foundation of our civilization. This is like setting the clock back. Indeed, for the large body of men big government has increased the worth of the state precisely because of the enlarged public concern with their welfare. But big government is good only in proportion to its actual performance. From this angle the question of general efficiency in public administration is something in which today almost everybody has a personal stake.

Changing Group Positions

If the enlarged presence of government in the affairs of industrial society be called bureaucracy, then bureaucracy is as much the shadow of industrial society as is big government itself. Conversely, if big government is to be condemned, then bureaucracy must be condemned for the same reason, irrespective of whether or not the administrative system in fact shows integrity and efficiency. On such grounds we might even insist—as some spokesmen of private business have—that an efficient civil service is the worst, because good men in government offices are not easily pushed over.

But it should not be assumed that the lines of partisanship can be drawn so simply. Political attacks upon bureaucracy—in particular, *the* bureaucracy—have often come from those who sensed in it an unsympathetic predisposition toward them. Thus such attacks have frequently come from organized labor. Moreover, depending on time and circumstance, private business may actually look upon government as its partner or its defender. Up to the Civil War, for instance, American government, especially in the eastern seaboard states, was deeply involved in economic planning and the promotion of private enterprise. Henry Clay's "American System" was meant to rest squarely on an alliance between government and private business. Needless to say, under such auspices it did not matter how big government was as long as it was big enough to do its part. In somewhat the same manner, private business generally looks upon government with less critical eyes when government acts in the role of a large-scale dispenser of contracts. This is true of wartime conditions, for example, when government becomes the key customer of private enterprise. But we may also notice the spirit of partnership in the contractual relationships between government and private business in the vast and expanding field of research and technical application, in its present-day scope the most recent addition to big government.

Censure of the Executive Branch

Big government, with its stress upon continuing administrative functions, gives increasing importance to the executive branch as the logical place to lodge these functions and to provide general direction and co-ordination for them. As a result, the civil service has physically grown in a substantial manner. These two interrelated facts have furnished grist for the mills of those who regard both as adverse to their own interests.

On the one hand, the executive power has been portrayed as usurping control of the government and outflanking the position of the legislative branch. There is superficial plausibility to the charge, but the facts, for the most part, are not on its side. In particular, this line of criticism neglects the enhanced importance of the legislature in supplying statutory guidance to the executive establishment and in imposing political accountability upon it. Moreover, it was usually the legislative branch itself which gave the executive power the task to assume leadership in the formulation of basic policy proposals so as to make for more effective legislative consideration and action.

The civil service, on the other hand, could be presented, with some poetic license, as a hydra growing new heads faster than anybody could hope to cut them off. The permanent officialdom has often been pictured as engaged in unproductive routines when not indulging in its favorite sport of bullying the helpless citizen, as both intolerably meddlesome and bogged down in inertia. This seemed to come to light in the limited ability of large-scale organizations to give adequate attention to the human aspects of each particular case to be dealt with. The magnifying effects can easily be imagined when it is borne in mind that it has become a common experience for contemporary man to be a frequently unwilling visitor in government offices.

BUREAUCRACY AS INDICTMENT OF MODERN GOVERNMENT

A New Absolutism?

As modern government was called upon to widen the range of its responsibilities in the interest of industrial society, it extended its administrative operations to the point of touching ever larger parts of the public. As a result, the impact of today's career bureaucracy has become one of the familiar facts of life for the ordinary citizen. But some obstinate questions remain unanswered. Are we on the road to a new absolutism more ruthless than the old, which was often moderated by the philosophical currents of enlightenment? Can we be sure that nations or leaders can maintain control over the growth of government?

It is no acknowledgment of defeat or despair to allow such questions to stand instead of brushing them off as pointless. As an act of caution it may profit us to doubt when doubts alert the mind to dangers that otherwise might be ignored. Blind confidence that "things will work out somehow" is not a good guide. On the other hand, inability to answer large questions conclusively need not lead to a loss of that sturdy confidence that stems from mature reflection and an experimental approach to practical problems.

Effects of Reckless Criticism

It is quite a different matter to indict modern government for alleged encroachment upon inalienable liberties. The central premise of this denunciation appears to be the liberty claimed by some to ignore the obligations of man toward fellow man, especially in the pursuit of private gain. Thus there will be those who use "bureaucracy" as a word from the dictionary of contempt. Whether viewed as political power that somehow got into the wrong hands or as a conspiracy of irresponsible officeholders eager for complete control, "bureaucracy" then adds up to only one thing—a damnation of government for its capacity of enforcing change unwanted by the critic or of resisting change demanded by him.

The indictment flung at modern government for embodying and promoting bureaucracy is addressed to the contemporary role of government in the life of industrial society. It has little reference to the institutional characteristics and the working processes of public administration, but it has done much to lower the esteem in which government is held. It has exerted a detrimental influence upon both the performance of the administrative system and the behavior of civil servants.

CHAPTER 3

ESSENTIALS OF PUBLIC ADMINISTRATION

Previously we discussed the connection between the evolution of industrial society and the emergence of big government—government big in terms of both the scope of its responsibilities and the size of its administrative machinery. It was shown that industrial society, in its own interest, is bound to press for efficiency in the operation of that machinery. The pressure for efficiency favors a structure of organization characterized by vertical relationships of command, lateral relationships of advice, and complementary relationships of accountability. More specifically, as indicated in the second chapter, this type of organization combines several distinctive features: hierarchy, jurisdiction, specialization, professional training, fixed compensation, and permanence.

Each of these features represents a response to the basic requirement that the administrative machinery of government function effectively. Indeed, without these features the machinery would fail to accomplish its purposes. The rise of the modern bureaucracy can be understood only when we recognize its superior capacity for attending to the essentials of public administration. What are these essentials? Broadly speaking, they may be listed as (1) the essential of rationality, (2) the essential of responsibility, (3) the essential of competence, and (4) the essential of continuity. We now turn to consider in this order each of the four.

THE REQUIREMENT OF RATIONALITY

Rationality as Pursuit of Purpose

The abstraction called "rational man" is not a recent invention; it has performed marvelous tricks as an endearing spook for ancient philosophers as well as for contemporary social scientists. To associate the conduct of public administration with anything as demanding as the requirement of rationality may therefore seem to be a very dubious undertaking. A consideration of bureaucracy as a living thing cannot fail to cast light on the irrational as well as the rational factors in human behavior. But even when looked upon as an operating process, as a pattern of behavior, public administration is governed by a strong sense of purpose. The bureaucracy is an instrument for the attainment of specified aims by application of specified means—that is, a device for discharging the functions of government. For this reason, when we examine the bureaucracy at work, we observe human beings as they act in the context of predetermined objectives, of given organizational arrangements, and of prescribed operating methods—in short, in an institutional framework that is largely external to their personal choices.

The presence of this discipline is of greatest significance in accomplishing control over an organization and in maintaining efficiency in its operations. The ability and willingness of the participants to shape their conduct in acceptance of the discipline of acknowledged institutional purpose provide the key to effective as well as responsible administration. Each participant must learn to act as part of the agency he serves and in accordance with the policies laid down by the agency's top command. In the widest sense, therefore, the requirement of rationality arises from the need for getting things done that *have* to be done, fully, quickly, and economically. This need is answered in the instrumental character of the bureaucracy, by the fact that the bureaucracy itself is a means to an end. Its task is to serve government by administering the government's continuing functions and by giving advice on policy as well as operations.

The discipline of acknowledged institutional purpose is in sharp contrast to the freedom to do as one pleases and even to the freedom to do as seems best. We shall consider later the limits to the practical reach of this discipline, for man cannot be kept under the domination of rationality either completely or continuously, whether it be institutional or individual rationality. We shall consider also the factors that determine the relative strength of the discipline of acknowledged institutional purpose in the general setting of public administration. But it is well to recognize at the outset that the operating doctrine of the bureaucracy centers upon the obligation to *serve*. It follows that the bureaucracy must combat within itself the divisive irrationalities of human nature and employ its collective ingenuity in a systematic search for the best road to the goals marked by public policy. Even partial success secures large benefits.

Rationality as Source of Cohesion

Considering the magnitude characteristic of modern administrative systems, the discipline of acknowledged institutional purpose is doubly important. It is like an electric current that runs through the whole system, connecting all points. Short of this discipline, and hence short of the rationality it imposes, the administrative machinery would fall apart into countless separate clusters of personal influence. Control would become impossible. Responsibility would disintegrate. These consequences could not be prevented by organizational structure alone. Organizational structure is no substitute for the discipline of acknowledged institutional purpose and affects it only in a secondary sense, by encouraging and conserving it or, as the case may be, by ignoring and dissipating it. The crying need of large-scale organization is for cohesion. To the extent that large-scale organization can be a single, unified thing, it gains such unity from being held together by the rationality imposed by the pursuit of its purposes.

In the overshadowing need for cohesion today's large-scale organization is distinctly different from its historic counterparts, which reflected little experience in combining great size with close control. In government a rudimentary type of bureaucracy was brought into existence as soon as authority was spread by delegation. This happened, for instance, when rulers assigned part of their power to regional and local agents, who then acted largely on their own, communications being what they were. Even on the basis of relatively simple organizational arrangements it proved possible to build up considerable competence in the conduct of administration, of which examples can be found in every century. Especially during the Middle Ages secular chancelleries and monastic establishments often achieved a substantial degree of efficiency in the organization and the conduct of such activities as land management, fiscal control, and record-keeping. But each of these establishments remained essentially a self-contained unit without sufficient connecting tissue to form anything comparable to the far-flung administrative system of modern government.

In this sense, therefore, it may be said that the feudal age was free from bureaucracy. Feudalism employed as its principal organizational form a mutual relationship between lord and vassal. This man-to-man relationship was repeated in descending order on the various rungs of the ladder of dependence. Hence the total picture was one of personal ties between individual points of power, compared with a line of control running from top to bottom. Such an arrangement would be entirely unsuitable for today's large-scale organization, which resembles feudal relationships only as a symptom of weakness. In addition, feudalism leaned too heavily on personal fealty to accept the idea of a salaried officialdom pledged to institutional purposes. By contrast, the contemporary industrial order has generated an unabating drive into a type of organization both large scale and closely knit. To be of use, this type must overcome the stresses and obstructions that come with its size. The strength of cohesiveness is in direct proportion to the degree in which large-scale organization is imbued with the discipline of acknowledged institutional purpose.

Rationality as Application of Knowledge

As government was pushed time and again to "do something" to allay the roughnesses and the risks inherent in industrial society, it had to increase its knowledge of causes and effects. In policing the industrial order, in heaving it back into balance by broadening the social incidence of its advantages, government had to know what it was doing. Inevitably, knowledge was bought by learning, interrupted by uneasy temporizing, erratic groping, and costly errors.

Knowledge about means to accomplish ends is in equal demand throughout the administrative system. It is needed in the drafting of regulations as well as in the planning of operations, in the handling of particular issues as well as in assuring expeditious disposition of a steady flow of routine cases. It is needed in the agencies that form the chief executive's over-all organs of general management and in the departments that centralize control over the conduct of the various governmental functions. It is needed at each of the several levels of determination: on the level of advice in the making of policy; on the level of day-to-day direction of departmental activities; and on the levels represented by the regional or local offices in the field, where we find, as a rule, the main body of governmental personnel, corresponding to the distribution of total workload. Knowledge about means to accomplish ends is needed, finally, not only at the point of the final signature but also in the concentric circles of preparatory action grouped around each such point. What is even more important, knowledge about means, by and large, requires equal knowledge about ends. Analysis of ends is often a prerequisite of the choice of means. Moreover, analysis of ends and formulation of reasoned alternative proposals for action as steps toward responsible decision are usually tasks for which political officials lean upon the career man in public administration.

Rationality as Application of Reason

Although it should not be assumed that in these matters we must think first of the role of the higher civil service, much of what has been said has particular relevance for it.[1] When the higher civil service is recruited from the colleges and the universities, it carries with it both a mental disposition in favor of a rational approach and a basic skill in the use of tested methodology for reaching conclusions. From this background it is natural for the career man to accept reason as the controlling standard of his professional judgment—not authority, much less sheer power. Reason is his guide in resolving the issues of administration, in carrying out assignments, and in advising policy-makers. The civil service finds in the canons of rationality the fundamental ground for its existence. There is never a dearth of partisans, but none could be given the continuing task of caretaker of the public interest, looking at the merits of each matter in administering governmental functions and in supplying impartial counsel.

To get well-informed minds for the higher civil service was one of the incentives for the rulers of Brandenburg-Prussia to become founders and patrons of universities. In the rise of the British civil service during the last hundred years to the stature of a model in institutional strength and in sensitivity to the principles of representative government, a decisive factor was the use of the univer-

1. The role of the higher civil service has been described briefly in the first chapter (see pp. 10 ff.). We may think of the main function of the top cadre as threefold: *first,* to keep the machinery of administration in good order so that it is readily useful for the political leadership of the departmental system; *second,* to operate the administrative machinery so as to accomplish the aims of the political leadership; and, *third,* to advise that leadership about the best ways and means of using the administrative machinery for the accomplishment of its aims. The political (or, better, the politically responsible) direction of the department falls to the department head as the agent of the government of the day to put into effect its programs. But the administrative (or, perhaps better, the technical, or the institutional) direction of the department is properly the task of the ranking career men. In this capacity they give general guidance also to the activities of the professional groups in the more specific sense—say, the economists in the economic analysis section and the accountants in the fiscal reports section, each such section being headed usually by a member of the particular professional group. Whether or not the higher civil service is ordinarily used as the body responsible for departmental management; whether or not its members show a professional point of view; whether or not they have sufficient intellectual breadth, on the one hand, to comprehend the mission of the department in the context of the government's policies and, on the other, to serve as the department's "generalists," bringing about a concert of action from the output of the various groups of departmental specialists—these are basic questions for the effectiveness of the bureaucracy as a whole.

sities as the source of supply for the top group. Objectivity of perspective came easier with training in scientific deference to facts, figures, and findings. This perspective also influenced the development of the technical side of public administration. Historically, it was for the most part the civil service itself that elaborated the mechanisms for the conduct of its work. In many instances it was the civil service, too, which sparked the ideas that influenced governmental reform.

Despite all his reservations toward an excess of government, Jeremy Bentham, true to his utilitarian philosophy, insisted on a centrally administered system of statistical information to make policy intelligent. But this was a continuing task. The civil servant's attachment to rationality gave him an important role in the empirical approach to an understanding of the problems of industrial society. Academic study and the opinion of practical men alone would not have been sufficient, for an underpinning of inferences in terms of detailed evidence and technical appraisal was needed also. The bureaucracy, in time, amassed statistical data as a by-product of conducting administrative functions, being able to hold out a mirror to the economic and social realities of the industrial order. In the alternation of political control normal under popular rule, the civil service represented the element of continuity in planning—a resource available to bolster the effectiveness of every government as long as loyalty was not partisan.

Rationality as Intelligence Service

The bureaucracy thus contributed a new dimension to government. It added administrative strength, especially by greatly increasing the government's capacity for influencing the economic and social order in the general interest. It also showed considerable success in dredging up the facts needed for the formulation and execution of public policy. Debate on the political stage could no longer be won by rhetoric. In the bright light of factual analysis, one-sided claims did not stand up well even when advanced by superior force, whether of money or ballots.

Indeed, when a bureaucracy found itself in the dark, because of uncertainty either about the facts or about how to interpret them, its natural inclination was to call for special fact-finding machinery. Thus in Germany, for instance, the career bureaucracy promoted ambitious official inquiries into unsolved economic problems in the closing decades of the past century. A similar part has been taken by the British civil service in helping to launch full-scale inquiries, in the form either of the so-called departmental committee, usually made up of outside experts, or of the royal commission, normally composed of public figures or representatives of rival interests. By its response to the requirement of rationality, the civil service served the public as well as the government as a general intelligence agency. Nations came to know themselves in their economic and social structure with increasing accuracy through the scouting eyes of the bureaucracy.

Distortion of Rationality by Social Bias

There is another side to the matter, however. Rationality neither develops nor functions in a void—social, emotional, or intellectual. Ultimately, it is controlled by its conscious premises or its unconscious predispositions. When the civil servant affirms in thought and action the guiding influence of an objective point of view, he may actually give free play to underlying assumptions or unacknowledged values that he shares as a matter of background or indoctrination. When these submerged assumptions or values harmonize with those of the public, there is no likelihood of difficulty. But when a discrepancy arises between the points of view, the rationality of the career bureaucracy will be denounced as the sophistry of a sheltered oligarchy.

The attitude of the political leftists in Great Britain toward the higher civil service has long reflected this critical judgment. It subsided only as a result of the practical experience of members of Labor cabinets who discovered that the career service served them well. In Germany under the monarchy, the tacit assumption was that the bureaucracy would not sympathize with republican or left-of-center sentiment. Organized labor and its political instrument, the Social Democratic party, consequently regarded the higher career service as biased against them. Colonial civil services, especially in our time, are suspect among the native population essentially because the premises of rationality on either side are colored by different habits of thought as well as conflicting values. The district officer may be a warmhearted humanitarian and identify himself with his public, but his objectivity will never pass for more than white man's reason.

Social Bias and Advanced Education

In good measure, self-isolation through a set mentality arises from a common social background, especially as a result of a prescribed higher education. It is easy to see why well-educated men and women are so frequently sought for top posts of the civil service. But few countries would claim that access to higher learning is truly equal for youth of every economic and social station. As a rule, the civil service tends to have a middle-class complexion, and the higher ranks, by and large, are weighted toward the upper middle of that class. Except for societies with unusual social mobility, the rise from the bottom of the social pyramid to the top is not accomplished in a lifetime. In most European countries, generally speaking, it is a matter of two or three generations. The educational system is not a readily accessible ladder; rather, it reinforces social division. In France, for example, in the graphic phrase of Raymond Cayol, who frequently cried out about it in parliament, the student body is the "inverted image" of the population, two-thirds of the active population providing one-ninth of the students and the other third providing eight-ninths. But France is not an exceptional case.

Where social divisions are relatively permanent, the civil service is likely to draw criticism when its top cadre shows a very homogeneous outlook. However he may strive for scientific detachment, the career man cannot expect to appear to all in the shining armor of rationality. Hostile political parties or social groupings may respect the basic integrity of the civil servant and yet be totally unimpressed by his intellectual approach. To his embarrassment he may become the object of enthusiastic support from certain quarters precisely because he appears to be the standard-bearer of the right class orientation.

Political Rationality versus Administrative Rationality

Entirely apart from differences of background and education, administrative rationality often has little appeal to the political mind, whether in the executive branch or in the legislative body. The political decision-maker, bent upon his aims, is often impatient with dispassionate reasoning, except in small doses. He does not like to face the dreadful array of pertinent facts, especially when he is cast in the role of the special pleader. To him, the civil servant— talking professorially of what the public interest demands but exempt from facing a constituency on election day—may well become an obnoxious figure, with all his stubbornness in making the most of cold facts.

To the very degree, therefore, to which a bureaucracy asserts its institutional rationality, particularly in the face of political choice, the administrative mind may part company with the policy-making mind. This, in turn, can have a weakening effect upon public administration. Exceptional political maturity is required for public opinion and party leaders to welcome the role of the bureaucracy in putting proposed policy to the acid test of cause-and-effect relationships.

Rationality as Constructive Challenge

On all the evidence, however, it cannot be denied that a career service is able to cultivate great self-discipline. The ideology of service can be so firmly rooted as to overcome class bias and unequal responsiveness to the government of the day. As the scholar seeks to identify his personal bias in order to conquer it, so the civil servant can train himself to pay little attention to the whisperings of his preference or predilection. Hence it would be a vast oversimplification to assume that a bureaucracy, especially in its higher ranks, necessarily acts according to the presumed dictates of its social background.

In Spain before the advent of the republic, the artillery officer—then still the military intellectual—was often found among the plotters for reform. Prompted by the same motives, civil servants coming from the peak of the social structure have turned into protagonists of social justice. What matters is how a bureaucracy comes to think, especially at the top. This may be the result of many influences. For one thing, a civil service drawn in its higher ranks from the universities is likely to be affected by the prevailing currents of ideas. This is why Bismarck, during the constitutional conflict in Prussia between king and parliament, found the career men in the more important ministries disgustingly liberal from his point of view. When receptive to the thought of his time, the civil servant has challenged the policy-makers by holding forth necessary choices that otherwise might have been delayed dangerously or not been made at all. In this sense a bureaucracy can both sharpen the sensitivity of government toward issues that must be met and supply a safety valve by putting matters on the national agenda that otherwise might develop explosive power.

THE REQUIREMENT OF RESPONSIBILITY

Control and Responsibility

Despite its massive appearance, large-scale organization is an artificial and delicate structure, which for its effectiveness and even its existence depends on the correlation of many individual wills. Without the reinforcement of rationality in planning, direction, and performance, such a structure could not serve as a framework of co-operative action involving large numbers of men. On superficial examination the essential thing may appear to be imposition of control. But control comes from above; it is an external factor for those to whom it is addressed. Unsupported by acceptance, control is an intrusion, a thing piercing from the outside into the personal sphere, and thus a force to be resented and defeated. In structures as elaborate and hence as rich in opportunities for obstruction as is large-scale organization, control could not accomplish co-ordination in the interplay of human wills. Although control cannot be dispensed with as a convenient regulator, it is bound to operate in a haphazard fashion without well-formed habits of deference sustained by reason. The device for developing, perfecting, and maintaining such deference is responsibility.

Institutional Responsibility

Several meanings of responsibility must be distinguished. Responsibility may be thought of as institutional, public, or personal. The first, institutional responsibility, finds typical expression in the acceptance of orders. It flows directly from man's place in the organization. In a hierarchical structure the idea that the superior's order is to be followed in one's own behavior is as elementary to all participants as the sequence of night and day. Under normal circumstances such response is almost automatic, resting largely on ingrained habit. Obedience to orders is supported by man's collective sense, by the value he attaches to the group. Obedience also endears itself to him for the way it helps him across the hurdles of indecision.

On the side of reason, those within the organization find it easy to acknowledge the logic of somebody's final say. Even when confronted with a disagreeable order, they still acknowledge the merit of institutional responsibility in preventing the organization from dissolving into a mob in which everybody would be a nuisance to everybody else. Furthermore, in the execution of the order there is the compensating satisfaction of being assured of deference on the part of those farther down. We must also recognize the peculiar exultation felt by the participants when the organization performs effectively. Finally, institutional responsibility is a splendid tool for breaking deadlock and stalemate. The order may seem stupid or exacting, and in the end it may lead to nothing; yet peace of mind often follows consent to the dictum that "orders are orders."

Public Responsibility

Institutional responsibility in this sense enlists rationality to give full effect to hierarchy. All within the organization are responsible *to* somebody, and responsible to him *for* something. They must answer for their actions. They must submit to review, inspection, and evaluation. They must learn to act as conscious and unconscious custodians of institutional discipline, which requires them to do as they are told to do. But there is also a broader concept of responsibility. This concept projects responsibility toward the outside, transcending the internal affairs of the organization. For want of a better term, we may call it "public responsibility."

Public responsibility requires devotion to the public interest. It asserts the necessity of providing demonstrable public benefits and of meeting public expectations about the provision of such benefits. The first requirement of public administration is that the bureaucracy recognize its character as an obedient arm of any government lawfully in power. But public responsibility under popular government further includes respect for the rules imposed upon the civil servant by the character of the representative system itself, especially in giving full effect to basic political choices. Public responsibility demands the willing subjection of the bureaucracy to the laws as the general instructions of the representatives of the people. This is a matter of the spirit of the law as well as of the letter. For example, the German civil service, regarding itself as a pillar of the rule of law, has long shown a deep concern for lawful authority, for legality as the basis of administrative action and as a restraint upon administrative discretion. Finally, public responsibility expresses itself in a recognition by the civil servant of the need for rules of professional ethics to indicate what is expected of a servant of the public.

Personal Responsibility

From these observations it will be apparent that the demands of institutional responsibility frequently conflict with the demands of public responsibility. The institutional world with its immediate, pragmatic urgencies may subvert the higher maxims of public responsibility. Bureaucratic power struggles within an agency may be fought to the detriment of the public. Institutional discipline has the sharper claws of enforceable punishment for causes good and bad. By comparison, the public interest is often not directly enforceable.

Fundamentally, a satisfactory reconciliation between institutional and public responsibility can be attained only by reference to a third concept of responsibility. That is the concept of personal responsibility—a responsibility lodged in the civil servant's individual conscience. Personal responsibility will usually work as the critic of institutional responsibility and as the ally of public responsibility. But it obviously makes a great difference whether conditions encourage frequent opportunity for practicing personal responsibility. Where institutional responsibility in the full bloom of its self-sufficiency overwhelms public responsibility as an active force, it ordinarily suppresses personal responsibility at the same time. In turn, where the concept of public responsibility flatly ignores the idea of institutional responsibility, the unity of the organization and thus its basic efficiency may seriously weaken. Where personal responsibility bears little relationship to either institutional responsibility or public responsibility, we might expect considerable organizational anarchy, one concept of responsibility getting in the way of the other.

THE REQUIREMENT OF COMPETENCE

Education—Cost versus Need

Public administration in our day cannot do without trained personnel. But what is training? How is training to be accomplished? How far do training requirements prescribed for entrance insulate the bureaucracy from the outside world?

It would be entirely possible for government itself to administer or finance a comprehensive training scheme geared to the needs of the public service. An arrangement such as this would conform to the idea that nobody showing promise should be barred for economic reasons from entering the government service—an idea which has been advanced both on grounds of equality and for the good of society. The idea has been treated with particular reverence by spokesmen of democracy, but it has also appealed to rough-and-ready common sense. Not surprisingly, it has found equal support in the Soviet Union's ideology of the classless society. Even in political systems without equalitarian ambitions, such as tsarist Russia, unduly narrow class representation in the bureaucracy has generally been regarded as undesirable.

It is a conspicuous fact, nevertheless, that nowhere has government taken charge of training for the public service to the extent of doing the whole job itself or assuming complete financial responsibility for it. Even where public education is free, including the higher learning, loss of income as a result of study is not compensated for. Hence the limited opportunity for lower-class aspirants is reflected in the middle-class flavor of the modern Western bureaucracy, especially of the higher civil service, and the upper-class air of its counterpart in many of the newly independent nations.

Occupational Structure of the Civil Service

In the Western world public employment has come to mirror in its composition the nation's occupational life. The number of occupations needed by government in the exercise of its diversified functions has continuously increased. For certain occupations, moreover, government is the principal or even sole employer. We may think of forestry in the United States or railroading and communications in continental Europe, not omitting a country as sympathetic toward private enterprise as Switzerland. Most of the occupations needed by government have nothing to do with administration, properly speaking. That is true of a physicist, for instance, doing research work and of a lawyer serving as part of an agency's legal staff. The government's need is met simply by getting qualified physicists, lawyers, and the like. For these groups—in total numbers now a substantial part of the whole public service—government is but one employer and not always an attractive one.

It is quite a different matter to recruit individuals for administrative work in the specific sense. Here the key group is the higher civil service. Generally, it consists of those who, under politically chosen leaders, direct the operations of the departments on the various upper levels of control. It also includes supporting staff charged with the planning of programs, the study of problems, the analysis of progress, the review of performance, and the conduct of other management functions (see pp. 10 ff.).

The importance of the higher civil service springs from the fact that collectively the upper ranks represent the bureaucracy's outlook for most purposes. Although the other service groups often lean toward an unflattering opinion of the men higher up, and although the public may censure the top cadre for lack of common sense or for an ivory-tower attitude, there is no question about the formative influence exerted by the top group upon the bureaucracy as a whole. Indeed, the characteristics of the top group have generally formed the model for the civil service at large.

It would be wrong, nevertheless, to assume that the higher service is one and the same thing in different countries. Even where the practice of career promotion extends far upward toward the political level of responsibility in the administrative system, considerable variety exists from nation to nation in the degree of formal recognition of the top group. When it is given full recognition, the higher service forms a self-contained career within the bureaucracy, separately recruited and ordinarily not entered either from below or from the outside. This sort of a career within the bureaucracy is exemplified in England by the Administrative Class (see pp. 10 ff.). It is exemplified in France by the new category of "civil administrators" and by the traditional category of the functional "great corps," such as the Financial Inspection Service. The German higher civil service has long been a strong career group, numerically larger than the British Administrative Class and without the vertical cleavages brought about by the "great corps" in France.

By contrast, the higher positions in the civil service may have no special identity where they lack formal organization into a distinct career group. Then they will usually be filled by promotion from the ranks, mostly without resort to a special channel of recruitment. One illustration is the Swiss civil service with its almost complete absence of educational entrance requirements, which are frowned upon by a public steeped in equality. Another example is the classified service in the United States. There the aspirant normally moves toward the top from an entrance level rather far down, although modifications in the examination system introduced in recent years have made it easier for young men and women from the colleges and the universities to enter the federal service at the bottom of the middle grades.

Academic Preparation

Not surprisingly, in countries where the higher civil service is constituted as a specific group, the entrance level of this group generally is reached from the higher learning. The top positions are occupied by the "university man." But what is the desirable course of academic preparation? The answer common to each civil service system is that the study program should aim to produce a good public servant. The question of which study program is best has been answered differently by different nations.

The Germans, with their concern for holding public administration to legally defined authority, have favored the study of law, with social science trimmings, especially from political science, economics, and history. The British have favored a program suitable to a gentleman with a taste for scholarship. British study is therefore intended to be an intellectual venture rather than a practical preparation, with considerable leeway granted for high attainment in any chosen field of knowledge. The French, in the main, have relied upon a rather formal type of general education comparatively rigid in its organization and lacking a resourceful approach to contemporary problems. With the foundation of the National School of Administration after World II, however, a promising start has been made in France toward a thoughtfully planned program of advanced study aimed at producing a first-rate brand of newcomers to the higher service.

In the absence of a formally constituted higher service, the "university man" usually neither stands out as a standard commodity nor functions as the keeper of the departmental mind. In Switzerland, for example, where educational requirements are held to a minimum, recruitment for administrative work draws more on the technical and commercial schools than on the universities. In the United States, where the idea of a higher career group has not taken root either, the influx into the federal service of young men and women from the institutions of higher learning has increased in recent years, but their placement does not yet put them into any such well-defined category as the Administrative Class in England.

Learning the Ropes

In defiance of the faith that many American entrants put into study programs centered on public administration, it has been suggested that "vocational study" is not a very satisfactory preparation. Speaking as chancellor of the University of Chicago, Robert M. Hutchins argued on the authority of educational theory that, to become a civil servant, one should start being a civil servant. Behind this advice to learn by doing and to get better with seasoning is an acknowledgment of the limitations faced by colleges and universities in trying to turn out practitioners of public administration. As a matter of fact, the whole issue of whether public administration can be taught academically has been the object of recent lively debate in England—a debate that ended inconclusively. Even if we have no doubt that public administration represents a field of knowledge in need of attention at the universities, the question of what to teach —and also when and how—is not easily answered. The practical world of public administration is so complex that no study program can provide a reasonable expectation of success in the government service when it comes to the test of application. All we can hope for is good minds.

We may circumvent the dilemma of training by using practice as a teacher, by introducing the novice into the mysteries of the administrative environment after his entrance into the service. Formal or informal, there is great advantage in a properly organized probationary service. A probationary period is often justified on the premise that there must be an easy means of getting rid of obvious or likely failures right away. But a probationary service may also be used as a sort of apprenticeship if carried on for a sufficiently prolonged period. The candidate is given tutorial guidance by his supervisors. He is shifted about in a set sequence of tours of duty to become acquainted with various administrative activities at different places, including field offices. This is the time-honored German formula. Candidates for the higher service spend about three years in the probationary service, which is roughly the equivalent of the time they have devoted previously to university study. Part of the program of the new National School of Administration in France represents an elaboration of the same idea. There the successive duty stations may even include a period of time spent in training status with industry, possibly right at the assembly line. A proposal to add this feature to the probationary service was discussed in Germany before World War I, but nothing came of it.

In countries where the probationary service is not used as a means of making newcomers familiar with the practical phases of public administration, the only alternative is in-service training. Actually, this alternative is usually far less adequate. In-service training is not easily worked into a government-wide pattern because it is too much enmeshed in departmental self-interest and discretion. Moreover, budgetary stringencies and the pressure of work in the departments, as a rule, do not dispose them favorably toward a full-fledged in-service training program. In most instances a few special courses make up the whole effort, but there are exceptions. In Switzerland, for example, a showpiece of in-service training is found in the customs service, which uses its own service schools. In the United States comparable in-service training programs have been organized by the Federal Bureau of Investigation and the Internal Revenue Service, to name but two. For policy officials as well as top civil servants an experimental kind of conference program is being administered, with the encouragement of federal authorities, by the Brookings Institution in Washington.

Gaining Experience

Regardless of the probationary system or lack of one, full training has been achieved only when the apprentice has learned to be productive in the institutional context, when he knows how things are done. But the real benefit of experience does not come from anything other than personal experience. We may listen with great advantage to what a veteran of the public service has to say about *his* experience; and yet, compared with the listener's own experience, this is rather like reading a book.

The administrative activities that make up a normal day of work are sustained for the most part by experience. Experience tells the individual what to do, how and in what order to do it, and which other individuals to draw into the handling of particular matters. This is true in large-scale organizations to a greater extent than elsewhere. The reason lies in part in the elaborate division of labor, which requires conscious assimilation. Another part of the reason is the fact that the success of the entire organization is dependent on each individual's doing exactly what he is expected to do without improvisations. Despite the pile of written instructions that large-scale organization requires in order to live, the controlling factor in day-by-day performance is the participant's almost subconscious familiarity with the things under his nose. If this familiarity were suddenly destroyed, the organization would immediately come to a halt. Experience keeps the institutional capital of learning and knowing advantageously invested for good and steady returns.

The stock of experience consists of many things. There is, first of all, the practical knowledge of procedure, usage, and routine. Control and accountability, as policemen of responsibility, have showered the civil servant with regulations going into the most minute detail. On the other hand, as with parliamentary procedure, the expert at the game is often able to achieve miracles by adroit maneuvering. Thus there is strong incentive to keep in mind how all the little wheels turn. To do so is both a rule of personal safety and the mark of the "smooth operator" who knows how to cut corners. But the working knowledge that comes with experience also extends to the human environment. How to approach particular superiors—and sometimes also particular subordinates—can be a decisive thing in "getting action."

Of still greater importance, especially in the higher positions, is a sharing of the institutional memory of the department—what was done when, way back, and for what reasons. A man who has seen many files and can find his way back quickly to the specific thing he remembers becomes an asset to his colleagues and the organization at large. He will be able to tell on short notice how a particular proposal for changes in policy or procedure would stand up to the test of precedent and the past thinking of the department. On this

score, it is not difficult to see why seniority, as a measure of experience, carries so much weight in promotions—quite apart from the
fact that the seniority rule is favored by institutional inertia.

Experience provides access to the institutional memory on still
other points. Weathering high winds on previous occasions conditions the veteran in such delicate matters as how to deal with the
problems of changing political control, legislative and executive. No
less troublesome, in many instances, is the succession in the departmental leadership without party change. A new man at the helm
may have quite different predispositions even though he is of the
same party. Again, experience may teach how to give coherent application to the ethics of public service amid the exigencies of
pragmatic choice that constantly arise in the administrative environment. No organization can afford to squander the assets of experience. There is nothing new about that. Leonard D. White. in his
great history of administration in the government of the United
States, has shown recently how frequently the chief clerks in the
federal departments survived the political risks of the Jacksonian
period simply because they could not be spared.

THE REQUIREMENT OF CONTINUITY

Importance of Status

To attract and retain promising aspirants, to build up the level of
competence, to husband the accumulating practical experience, to
cultivate a sense of responsibility—for these purposes the bureaucracy must be more than a place for making a living, to be relinquished for a better place whenever opportunity beckons. There
must be considerable stability of employment. Stability increases as
the bureaucracy is put on a career basis. Where admission to the
bureaucracy is governed by standards of qualification, under the
so-called merit principle, government employment absorbs into
itself elements of the career concept. The more this is so, the greater
the bureaucracy's gain in status. It is on the basis of its status that
the civil service develops its capacity for functional continuity, for
carrying on its administrative tasks without interruption, for operating as an establishment having institutional "permanence."

Status may be a social thing, indicating a reasonably fixed position
in the informal social rating recorded by public opinion. Usually,
however, the meaning is more specific, relating to safeguards of
existence, to the institutional status of the civil service, and thus
also to the status of the individual civil servant. In this more specific
sense, status is expressed in law, not solely in social esteem. To be

sure, a purely legal status without social affirmation may not amount to much. Conversely, social prestige may boost a feeble legal status. Normally, however, legal status, especially when it reflects social rating, has the effect of a strong reinforcement. Such interplay can be observed also in the definition of the status of the bureaucracy.

Status Concepts

Definitions of legal status naturally vary as much among different countries as does the pattern of training. Switzerland is perhaps the example of the most gingerly expression of civil service status. There the bureaucracy is "elected" every three years by executive action—that is, by passing out a paper to each civil servant to this effect. Nominally, therefore, civil servants have no tenure, as the term is commonly understood. Of course failure to be "re-elected" seldom happens to a civil servant, but it does happen in some instances despite the availability of statutory authority to make dismissals for cause at any other time. The Swiss bureaucracy, however, does not lack the characteristics of a career service in institutional stability. Specifically, this comes to light in the spirit in which safeguards against arbitrary enforcement of discipline are observed. It is also evident in the arrangements for joint consideration by government representatives and civil service representatives of the problems affecting public employment. Perhaps the best proof is found in the very high frequency, even on touchy issues, of unanimous recommendations made by these joint bodies.

Although the Swiss approach gives the impression of a backhanded concession of status to the civil service, it is nonetheless written out as a statutory arrangement in a civil service act. By contrast, the British alternative is one of executive initiative. The career service has evolved almost entirely under crown auspices, and the formalization of its status occurred in orders-in-council and supplementary regulations. In other words, the British career man has little to stand on should he want the assurance of statutory clauses.

At first glance this would seem to make a very wobbly structure, but the exact opposite is true. The status of the civil service in England is like a foundation of rock. The explanation lies perhaps for the most part in the high degree of public appreciation of the guaranties that allow the bureaucracy to function with greatest effectiveness. Parliament and the civil service have long stood in a complementary relationship. In addition, the British constitutional spirit has fostered great respect for the machinery of government as the visible side of the operating constitution.

As one might expect, in reliance on statutory provisions Germany occupies a place almost at the opposite end of the scale. There the status of the bureaucracy as a lifetime career is articulated in civil service legislation amplified by an extensive case law of the independent disciplinary courts. But this legal status is not without a strong counterpart in social status. It has proved so strong, indeed, that modifications of the accepted civil service pattern launched by the occupation authorities at the end of World War II went out the window as soon as the external pressure ended.

No less significant as an illustration of the interrelations of social and legal status is the experience of France. Critics once blamed French administrative inadequacies and the conduct of the bureaucracy on the absence of a comprehensive civil service act. Yet, despite the passage of a "general statute" after World War II, the familiar mold of French public administration has not conspicuously changed, except for the bolstering of its spirit by the new-style "civil administrators" coming from the National School of Administration.

For effectiveness of performance, the strength and the stability that status gives the civil service are indispensable factors. But it is also true that the bureaucracy can be unduly preoccupied with the legal foundations of its existence. Its own conduct as an agency of the public interest is the best guaranty of its status—which it cherishes as an institutional basis and as source of its functional identity in the structure of modern government.

CHAPTER 4

TYPES OF BUREAUCRACIES

As shown in the preceding chapter, status is a source of strength for the bureaucracy in three ways: as a reflection of public esteem, as a legal foundation, and as a basis for a sense of identity. Such institutional self-identification gives to the bureaucracy a clearer view of its role in the public life of the nation. That role separates the bureaucracy from the forces that compete with one another in the contest for political control and thus also separates it from private enterprise—that is, the profit system. In this perspective the agents of politics and the agents of administration are seen to be in a necessary interplay, which ideally favors both more effective policy-making and more responsible administration, as Gaetano Mosca explained in the nineteenth century (see p. 18).

But bureaucracy, despite its homogeneity, is also shaped by varying external influences, political, social, and economic. Still more important may be cultural influences, such as the German devotion to order and orderliness and the American love of mechanical devices. Each bureaucracy is thus likely to see itself as a type and to behave accordingly. In broader outline it is possible to distinguish at least several types of bureaucracies, depending on the predominance of certain characteristics. Four types will be sketched here: the guardian bureaucracy, the caste bureaucracy, the patronage bureaucracy, and the merit bureaucracy.

In describing "types," we must bear in mind that the thing called type is not encountered in reality. "Type" is at once an abstraction and a generalization, a magic box into which we can throw things that look alike and have them come out again as a single composite. Moreover, by distinguishing types of bureaucracies, we are bound to exaggerate unities. Each type is usually most clearly expressed at the top level of the bureaucracy. Although the influence of the higher service extends downward to the base of the pyramid, more and more of the day's interest shifts in the lower ranges toward routine work which is relatively unaffected by the institutional doctrine embraced by the top cadre.

THE GUARDIAN BUREAUCRACY

Dedication to the Common Good

Although today the British civil service is widely admired as a prototype peculiarly well adapted to the needs of representative government, it looked like a very outlandish thing to many influential Englishmen a hundred years ago, despite Macaulay's eloquent advocacy (see pp. 10–11). Criticism mounted when in 1855 the public was given access to the epoch-making report on civil service reform linked to the names of Sir Stafford Northcote and Sir Charles Trevelyan, Macaulay's brother-in-law. The London *Economist* said icily of the principal proposals: "They have all the air of having been borrowed, cut and dried, from Berlin or Pekin."

Allusion to the administrative models of Prussia and China must have aroused the contemporary reader; but, with some juggling of the time factor, the matching would make good sense. In some respects there was a remarkable kinship between the Chinese bureaucracy up to the advent of the Sung period (A.D. 960) and the developing civil service of Brandenburg-Prussia during the hundred years following the ascent to the throne (1640) of Frederick William, the Great Elector, grandfather of King Frederick William I (see p. 14). These two examples could be picked to illustrate a type perhaps best called the guardian bureaucracy.

What is a guardian bureaucracy? Plato's guardians were not simply meant to go about doing things as directed. More important was their capacity for personifying in their actions the essence of the public interest. In this sense they were meant to be custodians of the ideas and assumptions about justice and welfare that held together the city-state—the political myth, as Plato saw it, which was the ultimate foundation of the community. The guardians were thus to serve as the physical representation of the approved ideology and as its devoted instruments too. Yet in the Platonic scheme qualification for guardianship was not supposed to be one of the mysteries of divinely guided revelation. On the contrary, Plato sought to put selection for guardianship on a rational basis by systematic utilization of a carefully planned course of education.

The Living Example

Whether or not during the preceding century the teachings of Confucius had somehow come westward to influence Plato, the concept of government reflected in the Confucian tradition of ancient China shows a remarkable resemblance to the Platonic blueprint. Chinese government did have certain administrative functions— mainly the purchase and storage of crops in the interest of an "ever-normal granary," the regulation of prices as a way of defining fair profit, and the planning and execution of public works. Fundamentally, however, government was not a regulatory agency. The effect of regulation was achieved by the pervasive force of a body of social doctrine, essentially the Confucian teachings as a comprehensive code of righteous conduct. Although criminals were punished, primary reliance in enforcing this code of righteous conduct was placed on education, in the sense both of schooling and of filial attention to paternal instruction.

The social system of ancient China, in consequence, made it the first duty of each official to demonstrate the exemplary life. This was a matter of knowledge rather than of judgment. Hence the bureaucracy was a scholastic officialdom trained in right conduct according to the classics. The same basic responsibility was supposed to rest on the highest organ of government, the emperor.

In seeking to gain for public office the best men available, the first Han emperors (206 B.C.–A.D. 25) made it a practice to use their governors as purveyors of talent. The governors sent candidates to the capital, where they would be questioned by the emperor and awarded with posts according to their merit. Beginning with the Sui period (A.D. 581–618), a system of civil service examinations came to replace the palace interview. These public examinations, held at regular intervals, became increasingly elaborate in the T'ang period (A.D. 618–907), China's great age of administrative sophistication. Quite in keeping with the accepted view of the highest duty of the official, the examinations were not geared to administrative needs. On the contrary, especially for the more important positions, they gave great weight to the classics as a guide of conduct and to rigid literary standards in dealing with the old texts. Although policy questions were not absent from the examinations of the T'ang period, as time went on the entire system developed highly formalistic features and degenerated into stupendous memorizing stunts. Such excesses, however, do not invalidate the underlying concept—

that is, to achieve an understanding of the common good by learning. This concept is well expressed in the following passage from *Li Chi,* one of the Confucian texts:

An educated man, familiar with both the appropriate steps toward the attainment of learning and the standards of sound discrimination, is capable of insight. Having acquired insight he can indeed be a teacher. When he can be a teacher, he is qualified for high government office. Being qualified for high government office he is able to be the ruler. Hence it is from the teacher that one learns to be a ruler, and the choice of a teacher must be considered of greatest importance. As it is said in the Record, "The three kings and the four dynasties were what they were by their teachers."

With its monopoly of classical learning as the source of rules of conduct, civic and official, the Chinese bureaucracy was bound to put great emphasis on rank. To be right in matters of conduct, after all, was not determined by observable results or the application of procedures intelligible to the common man. The basis of being right was scholastic mastery of voluminous writings. The decisive point was not *what* was said about a particular point of conduct but *who* said so. The more elevated the place from which the pronouncement came, the more weight it carried. Wisdom, authority, and seniority were therefore all linked with one another by order of rank. Those of low rank, as in the comparable case of a hierarchy of ecclesiastical offices, actually honored themselves by an unwaveringly deferential attitude toward those of higher rank.

Several conclusions emerge about this kind of guardian bureaucracy built around the political myth as the matrix of ideas supporting the system of government. In the first place, such a bureaucracy can develop and retain great moral fortitude because its ultimate guide is an unalterable body of doctrine untouched by the fickle winds of current preference. In following this guide, the officialdom is capable of exerting considerable influence upon the exercise of power, even the ruler's power, by insisting on the subjugation of power under righteousness.

On the other hand, a public service without significant responsibilities for public management, a bureaucracy dedicated to the teachings of an increasingly distant past, is apt to idolize obsolete practices. It is likely to become traditionalistic, conservative, ceremonial, and literal—all, indeed, characteristics of the Chinese scholastic bureaucracy. The result was an aloofness from the affairs of the common man and the political problems of the day. Correspondingly, in the long run the officialdom tended to huddle under the cloak of the emperor. The final step was taken by the philosophers of the Sung period, who raised the emperor, by adroit interpolation of the Confucian teachings, to an unchallengeable position of supremacy. According to the new version, the emperor could do no wrong.

The Creed of Unity

In accomplishment and in failure alike, the officialdom of ancient China stands out as a guardian bureaucracy committed to the preservation of the accepted ideology—the political myth of the entire society. The rising civil service of Brandenburg-Prussia during the second half of the seventeenth century and the opening decades of the next was a guardian bureaucracy pledged to the cause of the new state. During this period the crown succeeded in making Brandenburg (after 1701 the kingdom of Prussia) a military power of the first order and a model of effective administration. The new state was brought into being by the superimposition of both centralized machinery of government and the idea of the common good upon a geographically scattered realm previously split apart by local and feudal self-interest.

In undertaking this task, the Great Elector had to gain recognition of Brandenburg's growing strength from the great powers of that era, and, equally necessary, he had to overwhelm his domestic opponents by breaking their stranglehold upon public policy. The first aim he accomplished by raising and training a military establishment which in 1675 at Fehrbellin met the test by defeating Sweden's magnificent army. The second goal required the displacement of the estates—the powerful organs of consent, dominated by the nobility, which shared in the exercise of political power. To reach around the estates and to finance the army, the Great Elector erected a unified administrative system intrusted to men who gave promise of competence as well as of allegiance to the monarchy.

With the internal struggle for control at its height, the men the state needed could not be drawn from the aristocracy, the hostile camp. The new public service thus became an institution of the middle class, the ally of the crown. In point of view, the bureaucracy came to stand for the unifying and equalizing influence of the state. Like the Great Elector, his civil servants bore down upon the defenders of privilege and obstruction. One of the most important factors in this development was the public spirit shown by the ruler himself. He personally drilled into his princelings the Latin maxim that government obliged the ruler to promote the common good and to ignore his personal advantage. This was the rule the Great Elector demonstrated in his own example, and he expected his civil servants to observe it too.

The Great Elector's grandson, Frederick William I, the second king of Prussia, had the same kind of rational and disciplined mind and the same kind of consuming drive. Although often rough-handed and stubborn, he was a man with a keen eye for administration. He gave final form to the machinery of government. Brandenburg's first complete budget had been brought together as early as 1689, within a year of the Great Elector's death; but Frederick William I found much still to be done, and he gave personal attention to the conduct of public administration, dictating many of the instructions himself. He also perfected the examination system.

The instructions of 1722, further elaborated in 1748, laid down specific requirements for the top ranks of the civil service. To qualify for an extensive probationary service, candidates were expected to get a thorough grooming in the cameralistic sciences at the universities—administration, political economy, agriculture, and forestry. Appointments hinged on the outcome of practical as well as theoretical examinations. Above all, the king was wary of allowing the nobility a foothold in the civil service. As he once wrote scathingly on the margin of a petition, he wanted the "best heads," but the sons of the aristocracy might apply for judicial office together with the "dumbbells" (die dummen Deuffel). This hostility, however, subsided under his son, Frederick the Great, who fought his wars with an army officered largely by the nobility.

Sprouting from the meager soil of the "Holy Roman Empire's biggest sandbox," as Brandenburg had been described condescendingly, her guardian bureaucracy shared with the monarchy the middle-class virtues of industry, economy, and pragmatism. If the state had a "temperament" of its own, as Frederick the Great contended it had, that temperament was one of frugality, self-denial, duty, and hard work. The monarchy considered itself conscripted for public service, thus making its civil servants peers to the king. Indeed, between 1640 and Frederick's death in 1786, three of the four rulers had been master administrators who at the same time had excelled in "impartial impersonality," in Ernest Barker's phrase.

The guardian bureaucracy of Brandenburg-Prussia became the king's partner in the victorious cause of "enlightened monarchy." At times the light was dimmed by outbursts of naked absolutism, but there was genuine devotion to the "republic," as Frederick William I had liked to call his state, in admiration for Cicero. But res publica was what the king said it was. In their concept of duty, therefore, the civil servants were as ready to determine the needs of the public, independent of what the public might say, as they were unyielding in the face of special interest. Precisely because of their responsiveness to the goals of the monarchy and the program of the state, they were necessarily unresponsive to such public sentiment as happened to run counter to the official course. Standing on the side of the king and through him serving the people, Prussia's guardian bureaucracy of this early period took pride in being inflexible as well as incorruptible in its mission, authoritarian as well as benevolent in its relations with the public, and unimpressed by outside criticism.

THE CASTE BUREAUCRACY

The Class Base

Although not made for popular rule, the guardian bureaucracy is distinguished by great strength. That strength comes from a creed of service which is alive within the bureaucracy and adamant to external pressures or enticements. By comparison, the caste bureaucracy has nothing to commend it. Whereas the guardian bureaucracy is brought forth in the wake of great movements of reform or redemption, the caste bureaucracy arises from the class connection of those in the controlling positions.

This tie with a particular class may be intentional, so as to have the "right men" at the helm, as in oligarchical political systems. Or it may be coincidental, as a half-deplored and half-accepted result of linking the qualifications for the higher posts with arrangements that amount to class preference. Such a link with the upper-income levels results from requiring expensive education of the appointees. When a society is so unified that it can deliberately promote a caste bureaucracy, public opinion will naturally support the logic of the leadership formula expressed in the composition of the bureaucracy. Then criticism will be brushed off as "irresponsible." On the other hand, when value judgments about the desirable kind of leadership differ widely within the society, a bureaucracy weighted toward a particular social group will be under attack for its caste features.

For more than two centuries the general trend has been toward making academic study an entrance condition in the recruitment of the upper service groups. As a result, the more highly developed a bureaucracy is in its intellectual resources, the greater the likelihood that it displays caste or class aspects in varying degrees. In addition, when the upper class is favored in the key positions, it is probable that a caste system will develop throughout the civil service. Social lines will be drawn between service groups, perhaps even to the point that rules will tell who speaks to whom. On the other hand, a modifying influence is exerted by the extent to which acknowledged competence leads to a rise within the service across the boundaries drawn for particular service groups. It does not follow, however, that mobility within the bureaucracy on the basis of personal accomplishments always works as an antidote to caste mentality. Ordinarily the "climber" can be expected to conform to the mentality prevailing higher up.

In all of this, however, it makes a big difference how far public opinion in a given society is accustomed to stretch the concept of the middle class as the class of "almost everybody." The more that concept is widened, the more it obscures class divisions. In most European countries the effect of a politically oriented labor movement has generally promoted the "class-conscious proletariat." The result is a feeling of social exposure in the middle class itself.

Caste Characteristics under Political Attack

The esteem accorded to popular rule in the contemporary Western world prompts the caste bureaucracy as a type to deny itself. It exists covertly. Being a reflection of social fact rather than of acknowledged purpose, it exists despite all condemnation. The degree of its actual presence would be a matter of detailed analysis in each national setting. Where that presence has become a subject of public debate, the occasion was furnished mostly by larger political battles, which caused the limelight to turn upon the metamorphoses that occur in every society.

The German civil service, for instance, came to look more like a caste bureaucracy about the turn of the last century than at any other time. But this appearance had much to do with the unhealthy contractive tendencies in German society that accompanied the steady political rise of organized labor. Irrespective of period, however, the foreign observer has always been amused by the way Germans use official titles as family credit cards. "Certainly, *Frau Oberverwaltungsinspektor*," says the man in the store. A still closer approximation of the caste bureaucracy was represented in the behavior of the higher service in France well toward the middle of our century. Here, again, the public service was but a mirror of the social structure. The greater stratification of French society; the social distinctions recognized by French mores despite the strong sense of political equality; the class spirit of the secondary schools —all these had a marked effect. Each had a share in preserving the profile of the ranking element of the bureaucracy as one of the heirs to the authoritarian half of France's political tradition. This awkward insulation, in turn, gave special incentive to the aggressive unionism of the rank-and-file service groups. In Great Britain, too, with the ascendancy of the Labor party during the same period, a great deal was made of the caste spirit among the higher civil servants. Were they not the natural partisans of the forces that tried to hold things to the status quo? In this instance political generalization for partisan ends probably outran concrete evidence. But the early predominance of the Oxford or Cambridge man in the Administrative Class furnished a fine target for those rising spokesmen of the left who thought in terms of class-consciousness.

The Ideal of Classlessness

The middle-class element that usually became identified with the top structure of the civil service had, however, certain redeeming traits. Perhaps more than other social groups would have been disposed to do, it showed sensitivity to the implications of its role in government. It was generally closer to the professions than to the commercial, industrial, and financial upper crust. No less pertinent, the older bureaucracies came to draw a considerable portion of their recruits from civil service families, with sons often entering a higher service group than their fathers. As one illustration, in the years after World War II more than 40 per cent of the students at the new National School of Administration were following their fathers into the French public service.

Class affiliation has come to be consciously underplayed and class administration to be viewed as a dangerous blunder, if not as a mortal sin against the spirit of service. As class lines grew sharper throughout the social order, it was a natural reaction for the upper groups of the bureaucracy to disengage themselves consciously as far as possible from their own class preferences. This took the form of a vigorous affirmation of the concept of neutrality—political, economic, and social. It is a remarkable fact that at the middle of the twentieth century none of the Western bureaucracies, especially with regard to the younger generation of "university men," is readily put down for its class position.

The Roman "Welfare State"

An early example of the caste bureaucracy can be found in the history of the Roman Empire during the century after Diocletian. The last emperor to turn upon the Christians, this brutal Illyrian was also a forceful reformer of government. Ironically, the legal, fiscal, and administrative reforms he introduced between 284 and 304 enabled the Christian empire after him to live on. But his successors clung to the shadow rather than the substance. Eventually, an all-pervading public status system pulled down the entire economy.

At first only the officialdom was affected by the spirit of caste. A precisely defined separation of functions degenerated into an extravagant scheme of ranks and titles, until in the end a vastly enlarged bureaucracy spent much of its time inventing and enforcing minute distinctions in official standing. The malady next spread among the citizens, who substituted titles and status for a more venturesome approach to economic and social security. As time passed, the conversion of private enterprise to public function extended across the entire body of society. Honorific status proved to be an impoverishing burden because each title, in an ever wider range of fine distinctions, carried an increasing load of public duty. Finally, a thoroughly bureaucratized economic order collapsed under its own weight.

Japanese Administration under the Meiji Constitution

For a modern illustration of the caste bureaucracy, we may turn to imperial Japan. The Japanese bureaucracy was the offspring of a marriage of convenience between the Prussian concept of civil service and the oriental idea of power. The impulse had come from the strong-willed Meiji emperor who pushed Japan toward Western ways in the closing quarter of the nineteenth century. Prince Ito, as imperial emissary and surveyor of Western models, had soon satisfied himself that the United States had nothing suitable to offer. But he was greatly impressed by what he saw in imperial Germany and by the realistic quality of Bismarck's congenial advice. The final outcome was Japan's constitution of 1889, together with a Western judicial system and a civil service structure designed along Prussian lines.

The zest for duty was something Japan did not need to import, and in the fierce single-mindedness of public purpose her civil servants had no rival. But in adopting German administrative ways, including the idea that the key to authority is law, some ingenious improvising was necessary to allow superior official wisdom to step across the legal fence whenever that was deemed desirable. Administration under law was accepted in a distinctly formal sense, in cautious avoidance of the restraining implications of the rule of law which was alive in the German concept.

For that matter, deference to form was economy in learning. Essence is not so easily grasped. When Japan was still a half-barbarian nation on the fringe of China's one-world civilization, so rich in intellectual and scientific achievements, the logic and the splendor of the T'ang bureaucracy (see pp. 56 ff.) had stirred the Japanese mind to similar form-conscious imitation. To both the T'ang and the Prussian models, however, Japan contributed her own raw zeal for putting the harness of authority on the back of the people. At first the civil service operated as a guardian bureaucracy at the beck and call of a reform-minded crown. When in the course of time the passion for public betterment began to subside, the caste bureaucracy developed as a natural successor to the guardian bureaucracy.

The social, economic, and political characteristics of Japan's caste bureaucracy were partly affected by the pattern of recruitment. The normal channel of admission to the higher service was through study at the law faculty of the Imperial University in Tokyo. Under such auspices, candidates had the best chance of passing the stiff entrance examinations, in which constitutional and administrative law greatly overshadowed social science subjects, especially public administration. Because competition was sharp, those who succeeded were usually young men with keen minds; but the social base was narrow, for most of the candidates came from well-to-do families in the urban centers.

As a group, moreover, Japan's upper administrative cadre was put on the defensive in the course of the national development. Like the business and other white-collar groups, the bureaucracy felt insecure, squeezed on the one side by agrarian resentment and on the other by the superpatriotism of the military. Apart from a good position in private management, the most appealing escape was upward into the dignity of the elder statesman. A top man, remembered at the end of his career for faithful service, could hope for a seat in the House of Peers. Holding tenuously to an official status of considerable prestige and looking forward to the reward of membership in an aristocratic assembly, the higher civil servant was induced to cultivate his self-esteem and to cast his lot with those who exerted the strongest political influence. He was happy to look up—and proud to look down.

A worshiper of formal authority, the Japanese career man did not mind prostrating himself in the face of political strength. When he did, he had few witnesses, for his official world was not under the eyes of the public. Indeed, the caste character of the bureaucracy showed itself very clearly in the degree to which the conduct of public administration was guarded from outside view, as if it were a black art. Each department was adroit in withdrawing from public scrutiny, in extending its discretionary authority, and in making the methods of administration the secret of the practitioner. Normally, procedures were not committed to writing. They lived in the minds of the officials. This personal knowledge about the ways of office work added to the bureaucracy's standing, making officials less replaceable. Small wonder that the spine of all administration was precedent, and precedent was rigid because of its authoritarian basis and because rules committed to memory are harder to change. In general, therefore, the conduct of public administration was antiquarian, formalistic, and heavy-handed. The citizen was reduced to a mere object of an enveloping kind of administrative benevolence. Needless to say, there was no effective public control over administrative agencies, especially over the broad flow of discretionary decisions.

This example suggests that the caste bureaucracy is intimidated by its own sense of insecurity. As a result, it is constantly in search of flank protection by strong political allies, whose handmaiden it tends to become. But it is likely to turn into a burden to the regime whose arm it fancies itself to be.

THE PATRONAGE BUREAUCRACY

Patronage as a Means of Political Control

In both Great Britain and the United States the campaign for a better civil service during the second half of the nineteenth century gained its momentum from a growing understanding of the importance of public administration. Statesmen learned that government would be unable to meet its responsibilities if administrative action remained enfeebled by the use of public appointment as a personal favor or political reward—that is, for patronage.

Despite the aspersions cast upon it, the principle of patronage in the filling of public offices has had a great past. Politically, its logic has been clearly seen and freely acted upon since the earliest times. Winning control, obviously, could be a very temporary thing unless it was accompanied by steps to take hold of the machinery of government. The simplest way of doing that was to pack the points of effective authority with partisans. Moreover, in Great Britain such vital developments as the emergence of the prime minister's position face to face with the House of Commons and the beginning of the modern party system were linked with the employment of patronage. Similarly, in the United States the history of the patronage principle cannot be divorced from the rise of democratic government. When President Andrew Jackson ringingly asserted the common man's capacity for public office, he had two ends in mind. He wanted to end all bureaucracy by initiating a people's bureaucracy. He also sought to get rid of an intrenched officialdom thoroughly unsympathetic to the new ways.

A Rational View of Patronage

The excesses of the Jacksonian spoils system have been portrayed so colorfully by the spokesmen for civil service reform that today the patronage bureaucracy is thoroughly discredited in the United States. It is for this reason rewarding to read again what a distinguished British journal had to say a hundred years ago in favor of a refurbished patronage bureaucracy. As part of its chilly evaluation of the Trevelyan-Northcote report (see p. 54), the London *Economist* set forth its own, "better" alternatives. The first of two articles entitled "Reform of the Civil Service" (March 3 and 17, 1855) gave a summary of the reasons why civil service reform was essential:

> All agree that numbers do find entrance into the Civil Service who, from one cause or another, are unfit for the performance of their functions; that the public suffers in consequence, either from work being ill-done, slowly done, not done at all, or done by others than those paid for doing it; and that some test or probationary examination, more effectual than any now existing, is desirable for the exclusion of absolute incapacity or unfitness on the threshold. All admit that some mode of proportioning reward to services and of making promotion proceed according to merit—*if any mode could be devised that would work, or would be self-acting*—would be most desirable; since it is generally conceded that the cases in which talent or diligence secures rapid promotion or indolence or incapacity prevents it, are deplorably rare; and that in order to avoid the Scylla of promotion by favour, we have fallen upon the Charybdis of promotion by seniority. All, or nearly all admit finally, that—from one cause or another, from the absence of high prizes, the lack of inducements, honorary or pecuniary, or the probability that high endowments will lead to high advancement—the Civil Service does not attract to itself either the best intellect, the greatest energy, or the most unquestioned worth, of the nation.

Having thus persuaded itself that reform was "urgently needed," the *Economist* proposed in the second article "two simple regulations" as a proper remedy—a qualifying entrance examination and promotion by merit. The first of these was explained as the establishment of an examination—*not competitive but absolute*—of the qualifications of every individual nominated to a clerkship in any department of the Civil Service. Something of this kind now exists in what are called the non-political departments—as that of the Inland Revenue, for example. We would extend it to all. It will not interfere with the existing system of patronage one iota beyond what simple justice and a regard for the public interest imperatively demand. We do not propose to do away with the power, wherever vested, of "nominating" any young man to any department. We merely propose that the nominee shall, before he is actually appointed, undergo such an investigation into his capacities and acquirements of all kinds, as shall satisfy those entrusted with the duty of instituting this investigation, that he is duly qualified to perform the functions of the post to which it is proposed to appoint him. We do not require that he shall be the *best qualified* young man who could be selected:—this it would be both difficult and needless to ascertain. It will be sufficient if he be fit for his work in capacity, instruction, and character. We need not ask if any one else would be fitter. It is obvious that if he be fit, the public should be satisfied. If he be not fit, it is obvious that it would be a downright fraud upon the public to appoint him.

The whole purpose of patronage is answered by the "nomination" of the protégé of the minister, member, or political partisan, or electioneering friend, who recommends him. No solicitor, however daring, can in these days ask the Secretary of the Treasury to appoint to a clerkship in the Public Service a youth who cannot do a clerk's work. That would be asking him for 100[£] a year *gift* out of the Treasury. The party to be obliged or served comes to the dispenser of patronage, and says: "Give me a clerkship for my son, or the son of my friend, or the nephew of my colleague, or the attorney who has managed my election." The dispenser replies: "I will—here is the nomination. Your protégé has only to pass the Board of Examiners, and his appointment will be formally made out. That is all I could do even for the son of the Prime Minister." And this would be amply sufficient. No solicitor would venture to come back and say: "My protégé is such an ass that the Board have declared him incapable:—give him a place in spite of his incapacity." The Secretary would have his answer ready: "I did all in my power: I conferred the nomination—if your son could not take it up, I cannot help it." The solicitor, too, would have his answer for the disappointed electioneering friend: "I procured the appointment, and am very sorry your son could not pass, but such are the regulations of the Public Service."

As a plea for better public administration which yet would keep England in the grooves of the patronage system, this reasoning was at once ingenious and superficial. For even in such a cleansed version, the patronage bureaucracy would continue to suffer from the defects of political influence and unrelenting pressure to bring down the level of any general qualifying examination. To be sure, patronage had the advantage of assuring the influence of the "right people." It would discourage the development of "a democratical

Civil Service, side by side with an aristocratical Legislature," in the words of an alarmed critic of the principle of open competition in selecting aspirants for the civil service. But placement as a matter of favor, irrespective of the requirement of a qualifying examination, would always hew too close to the line of mediocrity to produce an impressive yield. At the same time the need for individual sponsorship would normally block the great body of men of promise who for want of either political recommendation or an influential "sponsor" would never knock at the gate. Moreover, having begun his career in the civil service with outside help, the recruit would be likely to wear the color of his patron for the length of his official life, thus falling in naturally with the intrigues of nepotism and factionalism. All the while, the very character of the patronage system would be challenged by the nuisance of the qualifying examination, until the examination had been whittled down to nothing.

Luckily for England, the movement for the reform of the civil service had "originated with the Crown," as the *Economist* had to admit; and the crown, despite a highly unfavorable press, proved unwilling to relinquish the initiative. As a result, candidates were eventually (1870) required to pass an examination resembling that for university honors. This procedure displeased the many Englishmen who shared the conviction expressed by the *Economist* that such arrangements were "essentially foreign in their origin, scholastic in their character, and out of harmony with the spirit of our institutions and the peculiarities of our national character." A visionary spirit like John Stuart Mill might speak cheerfully of the democratic implications of these innovations, but their authors were treated as outcasts by the London clubs. The victory won in the end must be credited to the combination of statesmanship and astuteness in the government, fostered by Macaulay in much the same way in which an earlier generation of ministerial officials had been inspired by Bentham.

Jacksonian Democracy

Whereas in England up to the middle of the past century the patronage bureaucracy had served the purposes of an aristocratic social order, the accent in the United States was distinctly on the other side. To the fastidious, Jacksonian democracy looked like mob rule—a scourge sweeping in from the raw West, tearing at the foundations of the Republic, and leveling everything with its vulgarity. Respect for competence in public office far above contemporary British standards had been firmly implanted in the central departments during the presidency of George Washington. When Thomas Jefferson won control from the Federalists, he felt compelled to make cautious replacements so as to assure himself that he would not suffer administrative sabotage from underlings whose loyalty was with the other party. But Jefferson was too deeply steeped in the idea of merit as a condition to government service to slight ability and experience.

By contrast, the Jacksonian surge collided head-on with the established machinery of government. To the partisan point of view, the men in the departments represented an intrenched force eager to crush the common people in the name of a discredited eastern oligarchy. Efficiency and integrity? They were of the wrong kind. Experience in the ways of official work could mean only dexterity in blocking the will of the people or cold self-sufficiency flourishing in the maze of stupid routines.

Long after Jackson, Lincoln Steffens in his exploration of the patronage system never really satisfied himself that popular rule and effective administration could be brought together within a profit economy; but an influential part of the public did not share his doubts. To practical men the patronage bureaucracy was a dangerously defective instrument of government at a time when government was being pressed by industrialization to govern more rather than less. If governmental intervention had to be accepted, if public authority was being made the umpire of the free economy, then it was of utmost importance that government acquire the expert touch. The patronage bureaucracy stood condemned as an anachronism for its lack of technical competence, its slipshod discipline, its concealed rapaciousness, its erratic ways, its partisanship, and its want of spirit.

THE MERIT BUREAUCRACY

Efficiency of Service

As a type, the merit bureaucracy is more sharply set off from the patronage bureaucracy than from either the guardian bureaucracy or the caste bureaucracy. Even when it avows a vague allegiance to the people, the patronage bureaucracy is the product of special influence and is its willing tool. The merit bureaucracy, in contrast, is governed by objective standards, specifically by the principle of admission on the basis of prescribed qualifications as attested by the outcome of a written examination. Thus, by winning an appointment, the successful candidate does not incur a personal debt to any sponsor or patron. He remains a free man in this respect, and in particular he is left free to devote himself to the promotion of the common good without being bridled by special influence as soon as there is a conflict.

But entering the public service on a showing of fitness would not assure the appointee of staying there for any length of time. Certainly he would have little peace of mind if his tenure depended on the approval of particular groups or at least on conduct that would not bring down their wrath. For this reason the merit bureaucracy is usually buttressed by legal guaranties of status or stability, expressed in such concepts as life-appointment and regular position. Typically, the merit bureaucracy also draws compensation on the basis of a salary schedule that is not open to discretionary management. Administrators may not decree from payday to payday the amount earned by each subordinate or how much is to be deducted for various worthy causes, including the local party organization.

Merit Bureaucracy and Guardian Bureaucracy

Patronage bureaucracy and merit bureaucracy are opposites. It is harder, however, to distinguish the merit bureaucracy from the guardian bureaucracy. Although showing high regard for qualifications, the guardian bureaucracy puts self-dedication above formal safeguards of tenure. Self-dedication is the condition as well as the basis of tenure. And, because of the very nature of this dedication, the guardian bureaucracy is bound to keep itself aloof from the idea of alternating popular control. It is able to do wonders under a fixed symbolism of supreme authority, but it loses its verve and its sense of direction in the contest of changing majorities.

The merit bureaucracy, recoiling from guardian pretensions, is able to live by the rules of representative government. This is not to say that the merit bureaucracy will succeed in each instance. It is enough to say that the contemporary concept of the merit bureaucracy puts strong emphasis upon the primacy of political control over the administrative system.

Merit Bureaucracy and Caste Bureaucracy

The border line between merit bureaucracy and caste bureaucracy is even more fluid. The merit principle itself encourages a search for the best candidates throughout the educational system, including the higher learning. The more advanced the educational preparation required, the greater the likelihood that the normal flow of qualified aspirants will come from the economically stronger social groups. As a result, the merit bureaucracy has gained an increasing middle-class flavor in the Western world. The mounting friction between the advancing labor movement and the middle class at the threshold of our century was therefore bound to touch the very foundations of official impartiality. A class point of view intruding from both sides exposed the merit bureaucracy to suspicion and censure on the part of organized labor.

Although the deepening antipathies seemed to foreshadow a full-fledged class conflict, the prospects changed because of the dynamic growth of industrial society and labor's participation in the conduct of government. Perhaps one of the greatest political facts of our era is the resolution of the threatening antagonism between labor and the middle class in the course of a few decades. In the climate of contemporary political criticism the merit bureaucracy has ceased to be a thorn in labor's flesh. On the contrary, it is now usually the upper layers of society that complain.

The development since World War I is striking evidence of the degree to which the merit bureaucracy, far from being ground to pieces by the class struggle, has actually managed to muzzle its own class inclinations in the service of governments of the political left. The far-reaching interpenetration of economically comparable segments of the working population and the middle class has become one of the outstanding features of the maturing industrial society. It therefore seems reasonable to assume a continuing retreat of the caste bureaucracy in the Western world. During the first decade after World War II increasing attention was given in a considerable number of countries to ways and means of strengthening the higher civil service by enlarging the influx of able aspirants from the base of the social pyramid.

The Propaganda of Merit

If in our day the merit bureaucracy has about it an air of self-evident superiority, we are entitled to ask how much merit can be claimed for the merit bureaucracy. In the first place, the concept itself echoes the propaganda of the crusade against the spoilsmen. "Merit rule," "merit principle," "merit system"—these phrases were brought forth to press the attack upon the patronage bureaucracy. The prim, matter-of-fact manner in which proof of the required measure of ability is put down as merit still gives the impression of an argumentative edge.

As might be expected, where the lure of merit was held out to uproot a system of political placement that functioned under the banners of democracy, the reform movement could not fail to draw support also from those whose real target was democracy. Merit, in one sense, was a reflection of the aristocratic principle. Thus not a few who in the United States flocked to the cause of civil service reform in the second half of the nineteenth century did so in protest against "government by the rabble." They felt very much like James Russell Lowell, man of letters and every inch a Cambridge Brahmin, who in his correspondence unburdened himself to a friend on the subject of democracy by surmising that it was a thing "for the benefit of knaves at the cost of fools."

The Pendleton Act of 1883, still the basic law on the federal civil service, seemed a very innocuous beginning, with its limited coverage and its emphasis on practical examinations. But it could also be viewed as a landmark in the counteroffensive against administration by the common man. Of all men, he was thought to be least trustworthy and most thoughtless. In other countries, too, the merit bureaucracy, looking at the turbulence of the democratic process, has been glad to keep a safe distance away from it. In this respect, pride of craftsmanship, sense of rationality, and selection by an objective test of qualification have made for a distinctive point of view within the civil service. Its outlook is characterized by a tactfully concealed disdain for politicians and an apologetically admitted bewilderment at the odd ways of politics.

CHAPTER 5

SAFEGUARDS OF CIVIL SERVICE STATUS

Although the dynamics of politics confront modern government time and again with the need for decisive action, compelling it to adopt new policies or to change old ones, its outstanding characteristic is the continuing conduct of "processes" rather than the making of large choices. Comprehensive choices could be made safely by use of specifically convened councils brought together for each occasion. "Processes"—such as the regulation of private economic activities, the administration of public health, and the provision of unemployment insurance—make it necessary to have offices filled with employees who "handle" things day in and day out on the basis of their special knowledge.

Such "processes," far-flung and diversified, constitute the bulk of the activities of modern government. It was largely because of its superior capacity for keeping these "processes" going, without showing favor or accepting favors, that the merit bureaucracy superseded the patronage bureaucracy. As a means of sustaining the fitness of the merit bureaucracy, a place of occupational security is accorded by government to those whom it employs in the conduct of public administration. This grant of occupational security may be expressed in terms of civil service law, or it may be the product of protective traditions. Each alternative, as a way of safeguarding civil service status, deserves specific consideration. That is the purpose of this chapter.

CIVIL SERVICE LAW

Status Guaranties and Constitutional Principle

Typically, in a very inconstant world the civil servant is (in the British phrase) "permanent" or (in the equally definitive German term) *ein ständiger Beamter*. The logic of this arrangement became evident in our consideration of the essentials of public administration (chap. 3). It was shown to follow from the fact that effective performance of governmental functions is dependent on particular resources—above all, rationality, responsibility, competence, and continuity. To assure the maintenance of these resources—indeed, to make possible their initial development—institutional safeguards are needed as an operating requirement of efficiency.

But the matter goes still further, for it is no less clear that civil service status is a constitutional necessity under conditions of popular rule. Popular rule implies opportunity for popular choice, for peaceable change in the lawful exercise of power. The principle of alternation in political control would be put in jeopardy if the government of the day were allowed to make heavy partisan replacements in the civil service. It is not entitled to adapt the machinery of administration so closely to its own political ends as to make that machinery useless for another government by substituting a patronage bureaucracy for the merit bureaucracy. Both elementary fairness and the public interest demand that each successive government be provided with unimpaired instrumentalities for achieving its purposes. Under popular rule it is imperative that any government, when lifted to power by the electorate, should have all the equipment needed to tackle its program with equal hope for success.

The need for keeping the administrative system in good working order at all times supplies the controlling argument in favor of giving the merit bureaucracy the status of a permanent establishment. That such status confers tangible benefits on each civil servant, together with various duties, is a secondary consideration, however great the practical importance of those benefits in order to attract and retain entrants of respectable caliber. Status is a means to an end; it is not an end in itself. The difference is not always remembered. The bureaucracy naturally takes a keen interest in legislative or judicial battles over questions relating to its status; and it is by no means uncommon for rank-and-file associations of civil servants to exert as much pressure upon the government as any other interest group. In many instances pressure tactics applied by public employees have succeeded in maneuvering governments into decisions they would not have taken voluntarily.

Moreover, status guaranties make it possible in cases of extreme friction for civil servants to attempt to defy politically responsible direction. The career man may well regard himself as considerably more "permanent" than the government of the day, which by tomorrow may be only a dead episode. It is not easy in each such case of conflict between the government and the bureaucracy to determine which side has the greater grievance against the other. The political masters are not above myopic opportunism, whereas the civil servants tend to surrender fully to the self-righteousness of the professional mind.

Limits of Civil Service Legislation

Like the whole status system of a society, civil service status may be based essentially on social convention, on the mores of the society. A constitution can be equally effective whether in the form of an unwritten body of rules or of a written document. Status guaranties, too, might be anchored in usage rather than law. Most frequently, however, law is relied upon to define and buttress the status intended for the government service. Legislative enactments offer greater promise than mere assurances of self-restraint to stay the manipulative hand of the "fixer," be he found among politicians or among executive officials.

But it should not be assumed that civil service legislation somehow miraculously brings forth a merit system of attested purity. Evidence from the United States indicates that legislation cannot banish either the astute spoilsman or the single-minded official who is set to get around particular requirements of civil service law. As the old spoilsman dies out, a new one appears, invoking the canons of managerial freedom to juggle things about for his own reasons, often with the help of career men who do not mind being "realistic" about these matters. Civil service law may make such unprincipled twisting a little harder, but in itself it is not an ultimately effective bar.

The Canadian Struggle for the Merit Rule

The limited utility of civil service acts in providing safeguards against the encroachment of undercover influences upon the administrative system is well demonstrated by the record. In the United States illustrations abound in the history of civil service legislation in the field of state government, although there, too, the patronage bureaucracy has been losing ground in the course of the twentieth century. But the lesson is equally clear when we examine the rise of the merit bureaucracy in other countries where patronage flowered until relatively recently.

Canada, for instance, adopted her first civil service act in 1868, one year after the British North America Act went into effect. But the gain was slight. Little relief was experienced from the evils of political placement, especially upon change of the party in power.

An attempt to overcome abuses was made with the adoption of the Civil Service Act of 1882, passed almost simultaneously with the civil service reform initiated in the United States by the Pendleton Act of 1883. Nevertheless, as late as 1907 a commission of inquiry still complained about using the dominion service as a quiet corner for political favorites who did not seem to fit anywhere else. The next step was the legislation of 1908, which brought about additional improvements, especially by establishment of a civil service commission. But political patronage was slow to die.

It required the impact of World War I and another drive for reform—this time on the strong initiative of Sir Robert L. Borden as head of the government—to bring forth the Civil Service Act of 1918, which greatly strengthened the authority of the Civil Service Commission. This act is the foundation upon which Canada's contemporary dominion service is built, but the present-day character of the service is the product of influences more potent than statutory clauses. One of these influences, the increasing importance of government in the life of the nation, attracted to Ottawa a complement of able men to fill top offices, especially in the category of deputy minister. Equally competent individuals were drawn into the upper ranks of the civil service; these included economists with academic backgrounds, whose ideas about the role of professional judgment in the making of policy were fresh and ready for application. The result of these developments was a remarkable invigoration of policy-planning, which gave the cabinet greater stature and raised the prestige of the civil service.

The French Battle for a "General Statute"

The main lesson to be drawn from the Canadian example is that laws are what men make them. The same conclusion is borne out by the experience of France, although the French civil service is a considerably older institution than the Canadian. Throughout the lifetime of the Third Republic the administrative system had to put up with a never ending struggle for a general law on the civil service, setting forth uniform rules to govern recruitment, promotion, discipline, pay, and retirement. The failure of successive attempts at getting such legislation made it plausible to infer that inadequacies in the conduct of public administration were mainly the result of the lack of a civil service act.

Not until 1946, in the Fourth Republic, was the "general statute of the civil service" enacted, the same year in which the present French constitution was adopted. Both the statute and the constitution recognized the previously contested right of civil servants to form or belong to associations. Indeed, after the statute was enacted, the civil service unions were welcomed to the deliberations of certain consultative bodies: the Higher Council of the Civil Service, a government-wide advisory organ of twenty-five members under the chairmanship of the prime minister; the technical committee of each department, concerned with matters of management; and the administrative committees, authorized to deal with cases of promotion and discipline.

It cannot be denied that the "general statute," together with other reform measures of recent years, benefited French public administration. Compared, however, with the expectations once associated with the idea of a civil service act, the effect of the statute merits a considerably less sanguine appraisal. In retrospect the new legislation does not stand out as a turning point in official behavior.

The Case for Constitutional Protection

If executive regulation as a foundation of status is open to the suspicion that such status may be taken away as easily as it was given, it is equally true that lawmakers may freely change their minds about their own enactments. The practical consequences of this possibility are eliminated when status guaranties are written into the constitution itself. As a matter of fact, there are instances where the fundamental definition of civil service status is provided by the constitution, with legislation reduced to carrying out the constitutional intent.

At first glance, such reliance on the constitution seems to be an unmistakable expression of lack of confidence in the judgment as well as the self-restraint of the legislative branch. In the United States, in particular, the argument in favor of constitutional solutions has often been linked with the premise that the partisan spirit of lawmaking bodies must be bridled by irremovable restrictions. Although this point of view cannot readily be reconciled with faith in the democratic process, it is true that legislative assemblies have been indifferent guardians of good government. They have often failed to protect institutional arrangements designed to make government more effective when such arrangements became the object of factional intrusions. Lawmakers on numerous occasions have attempted to rip holes into statutory guaranties of the merit rule in order to gain some immediate advantage, however temporary or trivial. This has been true especially in the area of state and local government. Needless to say, although constitutional provisions make it harder to use the civil service as a political pawn, the result is rarely an unmixed blessing. For it is clear that the price of constitutional protection may be a degree of inflexibility in administrative practice at variance with efficient management.

Administrative Principles and the German Constitution

Constitutional safeguards of civil service status may also stem from a recognition of the vital importance of the administrative system for the political order as a whole. In other words, when civil service is seen as an essential element in the structure of modern government, it cannot be ignored by constitution-makers. This factor furnished the main motive for the incorporation of basic principles applicable to the civil service into Germany's republican constitution of 1919. It was made more compelling by the need for introducing a monarchical merit bureaucracy to the practical requirements of majority rule, to complete the transition from the empire to the republic. Released by the emperor from their oath to him, the civil servants had made their peace with the "given facts," as it was delicately put at that time. In the aftermath of the five exhausting years of World War I, which in 1918 had ended in defeat and revolution, face to face with conditions that were about to erupt in civil war, the new regime put a high value on continuity of administrative operations.

Anxious to restore law and order, the republic sought to express in the constitution a basic formula for making the civil service both responsible and responsive in the framework of popular rule. It was hoped that this would be accomplished by building upon the civil servant's traditional devotion to lawful government and impartial duty, thus transferring from the empire to the republic the high standard of administrative efficiency. As a result, the constitution undertook to present a full-scale charter for the civil service. Its importance received added emphasis from the fact that the constitution made the charter applicable not only to the national civil service but also to civil servants of the state and local governments.

In the matter of recruitment the constitution stressed the democratic maxim of equal access to the civil service. Article 128 declared: "All citizens without distinction are eligible for public office, in accordance with the laws and corresponding to their ability and accomplishments." But that was nothing new. In this respect the constitution of 1919 simply echoed a familiar concept, going back two hundred years to the selection policies of King Frederick William I of Prussia. The first Prussian constitution, promulgated in

1850, had said the same thing by stating: "The public offices are equally open to all according to their ability, provided the requirements laid down by the laws are observed." But neither the monarchical constitution of Prussia nor Germany's republican constitution of 1919 provided for economic assistance to individuals who on grounds of ability might have made desirable candidates for the higher probationary service, although the republic furnished a reasonable monthly stipend for those who did pass the entrance examination.

More important for the immediate situation after World War I than the principle of equality of admission was the ideological attitude of the bureaucracy. To underscore the idea of political neutrality, the constitution of 1919 proclaimed: "Civil servants are servants of the whole people, not of a party." This, again, was not a new principle, but the constitutional pronouncement made it explicit. The civil service was cautioned not to acquire a habit of performing well only when a particular government was in power, while functioning badly under any other. On this basis Article 129 of the constitution reaffirmed the concept of tenure: "Civil servants are appointed for life insofar as not otherwise provided by law." Nor was any loophole left for legislative inroads into the civil servant's existing rights face to face with the government. The same article said unequivocally: "The duly acquired rights of civil servants are inviolable."

"Duly Acquired Rights"

The "duly acquired rights," as the Prussian Supreme Administrative Court once put it, had their origin in "the civil service status itself—that is, the bond between the civil servant and the state as his employer." These rights included the rights to rank and title, to salary and pension, and to annual leave. Although there was no legal right to promotion, the civil servant, once promoted, "duly acquired" the rights to his new rank and title and to his higher pay. Except when passed with the majorities required for constitutional amendment, no legislative act, for instance, could deprive him of rank and title or of his precious non-contributory pension.

Fundamentally, these rights were a reflection of status and related to the concept of institutional permanence. The civil servant was to devote himself to his public duties; he was neither to worry about his economic condition nor to feel a corrupting dependence on his political superiors. This had been made quite clear much earlier, as soon as Germany had achieved political unification under the imperial constitution of 1871. In the official explanation with which in 1872 the government put before parliament its draft of a civil service act, passed the next year, it was said that life-tenure had the purpose of safeguarding the "administrative independence" of the civil service. In short, the merit bureaucracy was not meant to be a lackey. It was meant to perform its public functions without intimidation. We can discern in these ideas some of the legacy of the guardian bureaucracy of Brandenburg-Prussia (see pp. 58 ff.).

As a logical application of the constitutional guaranty of the civil servant's "duly acquired rights," the legislature was prevented, for instance, from lowering the compulsory retirement age for the purpose of effecting budgetary economies. Nor was the lawmaking branch free to decrease the civil servant's salary as it saw fit, even if the pay act expressly reserved the possibility of changes. On this point the German Supreme Court recognized an important distinction. It did not doubt that the legislative power "is entirely unrestricted in originally constituting civil service rights." Moreover, it "may determine whether it wants to grant rights without reservation or only for a period of time, or subject to conditions, to revocation, or to any other restriction." But, in doing so, the legislative power must not "otherwise violate any duly acquired rights." A "duly acquired right" is impaired

if the foundations of that right are withdrawn. This would be the case if the reservation clause of the salary acts should cause a reduction of pay in such a way and to such an extent that for the individual civil servant the maintenance of living conditions corresponding to his position was made impossible. For the official can fulfil his duty of devoting his whole energy to public service only when the state relieves him from anxiety about his livelihood. Depriving him of the means of support which correspond to his position would therefore be equal to abolishing the civil service status, which, as a matter of principle, the state is not entitled to do. The constitution, then, guarantees the continuation of the essential foundations of civil service against any inroads of state or national legislation unless, in the latter case, the procedure for constitutional amendment is observed.

At exactly what point the "maintenance of living conditions corresponding to his position" would be made "impossible" for the civil servant, the court did not say. Indeed, this point would have to be settled by the fictitious "reasonable man" from the legal museum of Mr. Justice Holmes. The decision did give due warning to the legislature that the Supreme Court might speak with the voice of the "reasonable man" on some other occasion, and possibly with considerable conviction, because the German judiciary was under the same salary legislation as the civil service.

Uprooting Civil Service Law by Law

All in all, therefore, it is not difficult to understand why informed foreign observers have seldom failed to comment on the strong legal basis of the German civil service. But history soon set out to show how heavily law—and even constitutional law—borrows from the tenor of its environment. A fundamental change was introduced in 1933 as soon as the swastika had been raised above all government buildings in Germany. Repelled by the violence and the emotional excesses of the Brown Shirt movement, the career man had stood aloof; with the collapse of the republic, he found himself a prime target of the new regime, quite in the same way in which ten years earlier the Italian civil service had been made the victim of Mussolini's "crusade against the bureaucracy." Indeed, Hitler's approach was a faithful copy. Immediately upon substituting one-party rule for his earlier collaboration with other parties, Mussolini had set out to purge the civil service of those suspected of "incompatibility with the general directives of the government." Promulgated with cynical timing on Christmas Eve, 1925, this change in status opened the way for the creation of a patronage bureaucracy which was supposed to operate as the guardian bureaucracy of Fascism. Similarly, when Hitler found himself installed as chancellor of the German Reich, one of his first moves was to empower the government to get rid of civil servants who were not deemed "politically reliable," together with those of Jewish descent. The authority was secured by the "act for the restoration of the German civil service" of 1933, dressed up as a reform measure against officials alleged to have crept into the merit bureaucracy by political placement under the republic. But the actual aim was the undoing of the politically neutral career man, to make him the servile tool of the one surviving party.

Hitler proceeded cautiously, step by step. On the one hand, he had a high regard for the merit bureaucracy as the government's efficient agent for the conduct of public administration. On the other hand, he had no illusion that a civil service unbroken in spirit would do his bidding. By placing his own men strategically in the bureaucracy, he succeeded as well as Mussolini had in Italy. In a formal sense the large body of civil service law remained unchanged except for a superstructure of Nazi ideology; but personal insecurity swept through the career service as the twin tests of "political reliability" and non-Jewish background were pressed upon the administrative system. It did not take long for these tests to engulf the whole people, and then the proverbial thoroughness of the German bureaucracy was enlisted in the sordid task of specifying in minute detail what portions of "Aryan" and Jewish blood would make an individual a "mixed type" of various degrees and what legal consequences would flow from this designation under the racial decrees.

Legal Processes under Political Pressure

One must add, however, that law does remain law when legal processes prevail, especially when standards of justice are not swept aside by power or by passion. On many occasions canons of law have stood up in the defense of basic rights and fair procedure even when the individuals invoking these rights were linked to unpopular causes. For example, in 1953 five applicants for the entrance examination at the French National School of Administration were barred on allegations that they were Communists. There was no doubt that admission to the school, legally, was not a matter of right but one of discretion. The manner of action, however, and the justification offered brought the decision in conflict with the principles of French administrative law and opened it to vigorous criticism in parliament. All this might not have had much effect save for the fact that the applicants could bring the matter to the legal test. The Council of State, in its role as supreme administrative court, set aside the decision as contrary to law.

Roles were almost reversed in a similar episode that occurred in Norway. In 1955 parliament precipitated the resignation of the minister of justice over a matter quite unlikely to become a political issue—that is, back pay to some two hundred civil servants. It refused to accept his recommendation (and presumably that of the cabinet) that money be made available for this purpose. The issue arose from the fact that these civil servants had been suspended for a time after World War II for their wartime Nazi sympathies. On the legal side, there was no question that all had resigned from Quisling's treason-tinged political organization, the Nasjonal Samling, before the Norwegian government, then in exile in England, passed its decree on collaboration with the German enemy in 1944. Looking at the matter on the basis of law, the supreme court had affirmed their claim.

Statutory Innovation, Restoration, and Conservation

For many European countries the impact of World War II and its aftermath have provided strong incentives toward a fresh appraisal of established political and administrative institutions. Like other things, public personnel administration has come in for extensive reassessment in both its concepts and its practices. The condition of the civil service has been given considerable attention in the councils of national policy. But civil service law has retained its central place as a guarantor of administrative efficiency, integrity, and continuity.

The outstanding example is the French civil service reform. As soon as France stood on her own feet again, she set out with unprecedented energy to strengthen the career service. Action started in 1945 with the creation of the National School of Administration and a central Civil Service Office, attached to the office of the prime minister. The Civil Service Office was charged with the tasks of planning general personnel policies, developing detailed proposals in specific fields like pay and pensions, co-ordinating departmental regulations, preparing and reviewing recommendations for improvements in the civil service, and assembling personnel statistics. The French civil service was given its first comprehensive legislative underpinning in the "general statute" of 1946.

These measures illustrate a breath-taking dash into new things, in sharp contrast to the inertia of the Third Republic. The reappraisal of the civil service occurring shortly afterward in Germany was hardly less thorough. There, however, it led essentially to a return to the old pattern that the Hitler regime had so cynically disembodied. The new civil service act of 1953—a full-scale codification like that of 1873—represented in the main a reconstruction on foundations deeply imbedded in the German administrative heritage. As predicted by those not given to wishful thinking, few of the artificial implantations attempted under the military occupation remained, for the Germans resented foreign inroads.

As a parallel in conservation, the revision in 1949 of the Swiss civil service act of 1927 amounted practically to a reaffirmation of the existing law. An administrative face-lifting followed with the detailed regulations issued in 1952, implemented further by the rules on entrance and promotion of civil servants of 1955. As a result, most of the immediately applicable legal provisions today governing the Swiss civil service are found in promulgations of the last years, but these are based on precedent. Neither the Federal Personnel Office nor the Finance and Customs Department to which it is attached plays as decisive a role in the administrative system as does the British Treasury. For example, the Swiss regulations of 1955 leave each agency entirely free to appeal the required formal "opinions" of the Personnel Office in classification matters to the Finance and Customs Department; and, if disagreement is not resolved at this level, the case may be carried to the collegial supreme executive, the Federal Council itself.

A more intensive search for the best approach to increasing the effectiveness of the civil service was undertaken in republican Italy. Perhaps one of the most powerful incentives was the growing public criticism of the government for its seeming indifference toward both unabashed political placement and the swelling numbers of public personnel. The civil servants, in turn, had an undeniable grievance in the lack of a satisfactory adjustment of the salary schedules to the rising cost of living. When finally an upward revision of pay scales was enacted, provision was made simultaneously for a study of the civil service to bring about desirable improvements. This study, carried on without self-defeating haste, furnished the basis for inaugurating a "general statute" like the French, made effective in 1956. This *statuto* created an Advanced School of Public Administration under the office of the prime minister as a new training center.

Continental European Civil Service Law

In Great Britain the historic development of the civil service as a crown establishment has been guided almost completely by orders-in-council or other executive actions, but in most countries comprehensive codification has been the order of the day. No less important, the recent recodifications have gone far to build up a common continental European body of law, considerably influenced by the German example. There remain differences, to be sure; but the general pattern is strikingly revealed when the several texts are laid side by side. In each case the basic rules are put together in a single source designated to serve as a coherent exposition of the civil service relationship in its various aspects. For example, the Italian *statuto* runs to about a hundred and fifty sections grouped systematically under eleven titles which in most instances are divided into subtitles. The language of these texts, by and large, is concise, readily understandable, and remarkably free from ambiguities and obscurities. As a result, the law dealing with the civil service has been brought closer to the civil servant, thus becoming more truly the foundation of his conduct.

Not surprisingly, the rights as well as the duties of the civil servant have received particular attention. In the Italian *statuto* this is the subject of the first title, consisting of more than thirty sections. No less conspicuous is the recognition given in the recodifications to joint consultative machinery. In these joint bodies, departmental as well as service-wide, chosen representatives of the civil servants and representatives of the government are brought together for regular meetings to discuss matters of common concern in an effort to establish agreement or at least to foster mutual understanding.

PROTECTIVE TRADITIONS

At the turn of the twenties the reorganization of its police department gave Berkeley, California, a first-rate police force. In building up this force, however, it was not found necessary to establish a formal merit system. In a well-to-do, mostly residential community governed under the council-manager plan, the balance of environmental forces provided the equivalent of legal guaranties. The caliber of the men coming in was high. The care taken in their selection and the evidence of able leadership made them feel that they were being invited to share in the prestige of a fine outfit. On the national level only a few years later, this was the appeal and the experience of the Tennessee Valley Authority, which was authorized by statute to pioneer with a system of personnel administration of its own making, divorced from the general civil service legislation applicable to the other executive agencies of the federal government.

These illustrations may suggest how far the essence of institutions develops in the cultural context and under the influence of political as well as social forces and factors. That explains why civil service law in one setting provides for effective regulation and in another is little more than window-dressing. By the same token, it is reasonable to expect that the merit rule may find a thoroughly adequate foundation in mere executive regulation, provided the national mores serve as watchman. This is borne out by the history of the British civil service.

Effective Executive Regulation: Great Britain

Great Britain's success in employing executive action for the building of a civil service that has earned itself an enviable reputation can be explained only as the result of a combination of factors. Of these, three appear to be the most important. First, it is part of the "British way" to sustain the logic of an institutional evolution without petty interference once its beneficial prospects have become evident. This complements the instinct for the traditional, which Edmund Burke immortalized as the genius of English statecraft. Second, pressures upon the British Empire in the middle of the nineteenth century led men like Macaulay (see pp. 10–11) to clamor for reform of the Indian Service; and serious administrative failures at home were revealed by the Crimean War. Moreover, application of the new recruitment formula to the home service was easier in a period when policy was still often settled simply by agreement among a handful of leaders across party lines. And, third, the development reflected a concept of long-range political responsibility akin to the "truer English doctrine," which "exalted the power of government because it represented the joint will of an organic body politic," as G. R. Elton has put it in his history of England under the Tudors (1955).

The working doctrine of the emerging British merit bureaucracy was that of service to an "organic body politic." Although divided along party lines for purposes of responsible government, the body politic showed basic social unity. The end of patronage did not produce a social separation of the House of Commons and the competitive civil service. The new career man shared the general background of the membership of the House of Commons in education as well as in economic condition. He was "sound" in every respect, thoroughly trustworthy, and very British. He did not have to fight for parliamentary confidence in his dependability as the servant of the government of the day; social kinship formed a bridge across party differences. As a result, an early foundation was laid for the remarkable unanimity with which the civil service is viewed by British opinion as a national asset to be guarded vigilantly against deterioration.

As from the outset, so today the civil service in England is essentially an establishment of the crown. Statutory provisions governing its affairs are the distinct exception, such as the retirement or superannuation legislation. The foundations of the British civil service were laid by executive measures. The Trevelyan-Northcote report (see p. 54) was the product of a Treasury committee. Parliament was an arresting force, and in the face of its antagonism the idea of open competition for the home service did not win out initially. Gladstone had to struggle for the cabinet's support in making a beginning with a system of qualifying examinations, which could hardly have amounted to much had it not been coupled with the creation in 1855 of the Civil Service Commission, the first of its kind in the history of modern government. This step was taken by order-in-council—that is, on the responsibility of the cabinet.

When in 1870 the qualifying examination for the home service was replaced by the open competitive examination as the usual method of admission, this far-reaching change, again, was put into effect by order-in-council. After World War I, executive initiative was controlling, once more, when another pioneer move brought forth a formal arrangement for continuing consultation between the government and the staff side on matters of joint interest affecting the civil service. The National Council for the Administrative and Legal Departments of the Civil Service, better known as the Whitley Council, was established without resort to legislation, as were the corresponding more than seventy department councils.

Restrictive Legislation

The most striking instance of statutory prescription for the merit bureaucracy in England came as a half-punitive gesture rather than as a sheltering one. This was the much-discussed Clause V of the Trade Disputes and Trade Unions Act of 1927, which reflected part of the shock effect of the general strike of 1926. Civil service organizations previously had been free to affiliate with outside groups, including the Trade Union Congress and the Labor party, but the act of 1927 prohibited any such affiliation and the pursuit of "political objects" by civil service associations as well. These restrictions were repealed only after World War II, with the return of the Labor party to control. In retrospect, the prohibitions of the act of 1927 can hardly be said to have had much more than a nuisance effect upon the civil service. Its record had been good. No civil service union had called upon its membership during the general strike to join it, nor had civil servants actually participated in the strike. On the other hand, as a result of affiliation with the labor movement, financial aid was furnished the striking workers in part from funds controlled by civil service unions. Moreover, largely on the basis of personal ties with the cause of labor, some leaders of civil service organizations had played a conspicuous role in the councils of the strikers.

The impact of the general strike of 1926 on the British civil service demonstrates that it is folly to impute to the bureaucracy a unity of political point of view or of basic economic and social motivation which it could not be expected to possess in view of the diversity of its composition. At the very outset the upper categories of the civil service took occasion to express their fundamental disagreement with any kind of involvement in the general strike. Four of the associations of higher civil servants later formally withdrew from the Whitley Council. As they saw it, they had not received sufficiently explicit assurances that all civil service unions would stay out of similar labor conflicts that might happen in the future.

Legislative-Executive Relationships

In appraising the operation of protective traditions, we cannot ignore the question whether the strength of executive safeguards of civil service status has something to do with the character of legislative-executive relationships. In a political system in which the legislative and executive branches are set apart as sharply as they are in the United States, executive regulation would be a feebler foundation to build upon. In such a system each of the coequal branches shows a persistent inclination to assert its separate point of view. The philosopher T. V. Smith in his temporary guise as congressman devoted his maiden speech in 1940 to civil service in the federal government as one of the "few causes there are that somebody is not opposed to." Yet many do not mind making a political football of it.

Such rivalry between the legislative and the executive branches would be inconceivable in a parliamentary system where the cabinet is the acting arm of the legislative majority. There the pledge of the executive can be as good as the enactments of the legislature. This means, however, that crystallization of civil service policy must occur at the highest executive level. In Great Britain, as in France, we can notice a tendency to link the general stewardship over the civil service with the office of the prime minister. That tendency is present, for instance, in the arrangements worked out in 1956 when the post usually referred to as "head of the civil service" was relinquished by Sir Edward Bridges—a career man who did much to demonstrate to the Labor party that it could rely on the unreserved responsiveness of the Administrative Class. General management of the civil service has stayed with the Treasury, but responsibility for basic personnel policy was linked with the cabinet secretariat. Thus a direct channel has been provided to the prime minister himself, comparable to a scheme experimented with a few years ago.

Protective traditions consolidate in the course of slow growth. They cannot be forced, but they can disintegrate fast. Unless the public is sufficiently astute and alert to take up the battle for principle, legal defenses of civil service status cannot be expected to hold up under counterpressures. Moreover, retrenchment and economy drives may cut around guaranties of status, as do administrative reorganizations aimed in the main at getting rid of incumbents so as to gain opportunity for fresh recruitment.

Illusory Permanence

All this casts a sharp light upon the view that the merit bureaucracy, being institutionally indispensable, is for that reason irreplaceable. It has frequently been asserted on the authority of Max Weber that it was the inescapable fate of modern policy-makers to be forced to live with the bureaucracy they happened to inherit. But Weber did not say that. Moreover, history did not give him an opportunity of observing how easy it is to make even a strong bureaucracy cower before the whip of totalitarian political leadership. He never saw how a career service could be pressed into lending a hand in its own undoing by surrendering its institutional morality and rationality.

Both Mussolini and Hitler showed the world that moral fortitude does not live long in a bureaucracy if a sword is suspended on a silk thread above it. Courage vanishes when each civil servant discovers how little stock he can safely take in fraternal solidarity and how easily he can advance his personal fortunes by blackening the record of his colleague. Within days, the corrupting influence of an environment of fear envelops the entire administrative system. Quite the same condition is present in the Soviet Union. The division is not merely one between administrative functionaries, on the one side, and ideological overseers, on the other. Indeed, everybody is in part the ideological overseer of everybody else, and successful performance as ideological overseer brings personal advantages.

Institutional Adaptation to Changing Environment

Generally speaking, therefore, the institutional permanence of the bureaucracy as a necessary instrument of government does not extend automatically to the situation of the individual civil servant even if he belongs to a key group in the service. Individually, he is expendable. The internal adjustment within the civil service comes about as external pressure continues. In the longer run the bureaucracy is bound to mirror its environment, for even a partial penetration of the administrative system by "new faces" destroys its resistance to changes forced upon it. Institutional adaptation to a changing environment is a normal development for the bureaucracy, especially when the incoming replacements for its top cadre carry into the service the ideas current in the universities.

An illustration is the profound change in outlook that occurred in Prussia's civil service during the half-century following her crushing defeat by Napoleon in 1806. Since the death of Frederick the Great in 1786, the kingdom had lived largely out of the stock of its legacy. In the opinion of Baron vom Stein, a civil servant who proved to be a farsighted advocate of political reform, part of the blame for Prussia's collapse fell on the bureaucracy for its stodginess and lack of public spirit. In his famous Nassau Memorandum, while outlining for the king his plan for a new Prussia based on civic participation in government, Stein wrote bitterly: "A hireling's spirit easily and commonly intrudes into the public authorities composed of salaried officials, a life in set forms and administrative mechanisms, an ignorance of the local area which is being administered, an indifference and frequently even a ridiculous antipathy toward it, a fear of changes and innovations, which adds to the work that overburdens the better officials because the others keep away from it."

Fifty years later many of the best thinkers in the bureaucracy stood on the side of liberalism. When Bismarck was appointed prime minister of Prussia on October 8, 1862, to fight the king's fight in the constitutional conflict between crown and parliament over the military budget, he had to pull hard for an unpopular cause. As he described it in his memoirs:

At the distribution of the ministries, for which the number of candidates was small, the Ministry of Finance caused the least delay. It was assigned to Karl von Bodelschwingh, brother of Ernst von Bodelschwingh, the former minister of the interior, who had resigned in March, 1848. Karl von Bodelschwingh had already held this position under Manteuffel from 1851 to 1858. Yet it soon became evident that he and Count Itzenplitz, to whom the Ministry of Commerce fell, were unable to direct their departments. Both confined themselves to putting their signature to the decisions of the well-informed ministerial civil servants and to mediating, as far as possible, any differences which might arise between the decisions of the civil servants—partly liberal and partly absorbed in narrow departmental outlook— and the policy of the king and the state cabinet. The majority of the expert officials of the Ministry of Finance belonged at heart to the opposition against the Conflict Cabinet, which they regarded as a short episode in the liberal development of the bureaucratic machinery. And although the ablest among them were too conscientious to curb the activity of the cabinet, they indulged in a not inconsiderable passive resistance wherever their sense of duty permitted. The strange consequence was that Herr von Bodelschwingh, who according to his personal attitude represented the extreme right in the cabinet, as a rule cast his vote for the extreme left.[1]

A particular civil service system is primarily the product of the cultural characteristics of its national environment. It may change slowly or rapidly in the course of time, but its enthusiasms and animosities will be directed toward what the nation as a whole finds important.

1. Otto von Bismarck, *Gedanken und Erinnerungen* (Leipzig: Cotta, 1905), I, 326–27.

CHAPTER 6

THE BUREAUCRATIC WORLD

In an era of large-scale organization public administration, too, is carried on in massive structures that extend from central head-quarters into the field without loss of each organization's basic identity. In such structures the individual participant is absorbed into a faceless collectivity: he becomes manpower. In his condition as manpower he is perennially subject to orders, but each order stands in the shadow of still higher authority, which conveys implicit or explicit directions about what order to give. Although each participant has his "boss," there is typically a "boss" behind each "boss." Even on the highest level where the major decisions are made, those in power are usually reduced to "taking part" in the making of these decisions. Employees rather than employers, they act under the compulsion of coming to an agreement among themselves, for only under the authority of substantial agreement is the decision safe from serious challenge. It is through his capacity for adapting himself to this group process that today's corporation executive rises to the top and retains his share of authority. It is through the same capacity that the career man in public administration gains his personal opportunities for promoting the general interest.

But a group process is a two-way thing. It allows man to multiply his resources by building upon the resources of others. It makes for achievements possible only through collaboration. But it demands a toll. It forces man's efforts into grooves, denies him the taking of chances the institution will not allow, and saps his initiative by pinning him down to compromises with those who look over his shoulder. This chapter takes an excursion into the bureaucratic world in order to see its two sides. Thus it will become easier to understand why, side by side with a great deal of unadvertised attainment in serving the common good, there is so much institutional stagnation, so much deflection of public action toward individual self-advancement, and so much gray routine. To put the matter in perspective, we need to look at it from three angles: first, from the angle of the participant's working place, in terms of what he may call the day-by-day grind; second, from the angle of the bureaucratic incentive system, in its influence upon human motivation; and, third, from the angle of concerted action to bring about changes, especially in the economics of civil service—that is, civil service unionism.

THE DAY-BY-DAY GRIND

The Participant's Small World

Hierarchy suggests up-and-down lines between "levels," described in the language of public administration as "channels of control." For the individual participant in the bureaucratic world, however, life characteristically is lived in circles. This is true in the dual meaning of the phrase. In the first place, although the individual participant knows the undeniable realities of the up-and-down dimension of authority, his institutional environment is envisaged by him as stretching all around, with himself at the center. In the second place, much of what happens in this environment has a circular drift, which becomes ever more marked when there is an abnormal increase in bureaucratic tendencies.

The day-by-day grind in the office is strongly affected by these "circles," as demonstrated when the individual participant is asked to indicate his place in the department. He will find it hard to show his position on the departmental organization chart with its neatly drawn boxes connected by straight lines. Unless he occupies a position of authority in any of the designated components, his finger will draw a tiny circle somewhere while he murmurs, "It's about here" or "It's in between these two." When he is pressed for further explanations, the relationships he describes will fit around him like a cocoon. He will talk of the "boss" and the boss's sidekicks, one of whom will be the boss's secretary, who may be a very important person to get along with and who is usually the best informed about office matters. He will also talk of the immediate work associates, who have no right to give orders except that what Dick and Jack say is equal to an order; for the boss almost never fails to uphold these two if a question is raised about their actions. The only trouble is that Dick and Jack carry on an odd feud of long standing. Then there are still others, a step down, who do what is asked of them.

Our witness appreciates the fact that his boss has a boss, but he has personally talked with the latter on very few occasions—once upon bringing him a draft memorandum marked "urgent," once as a result of being jovially addressed in the hall, and once in the men's room, where the conversation unaccountably dealt with the care of tulips. The boss of the boss is a controlling factor in many activities, for the immediate boss insists that things must be tailored exactly to the desires and peculiarities of his boss. But the detail is all hearsay, coming down through the immediate boss only, whose personal strength flows in large part from knowing what is on the mind of *his* boss. For these reasons it might be just as well to forget about the boss of the boss, for he is present anyway in what the boss wants done. As a matter of fact, when the boss specifically invokes the higher boss, it may be simply to put special emphasis on his own orders or preferences.

The same flattening of the perspective is evident when our witness turns his mental eye upon the organizational subdivisions adjacent to his own or even farther away. What is happening there is distinctly at the periphery of his experience. He neither knows much about it nor sees any reason why he should. But he is likely to have his suspicions. Beyond the fringe of his own work environment is the realm inhabited by a lesser humanity whom he calls "they." They have a way of getting by with less than their share. They always have some sort of pull. And they certainly know the tricks. Didn't they manage to kick that big mess this way so that "we" are now stuck with it? But when they thought they could make a hit with the Information Office and buy a lot of fine publicity, they doctored up our stuff and passed it on as their own.

Collectivity and Seclusion

Life in the individual circle weirdly combines aspects of inescapable collectivity and aspects of insurmountable seclusion. Within the particular work group everything that is being done, generally speaking, shows the fingerprints of many hands. Nobody works wholly for himself. Everybody concerned with proposed actions works in anticipation of the next move in the chain of indorsements, and each move carries with it the likelihood of changes. The work group thus actually functions as a plural body. Individual contributions are collectivized, and much of the information needed in this group process must be shared by the participants, including which turns of phrase are favored one step above in instructions, memorandums, or correspondence.

But the relative intimacy of collective operations comes to an end as matters pass beyond the confines of the particular work group. Knowledge of what is likely to happen next may be unobtainable except what is conveyed through a narrow channel normally represented by the boss alone. This explains the insatiable thirst for information within bureaucratic organizations, the perpetual cry for fuller communication. Yet each point of authority in the hierarchical structure acts like a dam in the flow of information, for to know is a privilege, a defense, a weapon—in short, something not to be surrendered without compelling reason. As a result, even an institutional policy of "full information" is quite likely to operate as a selective type of control over knowledge of what is going on.

Running Around in Circles

It is thus no play on words to say that life in circles provides an ever present temptation to run around in circles. On the one hand, it is a natural thing for matters to be passed around when their disposition is a collective process; and each participant's own burden of work and responsibility is minimized when he can think of additional places to which to shift part of that burden. On the other hand, when the eventual results to be accomplished or the purposes to be served are obscured, when they mean little to the participant, the inducement to push things around and around, if only to get rid of them for the time being, becomes constantly stronger. Running around in circles is a particularly satisfying outlet for those who instinctively guard themselves against the longer-range view because their vision is not equal to it.

To some extent, the tendencies here outlined are part and parcel of all large-scale organizations. It would be wrong to conclude, however, that nothing can be done to prevent such behavior from reaching uncontrollable proportions. The most effective therapy must be applied within the administrative system, out of the critical sense and the moral stamina of the bureaucracy itself. This calls for both insight and detachment of a high order, especially among the top cadre of the civil service.

THE BUREAUCRATIC INCENTIVE SYSTEM

Range of Incentives

In the competitive drive for increasing productivity in industrial society, it has become customary to talk about incentives as special spurs to action, effective over and beyond what is assumed to be a general inducement to come to work. For example, the personnel department in a factory may run an incentive system under which awards, bonuses, or pay raises are granted to employees who do exceptionally well or who have come up with a money-saving suggestion for improving operations. But such special incentives would not explain, by themselves, what brings the workers into the factory in the first place and what makes them do a good day's work.

An answer to these questions would have to delve into the complex combination of the worker's actual productive capacity in terms of what he knows he can do, his ideas about what that capacity should earn for him, the attraction of a particular line of work and of a particular work situation, the general condition of the labor market, and other similar factors. All these, together with any special enticements furnished, make up the total incentive system.

In a bureaucratic organization the mutual action of incentives in this broader sense is controlled, in the first place, by the character of the setting itself. That setting represents a combination of several factors—hierarchical structure, jurisdictional concern with specific functions, specialization, professional training, fixed compensation, and continuity of employment. These factors set the stage for the working of the bureaucratic incentive system.

The operation of that system has been variously described by practitioners as an artful alternation of bowing toward those higher up and kicking those further down; as a perpetual scramble for position; as an elaborate game of hiding behind the stout tree of procedure and of never getting caught out on a limb; and, quite differently, as a competitive dash of dedicated men for the sacred fountain of public service. Such epigrammatic descriptions are obviously incomplete when taken singly. But they convey much of the essence of the thing when put together.

The Missionary Spirit

It would be hard to find a bureaucracy without dedicated men. Their attitude may reflect a sense of mission as strong as that displayed by members of a religious order. How large this group tends to be in the individual national setting is a matter of great consequence. It is of immediate importance for the ground rules according to which the institutional incentive system operates. A strong sense of mission has a multiplying effect upon selfless duty. The strength of the missionary spirit is no less significant for the extent to which the career man is able to alert himself against the threat of the bureaucratic virus, thus gaining for himself a precious immunity.

Dedicated men, however, can be narrow-minded, even bigoted. A closed mind enlisted in a noble cause can do much harm. Likewise, a mind that shrinks from the broader view is a limiting influence. It will scatter itself over the day's burning issues, although they will hardly be remembered a week later. That kind of mind is bound further to stultify rather than to counteract bureaucratic behavior.

The Strategy of Position

Hierarchical organization carries with it a parceling-out of authority from the top to the bottom. Authority stands for effect, power, influence, and prestige. In hierarchical terms the participant gains on every score as he rises. His eyes are therefore turned upward, specifically upon what he can see immediately above him. But, in order to move, he must have the support of others who count. How he stands with these is important to him, and he will therefore try to make useful friends in the handling of particular matters.

The search for alliances leads to the formation of small clusters of individuals who seek to act together both in "putting across" decisions proposed by them and in attending to their respective interests in the institutional context. For the same reason it is necessary to hoard jurisdiction. The transfer of a responsibility from one participant to another normally is fought by the prospective loser because it may weaken his position in the organization. As a means of self-protection and aggrandizement, every fresh sprout of authority must be nursed along. Similarly, considerable time comes to be devoted to "empire-building." Each function corralled, each employee added, each office room gained, represents a step forward, which is a step upward. Again, it is essential to be constantly circumspect; to be alive to the danger of a raid on one's empire in the guise of a re-organization; to maintain the illusion that everybody within the empire is terribly busy; and to refuse requests for a loan of underlings to another division which contends that it is momentarily swamped. On the same grounds it is best to shun co-operative arrangements with other parts of the organization for fear that joint undertakings may end up belonging to somebody else.

Rivalry of Interests

Despite the strong conformist pressures that assert themselves in bureaucratic organizations, the existence of rival interests causes continuous friction. At its maximum such friction may paralyze the whole organization. It may take the form of disagreements over policy proposals or the manner of handling particular problems. Many clashes have their basis either in personal antagonisms and jealousies or in impregnable stubbornness based on fear. Within limits, these internal cleavages, whatever their actual cause, may be a source of institutional strength, however. Wise leadership is able to benefit from the clarifying effects of differences of opinion vigorously argued.

But all squabbling is usually forgotten when the jurisdiction or the survival of the organization itself is in peril. Then those on the inside are likely to close ranks spontaneously. This is often most conspicuous when a department is bombarded by public criticism or becomes the object of serious legislative disfavor.

All these conditions affect the play of individual motivation within large-scale organizations. In the last analysis, therefore, the bureaucratic incentive system is fashioned by forces both personal and impersonal that originate in considerable part within the institutional setting. But we must not lose track of the fact that this setting rests on a material foundation which in many ways affects the impulses running through the organization. It is therefore necessary to take a look at the economics of civil service.

The Economics of Small Chances

In the light of our examination of the bureaucratic milieu as well as of the safeguards of status, the economics of civil service may be summarized as the economics of small chances, each cautiously considered. In the first place, the ideology of service itself minimizes the unabashed display of consuming ambition. In some respects, indeed, service is its own reward. Moreover, the mass conditions to which personnel policy and procedure must be addressed in large-scale organizations cry out for recognition of the normal rather than the exceptional. Meteoric rise of the outstandingly able individual is therefore discouraged quite in the same way as favoritism and disregard of rules are discouraged. Advancement, if it is not to attract suspicious or unfriendly eyes, must generally stay in line with the "normal." Exceptions call for too much explaining. All this tends to make rewards for accomplishment something that comes in small packages at fairly long intervals. The large number of civil servants actually accrue such rewards with length of service rather than earning them by conspicuous effort or achievement.

The "Careerist"

The general rule, however, is usually modified by special instances; and in large establishments the number of such special instances may be beyond quick count. Ability is by no means ignored, and there is also the tenacious climber. Individuals whose personal interest is the measure of all things are found in every organization, public as well as private. They can easily dress their personal motives in the gown of public necessity, pushing on and on in single-minded pursuit of "success."

In the life of large-scale organizations the "careerist," in the familiar Soviet phrase, is a common plague. The only force that can contain this plague, even though it cannot completely conquer it, is the militant self-discipline that may be active within the bureaucracy. When this force is weak, we can be sure that for each climber who succeeds, ten others will try. To the extent that the "careerist" is allowed to set the tone, public purpose and public service will part company. Then the behavior of civil servants will be governed by the untempered profit motive, as it is with brutal candor in the administrative organization of many a dictatorial regime, which buys the allegiance of its officialdom by allowing it a cut in the common exploitation of the general public.

The Asset of Position

Outside the gains that come from subverting the idea of public service, the bureaucratic environment is crowded with abstentions, moral as well as economic. The career man must not get beyond the amateur's range into such extracurricular money-making activities as speculation, betting, and gambling. Unless he or his wife has independent means, his investments can mount only if there are savings from his pay. It is easier for him to fall in debt; and, if he gets too deeply enmeshed in it, he may have to forfeit his career or be fired as unworthy of public trust. He must not try to keep up with the well-to-do with whom he is brought in touch by his official activities. Above all, he must not use them as a source of credit or other economic benefits. In short, he lives in frugal righteousness without being either boastful or apologetic about it.

Accordingly, the civil servant is apt to have his mind on his position. The position supports him, reflects his prestige, and represents a precious investment in effort, time, and deference to institutional impositions, like putting up with an intolerable superior. Moreover, the position is the key to his pension rights upon retirement, and it is not an exchangeable commodity in the sense that it is an equally good asset in private employment. This may be aggravated by training requirements. As one illustration, the new National School of Administration in France has geared its training consciously toward public service, not toward turning out a general type of junior executive who would—if one could—be equally at home in government and in private business. Thus the civil servant's security is based upon his position, which in turn is moored to status. Even in transferring from one governmental position to another, he will evaluate the pros and cons with extreme care. If he were to take bold chances in this respect, he could not be called a normal civil servant.

By the same token, the civil servant's position is his Achilles' heel. When the position is imperiled, the shock effect may cause him to lose his morale and to surrender his integrity. As we saw earlier, by driving holes into the guaranties of status, Hitler was able to bend the strong German bureaucracy at his pleasure, even though the number of civil servants who did not yield in spirit should be allowed for. Similar reverberations have been noticeable in the Soviet bureaucracy, not only when particular purges were going on, but also when, as again in 1955, the regime abruptly pulled manpower from administrative offices to shift it to points of greater need in the economy. Here we should recall Max Weber's observation that the indispensability of the bureaucracy in the performance of essential functions means little in regard to its hold on actual power—as little as the indispensability of slave labor meant to the slaves in the power structure of ancient economies.

Economic Rank and Social Standing

One measure of the civil servant's economic rank and social standing is gained by looking at other occupational groupings. In comparing the top pay groups in the civil service with the earnings of skilled labor, we discover great diversity among different countries. For instance, in the United States the salary of civil servants in the upper ranges runs from two to three times that of the average skilled worker, who as wage-earner has no equal in the world. But in Great Britain the corresponding ratio is much more favorable to the top career man, giving him eight to ten times the pay of the skilled worker. Canada, Australia, and New Zealand show a ratio much like that of the United States, as do the Scandinavian countries. West Germany and the Netherlands, on the other hand, have a ratio closely comparable to the British. Between the American and the British ratios we find, in ascending order, Italy, Belgium, France, and Switzerland.

Partly reflected in these comparisons is the general spread of economic differences between various occupational groups in each country, but varying ideas about where the civil servant belongs

within the occupational structure are also reflected. To round out
the picture, we must compare the salary range of the higher civil
service with the pattern of compensation that prevails among executives in private business or the earnings of practitioners of the professions. In both these groupings top pay goes far above the salary
ceilings of the bureaucracy in each of the countries previously
named. As a matter of fact, in the professions as well as in private
business peak compensation may be ten times higher than in the
civil service, and the limit is fixed neither by law nor by usage. There
is, however, greater approximation between public and private pay
as we proceed downward from the very top to something like the
statistical mean for the occupational categories here compared. This
increasing approximation is true to a greater extent of the professions than of private business, in comparison with the civil service.
In the middle and lower groupings of the bureaucracy, on the other
hand, comparison with the same kinds of outside employment becomes progressively more favorable to those in the government
service.

How To Rise

More specific evidence of how one gets ahead in the bureaucracy
has been provided in a study made in the United States in 1955. This
study dealt with a sample of almost eight hundred federal civil
servants in top-range positions, the bulk being in Grade 15 and a
fraction in Grades 16–18. For the sample as a whole, more than a
third had entered the service in Grades 1–5, and one-fourth in
Grades 7–9. Before entering the service, more than two-fifths of
those included in the sample had been in private industry or professional practice, including their own business; another fifth had been
attending schools; while about one-tenth had worked for state or
local governments, and more than another tenth had been in the
field of education. Those who upon entry were not college graduates
represented almost a fourth, while an additional fourth had carried
the higher learning up to the Bachelor's degree; the other half had
proceeded further, mostly to graduate degrees. In age, more than
half of the civil servants covered by the sample were over fifty years
of age, almost one-fifth being above sixty; but another fifth was
forty-five years old or less. Of the entire group, no less than a fourth
had spent more than twenty-five years in the service, and a total of
almost two-thirds had been with the government for more than fifteen years. Very much like the present-day American business executive, who stays with one company, more than half had remained all

the time in the same agency; another fifth had changed agencies only once. As a matter of fact, almost half had even stuck to the same bureau in their agency, and a further fifth had made only one transfer to another bureau.

As might be expected, almost four-fifths had been in government employment without interruption. Of those who had a break in service, more than half had been out of the government for less than a year, and no one had been away longer than five years. Almost half of those not continuously in the service had gone into private industry, including their own business. Nearly half of the sample after entry into the civil service had taken either undergraduate or graduate courses, mostly to supplement previous academic work. Two-thirds of the entire group had not taken any academic courses in business administration or public administration. Among the courses preferred by the sample as part of an in-service training program for federal executives, public administration ranked highest (16 per cent), followed by business administration and personnel administration (10 per cent each).

The Advance of Equality

In speaking in economic terms about the civil service today, we need to stress that it is distinctly freer of the effects of social inequality than it was at the beginning of the twentieth century. As far as the higher service is concerned, a measurable broadening of the social base for recruitment since the end of World War I has pushed the center of gravity in the top cadre from the upper ranges of the middle class toward its lower ranges. This development, which is continuing rather than completed, gained considerable momentum in Germany during the republican period from 1919 to 1933, when it was helped along as a matter of democratic principle. Moreover, the Hitler regime, with its disavowal of the "Marxist" class struggle, intentionally advanced the lower middle class as its principal support. The parallel tendency in England was more even, if slower, but the cumulative effect has been significant in the changing social composition of the higher civil service. In France the establishment of the National School of Administration was meant to be in part a move toward making the higher service more democratic. A like orientation is being stressed among today's university-trained entrants into the Japanese civil service. These tendencies run parallel to the efforts of modern government to "modify the class chances of lower groups upward, and of higher groups downward," as C. Wright Mills has epitomized the social politics of our era.

The emphasis on equality has also run strong in the lawmaking bodies which after World War II set out to rebuild or reform the administrative system. For instance, in the legislative deliberation of the draft of a new German civil service act in 1953, provisions that smacked of discrimination of any kind fared badly. A clause authorizing the discharge of married women whose economic interests appeared satisfactorily taken care of by the family income was struck out, for "matrimony cannot be treated as a crime." Similarly, a modification was introduced into another clause under which the pension due a civil servant's widow was to be reduced if she was more than twenty years younger than her spouse and if they had been married only a relatively short time. The modification, urged on the theory that "men have grown a lot younger these days," made the clause inapplicable when there was a child, for then one could surely not speak of a "pension wedding."

The Settled Life

More democratic than ever before in terms of legal access and actual influx, committed to equality of basic standards, devoutly attached to procedural regularity, favoring permanence in order to maintain operating effectiveness—the merit bureaucracy is not the place for those who want to make money, to rise fast, to venture far, or to stand on their own. Entrance requirements of the service call for a demonstration of promise or ability that ordinarily bars the incompetent and may demand distinctly superior performance, as in the case of the entrance examinations for the British Administrative Class and for the National School of Administration in France. However, although generally one has to make a reasonably good showing to clear the hurdle of admission, the appeal of a government career tends to be strongest for the personality type called "solid"—as contrasted with the brilliant but restive, for instance.

This factor greatly adds to the pressure for extensive uniformity that in every large-scale organization is insisted upon in the name of control. Uniformity of procedure runs thickest in government, primarily because in the conduct of public affairs it is assumed to be best, as a matter of general political dogma, to cut down on discretionary freedom. When the common rule and the common mind combine, the natural consequence is a narrowness of perspective—a weakness more aggravating than mediocrity in administrative performance.

A contributing element is step-by-step advancement, which fosters the settled ways of seniority and the correlation of age with responsibility. It is therefore easy to see why the bureaucracy so often appears to trudge along in the rear of fresh thought and innovative change. Unless there is a fountain of regeneration in the spirit of the higher service, vital correctives have to come from the outside. Thus in agitated periods when government is dramatically pushed to the forefront of action, public service temporarily gains the aura of a great crusade joined by men and women from other walks of life. More important in the longer run is the presence of a favorable climate of opinion. Service with the government may have high prestige as a matter of national tradition, as it has had so long in Germany, for example. Institutional planning, by itself, necessarily has a lesser role. One remedy for narrowness of perspective lies in so formulating the entrance requirements and the career opportunities as to induce a fair share of the best minds among the younger generation to join the civil service. For full use of their intellectual contribution, they should be moved up to work near the points of decision before they have soured in the thicket of routines.

Predictable Returns

The economics of small chances magnifies the importance of each gain made. To be set back is a serious matter. It is not surprising, therefore, that in the parliamentary discussion of the draft of a new German civil service act the proposal to couple "diminishing performance" with a reduction in pay or grade did not get far. Similarly, in France delay or refusal of an automatic pay increase for less than satisfactory performance is viewed as an act of meanness unless the civil servant has managed to make himself a burden to his colleagues. Because in principle it is the same thing, the accelerated grant of an increment to a very good man, who thus would move ahead of the general timetable, is not regarded as desirable either.

But it is unnecessary to go to France to discover why special incentives in the form of honorific or money awards for superior achievement or constructive suggestions have not substantially quickened the institutional pace of work, despite a good statistical showing of employee participation. In another dimension the economics of small chances prompts the bureaucracy to take an unsympathetic view of general economy measures at its expense, such as the reductions in force and salary cuts that were enacted at the threshold of the thirties under the impact of the world-wide depression. The civil servant's reaction may be so strong as to get in the way of public policy.

This sensitivity to interference with the economic attributes of status is understandable in light of the fact that government as the sovereign employer is not known for generosity. In particular, government is notoriously slow in raising salaries in accord with a rising general level of prices and wages. One recent documentation of this point is the analysis of civil service pay in relation to private employment found in the report submitted in 1955 by the British Royal Commission on the Civil Service, headed by Sir Raymond Priestley. In the longer run, inequities in remuneration have serious effects. An even more striking example is republican Italy. There an equally long-overdue adjustment to the higher plateau of compensation in private business occurred in 1953, but the legislation simultaneously authorized the government to reorganize the civil service and thus to effect personnel cuts. We must remember, however, that the size of the administrative establishment and the use of patronage in filling regular positions have been two of the public grievances against the Christian Democratic party in the years since World War II.

Despite lagging salary levels, the depressed condition of Italy's south has made the civil service an insurance against unemployment for many holders of professional degrees from that region, especially those with law degrees. But the dependence of the intelligentsia on government jobs is a familiar fact in other places, too. There are many countries on the road toward industrialization in which the professionally trained individual finds it difficult to earn his living because he is not yet in great demand in the economy and because there are too few able to pay for his services.

Migration into Private Enterprise

In countries with a stronger economy, however, private business may become the object of a trickling or even pouring migration from the bureaucracy. Japan has been mentioned earlier. In France, too, commerce and industry have drawn on the higher service. More recently, this selective transfer of talent from the French bureaucracy has taken on the characteristics of an exodus of serious proportions. Perhaps there is a parallel in the dropping-off of exceptionally well-qualified aspirants for the higher civil service that occurred in the United States and in Britain in the middle fifties. Government may simply not stack up against more tempting conditions of employment elsewhere.

Another thing to be considered is the current easing of relations between private business and the civil service, going back to the forced partnership of World War II and continued in part as a result of nationalization measures, in part for defense planning, and in part as a matter of general policy. In the course of this development both sides have come to see more of—and in—the other. In the United States, for example, the evidence indicates that businessmen have a higher regard for the civil service than was the case before World War II. Trade journals and similar periodicals show fewer adverse references to those in public employment. In fields where government has a considerable portion of topnotch experts, as in the development and use of atomic energy, there is clearly a movement into private employment. To halt such drifts would require a substantial upward extension of the salary range in the civil service.

CIVIL SERVICE UNIONISM

The Shadow of the Sovereign Employer

If government as the sovereign employer were at once wise, attentive, and fair-minded, the proper self-interest of those in its service would be taken care of without much pleading. But to make such assumptions about the sovereign employer would be unrealistic in the light of experience. In consequence, civil servants nearly everywhere have resorted to organized efforts in promoting their self-interest, comparable to the pattern of collective action evolved by trade unionism.

The relationship between the sovereign employer's concern for his employees shown on his own initiative and the aggressiveness of collective action deserves attention. So does the fact that these two things are not opposites but alternatives. For instance, in Germany, where the sovereign employer has been traditionally a responsive employer, civil service unionism has not developed sharply militant tendencies. By contrast, in France the sovereign employer intrusted his determinations to many agents under auspices of departmental discretion and autonomy. It is no coincidence that French civil service syndicalism grew into a hard-driving force, becoming notorious abroad as well as at home, the bête noire of public administration.

What explains the responsiveness of the sovereign employer in Germany? It was mainly the result of the influence of the higher career men in policy formulation, especially in the Ministry of the Interior, which is officially concerned with the study, planning, drafting, and shepherding of proposed civil service legislation. Moreover, the public and the legislators had been educated, in the course of a long historic development, to give special care to the condition of the civil service as a vital factor in the nation's life. On the other

hand, during the lifetime of the Third Republic the French ministerial civil servants still stood in the shadow of the authoritarian tradition. They were accepted neither by the legislative body nor by their
own political superiors as trustworthy proponents of reform ideas,
and the rank and file of the civil service shared these misgivings.

The Course of Civil Service Unionism

In an occupational grouping of such size and in physical possession of such important functions, it is remarkable that civil service
unionism, by and large, has neither grown into an unruly giant nor
wavered much from a course of caution and moderation. This must
be laid to several causes. It resulted in part from the bureaucracy's
basically sincere ideology of service. It stemmed in part from an
awareness of the obvious limitations set to collective bargaining
with the sovereign employer. In part it also flowed from the knowledge that the support of the public is indispensable in bringing about
desired improvements in the conditions of government employment.

With their eyes on the public, civil servants have pressed for the
right of association and with it the right of affiliation with organized
labor, which in Britain was withdrawn from them in the wake of the
general strike of 1926 and which was not recovered until twenty
years later, in the same year in which the French civil service won
its "general statute" (1946). But the explosive issue of the "right to
strike" has usually been handled with kid gloves by spokesmen of
civil service unions. Perhaps all that needs to be said on this point is
that general civil service strikes have no acknowledged place in the
armory of collective tactics as a practical matter. All the same, scattered strikes or similar harassing actions must be reckoned with in
exceptional situations, especially in manufacturing activities or utili-
ties in government operation, where the common rules of public
employment collide abruptly with customary forms of labor pressure.

The French Development

Civil service unionism, generally, has showed a slow and steady
growth. In France the syndicalist doctrine took hold of the rank and
file of the civil service as early as the eighties of the last century.
The mailmen organized first, followed by government employees in
the arsenals and the state railways. For long, however, the legal basis
of such associations was in doubt. Even after postal-employee organizations were given formal sanction in 1899, the theory lived on that
the great body of personnel tied into the exercise of authority was
prevented from forming syndicates.

Resentful of the government's negative attitude, the rank and file was readily taken over by the labor movement. After the general strike of 1920, the government tried to undo this affiliation with organized labor. But it suffered legislative defeat, largely because of the resolute opposition of civil service associations. The resulting animosity increased as different cabinets took different positions, while the service unions came to show something like a persecution complex. This meant that untold grievances, which under other circumstances might have been settled within the executive branch, were pushed up into the parliamentary committees. A resolution of the issue, by affirmation of the right of association and affiliation, occurred only in the Fourth Republic.

Pluralism versus Unity

Elsewhere the evolution has usually not taken so long. In Great Britain, for example, after some repression during the seventies, official toleration had been extended to organizations of postmen by 1890. Recognition came in 1906, and in 1914 the right of collective representation had been granted generally. In Canada the landmarks fall a little later, the strongest push coming during the first two decades of our century. Typically, the pattern of association is set by historic chance rather than by considered standards of greatest effectiveness. Groups form in response to particular irritations as well as to strong leadership, and they often stay separate for no special reason other than organizational loyalty and the self-motivation of a full-time headquarters nucleus.

Although working agreements usually exist between various associations, the organizational divisions drain away strength and influence. This is true especially in France. What increased unity in collective action can do is evident from Germany's experience. There the united federations of civil servants, generally shunning a "trade-union aproach," have long known how to get full consideration in policy matters from the Ministry of the Interior and the legislative committees. There, also, the difference between the numerically thin voice of the higher civil service and the full-throated demands of the rank and file is reduced by the scope of a common service doctrine. By comparison, in England these two elements frequently seem to talk from different worlds.

Organized or not organized, however, civil service sentiment is reasonably predictable and predictably unified on certain points. It is generally inclined to view "Parkinson's Law" as divinely ordained— that immutable law of ever rising personnel figures so brilliantly invented by the London *Economist* (see pp. 7–8). As for "Parkinson's Law" in reverse, an illustration was furnished in France in the early fifties when the Financial Inspection Service sought to simplify and improve the administrative methods used in the tax system. Sounding like one voice, the civil service unions representing the bulk of the personnel in the revenue services defeated these attempts, despite deep and growing public discontent over the operating defects in the administration of taxes.

Organized Collaboration with the Government

Freedom of association among civil servants is channeled toward productive results when representatives of the government undertake to consult with representatives of the staff side as a regular procedure. This idea received a large impetus with the first meeting, on July 23, 1919, of Britain's National Council for the Administrative and Legal Departments of the Civil Service, better known as the Whitley Council. Together with the corresponding departmental councils, about seventy in number, this arrangement for continuous joint consideration of the "conditions of service" has proved eminently fruitful.

But similar arrangements do not always work the same way. Although the Whitley Council has its counterpart in Switzerland, the Swiss Joint Committee on Civil Service Matters is not an exact parallel. Like the Whitley Council, the Joint Committee is built on the principle of equal representation of the government side and of the staff side under an impartial chairman. But the character of its conclusions, usually arrived at unanimously, has given the Swiss Joint Committee in the eyes of the public the markings of an employee organ, rather in contrast to the reputation of the joint disciplinary review committee in each of the departments.

Still a different application of the same formula is found in Canada. Long gingerly talked about, a counterpart to the Whitley Council came into existence as the National Joint Council of the Public Service as late as 1944. It started slowly, partly because joint consideration of problems and issues requires a good deal of preparatory work from the staff side. The limited resources of the Canadian civil service associations were more adequate to the handling of specific cases before the joint appeal boards. These had been created in 1939 for review of grievances brought by civil servants who in a promotion felt passed over without sufficient reason. In 1946 the jurisdiction of the appeal boards was extended to cover demotions and dismissals as well. This procedure has been praised both as a source of greater confidence in the fairness of personnel determinations and as discouragement of acts of arbitrariness and manipulation.

In these respects the Canadian example is rather like the French under the Fourth Republic. The new French Higher Council of the Civil Service (see p. 77) has not yet got beyond a somewhat inconclusive beginning. But the joint machinery for consultation on matters of departmental management as well as on cases of promotion and discipline has been a greater success. To enter into joint consideration of broader matters demands capacity for marshaling supporting facts and figures, on the one hand, and self-control in refraining from playing to the gallery, on the other. Depending on their habits as well as their resources, civil service unions may find such demands too hard to meet.

CHAPTER 7

THE MAKING OF CAREER MEN

The picture of the bureaucratic world conveyed in the preceding chapter suggests that bureaucrats, by and large, are made by the contagion of their operating environment. To put it somewhat differently, nobody has good reason to think of himself as a career man unless he has tested his fitness for public administration over a considerable time. But he would not begin such testing without being guided into the civil service by some image of what it is—a brotherhood pledged to the general welfare; a life reverberating with the excitement of great decisions; a respectable profession; or simply a steady job.

That image is greatly affected by what qualifications are asked of the aspirant upon entry, by the general nature of the prescribed entrance requirements. Thus the career man is molded in part by what he believes he should be like as he passes through the portals of government service. In part, however, he is also influenced, and perhaps even more strongly, by the rules of proper behavior observed by those exercising public functions. We shall now turn to a consideration of these two formative forces in the making of career men, beginning with standards of selection and taking up next the canons of conduct that govern the bureaucracy.

STANDARDS OF SELECTION

Practical Examinations?

What is to be found out in the entrance examination about those who will eventually compete among themselves for key positions in the top cadre of the bureaucracy? Should they prove themselves experienced in "management" or at least informed about it? If they are asked to demonstrate experience, they must have gained such experience elsewhere. Here the first question is, Where could they acquire experience pertinent to the responsibilities of higher civil servants? The next question is, How satisfactory would recruitment of middle-aged experience be? And the third question is, What would the mind of this kind of entrant be like? But similar questions are raised when we substitute knowledge about "management" for experience in its practice. Obviously, the acquisition of such knowledge at the price of a fuller orientation toward the nature and the needs of our civilization is a doubtful investment.

By contrast, for sharing in the direction of government agencies a broadly trained mind is better than one filled with expert knowledge of a special field. The typical department combines in its functions a number of different specializations. Thus the principal thing in directing it is a capacity for looking beyond each specialization and for correlating all in the formulation of departmental policies and programs. The talent needed in this activity cannot be expected to come forth when entrance examinations are closely geared to the practical needs of particular administrative operations or even of particular positions. Indeed, then there will be little room for the career idea—a life's work with increasing responsibilities which do not culminate in a few routine promotions. On every score, therefore, it is distinctly preferable for these purposes that the entrance examinations focus on those resources of mind and personality that are of great value on every level of responsibility but of greatest value on the top levels. In the United States recruitment has long been in the grip of an examination system stressing particular lines of work. Progressive liberation from this system is only a recent accomplishment, one still far from completed.

The Legally Trained Mind: Germany

We saw earlier (pp. 46 ff.) that the question of what the "university man" should bring into the public service has been answered differently by different nations. The particular answer determines to a large extent the characteristics of the bureaucracy, for the "university man," gravitating to the points of greatest responsibility, has a strong effect upon the entire administrative system—in working methodology as well as in mentality and moral fortitude. One answer has been called here the German answer, although in fact it is an answer common to many European countries ranging from Denmark to Greece and relied upon also in other parts of the world. This approach makes a predominantly juridical study program the normal road of entry into the higher civil service, without ignoring additional paths for specified alternatives such as economics.

Juridical study, depending on what it actually is, can do more than merely lead to legal knowledge. Traditionally, juridical study in Germany proceeded with a background of Roman law—that great disciplinarian of logical and impersonal thought. Hence juridical study was also an induction into both the spirit and the mechanics of objectivity, into a manner of analysis, into the art of consistency. Moreover, legal study had a bearing upon how to deal with conflicting interests, which is the heart of public affairs. The recognition given to such fields as political science, economics, and history made the juridical course of study a still more useful preparation for the assumption of top responsibilities in public administration.

The requirement of completed juridical study could not fail to infuse into administrative responsibility a deep concern with legality. For the exercise of governmental powers such concern is no less important than efficiency. It concentrated on both the sufficiency of legal authority as a basis of administrative action and the observance of legal safeguards built around the citizen's interests. Thus in the entrance examination for the probationary service the aspirant could not afford to be ignorant of constitutional law or administrative law, but he was not expected to know much about technical approaches to work measurement, as contrasted to its general theory and use. Similarly, it would be highly unlikely that three years later a candidate for the final examination might be pressed for an enumeration of the "principles of management," although he would not commend himself to his examining commission if he knew nothing about the history of Prussian administration, the theory of taxation, or the practical significance of a point of procedure before the administrative courts. On balance, public administration gained greatly by being conducted in accordance with impartial rules, but simultaneously it became rule-minded.

"Gentleman's Education": Great Britain

The British entrance examinations for the Administrative Class, on the other hand, favor a good record of study, without undue limitation in subject-matter field. The classics, history, literature, and languages have long rated high. The social sciences—in today's sense —were welcomed relatively late and less warmly. As a result, intellectual strength ordinarily has been in greater supply than a forward-looking comprehension of where the world was going.

Needless to say, the British entrance examinations do not presuppose any special knowledge of public administration. The evidence of academic attainment looked for would be equally desirable for men meant to use their heads anywhere, as in research or in mapping the general course of action in business. Greater infusion of the social sciences into the examination pattern has been urged in recent decades by informed critics. One response is the new degree in politics, philosophy, and economics at Oxford. Even this degree, however, lies considerably closer to the British concept of learning than does a corresponding social science degree in the United States.

Institutional Traits

Expressed in institutional traits, the member of the higher civil service in Germany will generally lean on his assistants from the next lower career group to attend to the operating methods of public administration. He will ask questions when there is a special occasion, comment on new developments he has learned about, and insist on prompt remedies when something has gone wrong. Otherwise, however, he will leave these matters in the capable hands of the men of the middle groups of the service, who are the direct supervisors of departmental activities. To the higher civil servant, "management" is an inseparable part of performing each of the functions of the department. In this work he will regard it as his essential responsibility to assure himself and his minister at the helm of the department that its activities, including actions proposed by the minister himself, are in accord with law.

He will also employ his judgment and experience in shaking down the departmental operating methods into craftsman-like written procedures and regulations. Roman law being a teacher of economy of phrase, the regulatory language of German public administration is comparatively concise. In these matters it is of great consequence that the administrative mind and the legal mind are in the same rather than different organizational boxes. Perhaps mainly for this reason, economy in imposing controls, internal as well as effective upon the public, is a traditional feature of German administrative practice.

When not absorbed in a specific legal job, a legally trained mind functions as the "generalist" face to face with the functional specialists of the department—by getting them together and uniting them on a combined type of action, such as a departmental program. But acceptance of the "generalist" on the top level of the administrative system is still more explicit in England. There the higher civil servant is meant to contribute to the direction of his department and to the supporting planning process a mind prepared to probe into policy as well as operating issues and to convert findings into recommendations for action. That mind draws consciously on its cultural orientation, gained at the university. This is also the ideal pursued in the new National School of Administration in France. By comparison, the American civil servant on the higher levels of responsibility tends to remain a specialist in the administrative process. He is the man who knows how to put policy into effect but who is less often its initiator.

Routes into the Higher Service

European civil service developments since the end of World War II, generally speaking, show a strong inclination to maintain and strengthen the higher career as a key group in the administrative system. To illustrate, in England the novel route of entrance into the Administrative Class which was adapted from wartime experiments with officer selection has proved to be more than a temporary expedient. Originally popularized somewhat misleadingly as the "house party," the new evaluation procedure has been shaken down to a set of group tests combined with intellectual, psychological, and general interviews as well as with written exercises. Known as Method II, this alternative to the traditional literary examination has won praise for leading to a more incisive probing of the candidate's personality. On the other hand, most entrants coming directly from the universities have continued to make use of the older method. Graduates from Oxford or Cambridge are still clearly ahead in winning placement in the Administrative Class. In the last twenty years, however, there has been a measurable broadening of the social basis of England's undergraduate population, with the subsidized scholar becoming much more frequent in the old as well as the newer universities.

As a counterpart within the civil service itself, provision has been made in recent years for the conduct of examinations to enable civil servants in the lower grades to move into the Administrative Class as well as the Executive Class. Moreover, the Executive Class—the key management group below the Administrative Class—has been given enlarged responsibilities. This, in turn, has strengthened its co-operative bond with the Administrative Class and minimized the danger of undesirable insulation on either side.

In Germany, as in the past, the aspirant for the higher administrative career enters the probationary service from the university. There he has usually completed a type of juridical study which carries with it more of an introduction to the social sciences and public affairs than does law-school training in the United States. If he qualifies in the entrance examination, he will be moved about for three years from one work situation to another in the judiciary as well as in the administrative system, in each instance under the eyes of a senior who contributes his judgment of performance and prospects to the personnel record.

As in Britain, great reliance is placed on such practical learning under guidance for making trained minds into resourceful civil servants. At the end comes the final examination. Its outcome usually tells the aspirant whether and how soon he may expect an appointment "on trial" and subsequently a permanent appointment. To provide added opportunities for specialized study, the Administrative Academy at Speyer has been built up in the postwar period to a center for advanced training.

Training Preferences

Democratization was one of the fundamental goals of the French civil service reform. The spirit of the Resistance had been the spirit of the whole people, and the political as well as social exclusiveness long characteristic of the higher career seemed less tolerable than ever. The first classes enrolled in the new National School of Administration gave themselves such names as *France Combattante* and *Croix de Lorraine*. The halls were named for officials—including a woman—who by acts of self-denial had given their lives for France during the war. The only exception, the Council Room, bears the name of the chairman of the administrative committee in charge of the short-lived School of Administration founded in 1848. Such evocation of personal sacrifice is hard to extend into an administrative setting, but the available evidence points to the presence of high public spirit among the sixty or seventy graduates whom the National School has annually contributed to the civil service.

Competition for admission to the National School is very sharp, both from the level of advanced education and from within the service. Once admitted, the candidate passes through a three-year program of preparation that represents a very original combination of familiar concepts. During the first year he is sent out to struggle through the administrative brambles in the field, perhaps as far away as a Moroccan outpost. What is particularly noteworthy is that he is constantly held to the doer's direct responsibility toward the outside world, in contrast with the performance of staff work, where he could easily creep into the shadow of others. The next year is spent at the National School, where he faces a tough curriculum of courses and seminars. The study method is aimed for the most part at developing the student's skill in using broad knowledge to come forth with practical answers to policy questions in a week or two. In the third year he is meant to draw on his first-year experience in order to test the analytical competence he acquired during the second year. This begins with an observer's assignment in private enterprise, to see still another work environment and to learn about both the employer's and the employee's point of view. Thereafter, the student devotes himself to the kinds of projects, in conference sections or individually in one or the other department, that will occupy him after graduation.

As in the grooming of aspirants for the higher career in Great Britain and in Germany, the National School deals with public administration in the wider context of public affairs, rather lightly by American standards. It would be surprising should the new Advanced School of Public Administration in Italy move in a different direction in this respect, but greater emphasis on management subjects is evident in the recruitment for administrative responsibilities in Switzerland. Somewhat ironically, this is one of the results of the absence of a general higher career service. To fill the void to some extent, commercial training has been made to substitute in part for university study in the home service.

Such substitution is made easier because in defining and applying standards of selection great leeway is left to the individual departments. On the other hand, the Swiss regulations of 1955 prescribe that the candidate's "qualities as superior" be given due consideration, in addition to "abilities and character, experience, previous accomplishments, and conduct." Moreover, Switzerland has improvised another part-way solution by filling many of the top career posts at home from the ranks of the foreign service. It is in the foreign service only, specifically the diplomatic grade, that completed university study is recognized as a general requirement. According to the regulations governing admission to the diplomatic grade of the Swiss foreign service of 1955, the entrance examination for the two-year probationary term is to test the university graduate's "general education, his alert interest in political and cultural questions, and his ability to express himself concisely and accurately," together with his knowledge of Swiss constitutional law, international law, history, and economics. One subject reserved for emphasis in the final examination is the history and the importance of Swiss neutrality.

CANONS OF CONDUCT

Restraint versus Privacy

In Plato's outline of the best form of government the guardians held an honored place in the city-state, but their lives were governed by the public interest. For one thing, being maintained out of the resources of the state, they were not permitted to acquire property. Nor were they allowed the ordinary satisfactions of matrimony and parenthood. Although encouraged to have offspring, who might prove guardian material, they were neither to rear nor to educate them; both would be done institutionally. These rules were not intended to make guardian service tougher. They were meant to keep the guardians free from the distractions of personal responsibilities and private concerns.

Civil servants today are not under so severe a regimen, but the conditions of their status include considerable restraints, placed upon them principally in the name of compatibility. Where their public role and their private interests collide, the resolution of the conflict, as a general guideline, is accomplished by appropriate containment of these private interests. Exactly how to draw the line of compatibility has been a matter of historic evolution as well as of prevailing concepts of public necessity.

Related to the spread of democratic government, the tendency has been to reduce, as far as possible, the restrictions upon the civil servant's privacy that flow from his official position. That is particularly true of his civic rights—his participation, like every other citizen, in the political process, especially in elections, as we shall see later (pp. 143 ff.). More recently, however, a countertendency has asserted itself, which, without directly touching the civil servant as voter, has greatly sharpened the compatibility requirements imposed upon him. This countertendency had its origin in World War II and the vastly increased security-consciousness of governments as they faced a world divided and filled with unrelenting antagonism.

The Napoleonic Shadow: France

In the administrative system shaped at the start of the nineteenth century in France by the strong hands of Napoleon I, authority was made the taskmaster of efficiency. Authority was also the source of the legal relationship between the state and the civil servant—a relationship determined unilaterally. The discretionary implications of a unilateral determination of the civil service relationship, made solely on the authority of the state, have lived on into the twentieth century. They echoed in the stormy history of French civil service syndicalism as an extralegal counterdrive. They were a motivating factor in the dispatch with which the Fourth Republic adopted the "general statute of the civil service." As recently as in the closing period of the Third Republic, the carry-over of the French civil servant's official capacity into his private capacity was stated as follows:

> The duty of the civil servant consists essentially in devoting his work to the public service. He cannot content himself with doing his work like an ordinary worker, who goes off when his task is finished and has no connection with his employer outside the hours spent in the shop. The civil servant is attached body and soul to the public service. The status of civil servant does not leave him for a single instant even when distant from his office.[1]

Needless to say, this doctrine flew into the face of the rank and file of civil servants when they advanced their collective interest on the model of the labor movement. In full force, they were able to threaten cabinets and to negotiate parliamentary promises without being much bothered by the state's proprietary stake in their souls. On the other hand, it is equally true that the state's superiority in the civil service relationship was limited by legal principles. These legal principles had been developed in the judicial decisions of the Council of State, acting in the capacity of France's supreme administrative court. The easy and inexpensive access to the machinery of administrative justice was of equal value to each civil servant, however humble his position. It contributed to the gradual consolidation of the civil service relationship in terms of legal standards that could not be brushed aside by a superior acting in the name of the sovereign employer.

The Professional Spirit: Germany

The basic rule of conduct for the German bureaucracy was laid down in the civil service act of 1873. Section 10 read: "Every civil servant is obliged to fulfill conscientiously, according to the constitution and the laws, the duties of the office conferred upon him and to prove himself in his behavior inside and outside the office worthy of the esteem which his profession requires." Very much like the French doctrine, this fundamental provision was construed consistently to mean that the civil servant was at no time as unrestricted as the private individual. Only a few years before Hitler in 1933 dis-

1. In the introduction to the French civil service contributed by Aubert Lefas to Leonard D. White (ed.), *The Civil Service in the Modern State* (Chicago: University of Chicago Press, 1930), p. 238.

placed republican government, the traditional concept was restated by Prussia's Supreme Administrative Court when it declared that the civil service relationship "embraces the whole personality of the civil servant. Never is he merely a private citizen."

One important distinction between the German and the French doctrines should not be overlooked. The German civil service act did not impose rules of conduct by higher authority. The governing criterion for the civil servant was to show himself "worthy of the esteem which his profession requires." The appeal was to the professional spirit of the civil service, to "pride of outfit," in military language. Moreover, disputes over infractions went to the independent disciplinary courts, which drew part of the bench from the bureaucracy by permanent appointment. Thus the case law of conduct applicable to the civil servant was essentially the judgment of his peers.

This correlation of basic principle with the living ethics of the administrative profession proved persuasive in other countries, too. One example is Switzerland, where the issue of self-restraint outside as well as inside the office, in the German manner, was still hotly argued in the public debates that accompanied the adoption of the civil service act of 1927. In the years afterward, the propriety of the concept and its compatibility with legitimate civic interests have been accepted even among the spokesmen of the rank and file. The law reads as follows: "In his behavior on and off duty, the civil servant must prove himself worthy of the esteem and the confidence which his official position requires."

After World War II it was Germany's turn to borrow from Switzerland. The old Section 10 was no longer good enough. The new version in the civil service act of 1953 formulates the traditional rule thus:

The civil servant shall dedicate himself to his profession with full devotion. He must administer his office selflessly and according to the directions of his conscience. His conduct inside and outside the office must do justice to the esteem and confidence which his profession requires.

As developed by the German disciplinary courts, the case law of professional conduct, binding upon all civil servants, has crystallized answers to many specific questions. To begin with the most obvious, the bureaucracy must always be conscious of its essential task—to function as an agency of the general interest. The tenor of the German decisions was apparent in one of the leading commentaries on the civil service law (1931) as follows: "In his official capacity the civil servant must pursue the common good, and not only remain impartial but not even endanger his impartiality or give occasion for distrust of it." Or, as the German civil service act of 1953 puts it: "The civil servant . . . must perform his task impartially and justly and bear in mind in the conduct of his office the well-being of the general public."

But the act made plain that the necessary neutrality of the civil servant in the conflict of political, economic, and social interests stops short of any indifference toward the basic form of government. In the language of the act, "By his entire conduct the civil servant must profess his attachment to the free, democratic order in the sense of the Basic Law and exert himself for its preservation."

Sense of Propriety

Doubts about the civil servant's impartiality might arise from any political partisanship—a subject to be discussed later (pp. 143 ff.). But doubts could also be prompted by any careless involvement in money deals and other economic transactions based on knowledge or "contacts" acquired in official activities. In these matters a civil servant was expected to think twice and not simply to adopt the profit philosophy of private enterprise. Indeed, cautions applicable to him would also be applicable to the members of his immediate family. The safest line for him, on this point as on others, was to stay meticulously outside the shadow of doubt.

Despite all straight-laced righteousness, the law of conduct remained remarkably free, nevertheless, from the excesses of petty moralizing. For instance, unless unusual circumstances put a special slant on the matter, the disciplinary courts showed themselves disinclined to get into such questions as whether Jack was a privileged visitor in Mary's apartment. Moreover, with commendable firmness they refused to place women civil servants in a separate category in this matter. If the men were not to be asked questions, neither were the ladies.

Obligations of the Sovereign Employer

Still more important, German civil service law recognized a counterpart to the obligations of the career man, a counterpart consisting of the obligations that fell upon the state. The state was duty-bound to return the fidelity of its servants by being faithful to them. For example, let us assume that Herr Müller, in a condition of acute depression brought on by a string of trying experiences in the office, had submitted his resignation, taken to his bed, and refused to respond to any inquiries from his department. Let us assume further that the resignation had been acted upon, with the result that Herr

Müller was released from the service. But was he? If he changed his mind and sought reinstatement, the department could not simply hide behind the resignation as an accomplished fact. The critical point would be what the department had done to establish the seriousness of the intent underneath the resignation and how much concern it had shown for the condition in which Herr Müller had been during this period. Short of a showing that the state had actually lived up to its duty of fidelity in the particular instance, the department could not expect the court to let the matter rest on the strength of the resignation.

The state's duty of fidelity toward its civil servants carried with it a duty of care, in the sense of attention to their well-being. This, for instance, implied an obligation in law for the sovereign employer to provide working conditions that would not impair the health or safety of his employees. Although temporary overwork in unforeseen emergencies was not exceptional, the state's duty of care would not permit unreasonably strenuous assignments. According to the Supreme Court, the degree of consideration to which the civil servant was entitled depended in part on his general physical condition and the particular circumstances. Thus a partly disabled veteran was not to be employed in such a way that his handicap might become more serious.

The Ideal of Impartiality: Great Britain

From the very beginning, the British civil service has been in the keeping of the crown. That is to say, the bureaucracy came to share in the peculiar combination of detachment from party positions and of constitutional permanence reflected by the monarchy as the symbolic bond connecting not only the peoples of the British Commonwealth but also the strands of national tradition. This combination of detachment and permanence was strengthened, not weakened, by the fact that the monarchy was linked with the dynamics of political decision. For the authority of the crown is exercised constitutionally by the cabinet, which in turn is the executive agency of the legislative majority in the House of Commons. Because it is meant to be at the full disposal of the government of the day, whatever the party emblem, the civil service must attend to the affairs of each government with equal solicitude.

The concept is illustrated in an apocryphal story recounted of Maurice Hankey, long the career head of the cabinet secretariat. When he was told that the Labor government wanted a draft bill providing for the abolition of the House of Lords, he paled but calmly inquired whether he might take until Wednesday noon to do it, in view of the importance of the subject. Equally to the point is what Clement Attlee, from his exceptional experience as former prime minister and long-time leader of the parliamentary Labor party, wrote in 1954:

I do not think that this remarkable attribute of impartiality in the British Civil Service is sufficiently widely known or adequately recognized for what it is—one of the strongest bulwarks of democracy. I am often at pains to point this out and did so at a recent conference of Asiatic socialists in Rangoon where I told them, to their surprise, that the same men who had worked out the details of Labour's Transport Act were now, at the behest of a Conservative Government, engaged in pulling it to pieces.[2]

The axiom of impartiality and the supporting rules of conduct grouped around it were essentially the product of civil service self-policing in Britain. As in Germany, the nature of the thing, out of itself, furnished a practical guide. It was a guide implicit rather than explicit, accepted as plain enough without much legal specification, and regarded as too little in danger of abuse by superiors to warrant the sort of judicial review which in France is supplied by the Council of State and in Germany by the disciplinary courts. In Herman Finer's words:

No law or general administrative code lays down a scheme of disciplinary misdemeanors and accompanying penalties. A Civil Servant has no legal action against dismissal. His superannuation rights are ultimately determinable by the Treasury, for its interpretation of the Acts is not challengeable in the Courts.[3]

Disciplinary Procedure

What the British civil servant can demand is that he be given a bill of particulars in support of any charge against him before disciplinary action is taken. If this bill of particulars is actually the result of an inquiry into the facts thorough enough to satisfy a judicial body, subsequent court review might not add much to the fair disposition of the case. Such inquiry may be entirely informal or by official appointment of a special panel.

Without being required by law, examination of disciplinary charges by special panel is not an infrequent occurrence. When the

2. "Civil Servants, Ministers, Parliament and the Public," *Political Quarterly,* XXV (1954), 309.

3. *The Theory and Practice of Modern Government* (London: Allen & Unwin, 1932), II, 1444.

conduct of members of the Administrative Class is in question, the facts normally are looked into by a specially appointed board of inquiry composed of senior civil servants. Reports by such special boards, together with an occasional Treasury memorandum, have taken the place occupied elsewhere by other authoritative pronouncements. Although, in the British view, the scope of the civil servant's obligations away from the office is governed by a presumption of privacy which is different from the French and the German, the inferences to be derived are alike. This is evident from the so-called Gregory case in 1928, which had its origin in speculative activities involving foreign currency. There the board of inquiry declared:

The first duty of a civil servant is to give his undivided allegiance to the State at all times and on all occasions when the State has a claim to his services. With his private activities the State is in general not concerned, so long as his conduct therein is not such as to bring discredit upon the Service of which he is a member. But to say that he is not to subordinate his duty to his private interests, nor to make use of his official position to further those interests, is to say no more than that he must behave with common honesty. The Service demands from itself the highest standards, because it recognizes that the State is entitled to demand that its servants shall not only be honest in fact, but beyond the reach of suspicion of dishonesty. . . . A civil servant is not so to order his private affairs as to allow a suspicion to arise that a trust has been abused, or a confidence betrayed. . . .

Practical rules for the guidance of social conduct depend also as much upon the instinct and perception of the individual as upon cast-iron formulas; and the surest guide will, we hope, always be found in the nice and jealous honor of Civil Servants themselves. The public expects from them a standard of integrity and conduct not only inflexible but fastidious, and has not been disappointed in the past. We are confident that we are expressing the view of the Service when we say that the public have a right to expect that standard, and that it is the duty of the Service to see that the expectation is fulfilled.[4]

Restraint of Economic Self-interest

A comparable case of conflicting public and private interests occurred in 1936, when a special board of inquiry probed the conduct of Sir Christopher Bullock, then permanent secretary to the Air Ministry. The heart of the case was a number of informal conversations spread over some two years between Sir Christopher and representatives of Imperial Airways in connection with a government contract. During these conversations Sir Christopher had made allusion to his desire to leave the service and to his availability for

4. Cmd. 3037 (1928).

either the chairmanship or a directorship with Imperial Airways—
an arrangement apparently much to the company's liking. Moreover,
at the beginning of the contract negotiations he had suggested to
the Secretary of State for Air that the king bestow a high honor
upon the chairman of the company. In its detailed report the board
of inquiry declared Sir Christopher's actions "intrinsically improper."
It found these actions "completely at variance" with the standards
of conduct of the civil service despite the fact that none of the actions had actually influenced the negotiations for the contract. The
prime minister accepted these findings, and Sir Christopher was dismissed.

How does a career man take such a blow? A clue is supplied in
the personal statement that Sir Christopher made to the press, given
out at the same time that the report of the board of inquiry was
made public.[5] The discharged officer did not flinch. But while giving
recognition to the board's "impartiality," he said:

I do not seek to shirk responsibility for consequences which have flowed
from my own actions. But it is easy to be wise after the event; and fortu-
nate is he . . . who can honestly say that, if every private and informal conversation he has held were sifted and resifted months, even years, after-
wards in the rarefied atmosphere of a solemn and formal inquisition, no
passing phrase uttered in an unguarded moment could be held injudicious,
no word or deed be called in question in some degree by absolute standards
of taste or propriety. Whatever judgment your readers may pass on my
mistakes, I hope they may be charitable enough to temper it with that
reflection.

Perhaps Sir Christopher had a stronger point in a somewhat different sense. In sitting with representatives of private enterprise
around the same conference table, civil servants were faced with a
novel test of career ethics. In a way, what in this instance had happened would have been perfectly normal behavior among businessmen. With government becoming increasingly a negotiator in the
economy, rather than functioning solely as a regulator, old questions
begged for new answers. Not surprisingly, the Bullock case was followed in 1937 with the issuance of the official Memorandum on the
Subject of Acceptance of Business Appointments by Officers of the
Crown Services.

Without contradicting the conclusions reached in the Gregory and
Bullock cases, the rank and file has generally been in favor of keeping official duties from spilling over into the private life of the civil
servant, especially upon his freedom of organization. Thus, when

5. See the *Times* (London) of August 6, 1936.

Clause V of the Trade Disputes and Trade Unions Act of
p. 87) blocked affiliation with the labor movement, W. ,
the general secretary of the Civil Service Clerical Asso
pressed his opposition as follows:

The first thing which is clear is that the private view of the civil serva
does not absolve him from his obligations to the government as his em
ployer. Outside his official duties the position of the civil servant is that of
the private citizen—no more, no less. There ought to be no compulsion of
civil servants to act otherwise than as ordinary citizens. Most emphatically
he is not obliged by virtue of the fact that he is a civil servant to endorse
the view of the government of the day. Nor is there anything in the position of the civil servant which disqualifies him individually (or collectively
with his colleagues) from having relations with bodies outside the service
provided always that these relations do not involve any failure on the part
of the civil servant to carry out the duties for which he is paid.[6]

This statement, however, was not meant to be a plea for the civil
servant's "right to strike." Indeed, such a "right" has never been
claimed by the Civil Service Clerical Association. The range of substitutes for the "right to strike" has been outlined in the preceding
discussion of civil service unionism (see pp. 105 ff.).

Statutory Requirements: United States

A different approach to the matter of civil service conduct is represented by the example of the United States. In the federal government, and to an even greater extent in the several states, the absence
of an institutionally recognized higher career has arrested the formation of a professional sense of service ethics. By comparison, the new
city-manager profession in local government, product of the twentieth century, soon took the initiative in adopting a code of ethics for
its members. Historically, the United States Civil Service Commission saw its role in shielding the merit rule against the pressure of
the spoilsmen. Consequently, civil service regulations have been
more concerned with keeping those under the merit system politically sterilized than with fostering a career point of view that could be
trusted to acknowledge implicit restraints of conduct. The result
has been a sprouting of explicit requirements laid down by legislative enactments, helped along by the indigenous tendency that
"there ought to be a law" whenever there is a question.

What are the expressly prohibited actions? They are defined casu-
istically and often ambiguously. In the first place, no one who represents a private concern or is directly or indirectly interested in its

6. *Red Tape* (organ of the Civil Service Clerical Association), XV (1927), 385.

profits or contracts may act on behalf of the government in transacting business with the concern. In turn, a federal officer or employee may not receive private compensation for services rendered in relation to any contract in which the government is a party or directly or indirectly interested, or in relation to any proceeding, claim, or other matter in which the government is directly or indirectly interested. Moreover, he may not aid in the prosecution of any claim against the government nor do so for two years after leaving his public position in cases involving a subject directly connected with those he dealt with previously. No federal officer or employee may receive pay for services performed by him for the government from any source other than the government, except as may be contributed by a state, county, or municipality; and no contribution may be made from private sources toward his salary. Without authority, he may not release officially received confidential information or use it privately, especially for speculation. He may not ask or accept any money, check, promise, or gratuity with the intent to have his action on any question before him influenced by it. Finally, he may not engage in business activities that are incompatible with the duties of his office. As the Attorney General has put it in one of his official opinions, a government officer or employee "cannot in his private or official character enter into engagements in which he has, or can have, a conflicting personal interest. He cannot allow his public duties to be neglected by reason of attention to his private affairs."

Government Employment as Privilege

The legislative treatment of civil service conduct has been a mixed blessing. It had a dampening effect upon the development of a high ethical sensitivity out of the resources of the bureaucracy. This is not to suggest a lack of common virtues in the civil service. Quite the contrary—the merit system and "clean government" have come to be practically synonymous. But ordinary honesty is one thing, and alert awareness of professional canons of behavior, settling subtler things, is another. The subtler things were not touched when in 1954 all federal departments were instructed to set up within themselves special machinery for internal inspection.

One further factor that discourages the crystallization of civil service ethics is the tendency of American society to keep authority and office within the range of common man's rules. This is a thoroughly democratic tendency. The desirability for the official not to stand apart is asserted inside as well as outside the civil service. Civil

service ethics seem an exotic thing when the ordinary man's
have an aura of wholesomeness and sufficiency about them. Bu
"free-enterprise system" is not a good guide for official morality
close parallel, if not an inference, is the far-reaching axiom th.
government employment is at the sovereign employer's pleasure and
hence legally a privilege. In other words, government employment
is not a source of rights unless such rights be expressly granted by
legislation.

In this matter, ironically, the shadow of Mr. Justice Holmes looms
large, although, for once, it is an obnoxious shadow. In one of his
lightest judicial quips, while still on the Massachusetts bench,
Holmes helped to squelch an action brought by a fired policeman by
telling him that he "may have a constitutional right to talk politics,
but he has no constitutional right to be a policeman" (1892). Instead
of vanishing with time, this line of thought has held the ground. The
idea is widely accepted today that the work relationship of the civil
servant is dominated by the legal concept of privilege and that the
scope of the privilege is freely shaped as well as modified by the
sovereign employer. If in the definition of his status the civil servant
is thrown back upon the concept of privilege, he cannot use the constitutional shield of due process. In the language of a judicial decision later affirmed by an evenly split Supreme Court (1951), the
due-process clause "is not applicable unless one is being deprived of
something to which he has a right," and thus the clause "does not
apply to the holding of a government office."

Security Requirements

The doctrine of privilege has the most sweeping effects in the
sovereign employer's freedom to dismiss a civil servant or reject an
applicant for government employment for lack of "suitability." The
absence of a general basis of rights is made more dangerous when it
magnifies the striking power of discretionary authority in judging
the civil servant's conduct from the angle of loyalty and security.
When the appraisal of derogatory information is not governed by
specifically stated, generally applicable criteria but is left to each
agency; when fair procedure, in spirit as well as in form, cannot be
taken for granted; when public pressure may be brought to bear
upon an agency that insists on placing fairness above a record of
speedy disciplinary action; and when the security officer of the individual agency has reason for keeping himself on the safe side by the
widest margin—under these circumstances, civil service tenure may

come to rest on shaky foundations. The oddity of the situation is nicely portrayed when the drama critic of a Washington newspaper runs the following item in his column (1956):

Safety Note: Still trembling under security threats, Government employees have been phoning this desk to learn whether the Chinese film "Yang Oh" ("The Heroine"), to be shown at 12:30 and 2:30 Saturday at the Colony, is likely to be contaminating. . . . This department is assured that the picture was made in Hongkong, has an historical setting and has been shown openly on Formosa.

This tidbit suggests the strange ways in which contagion may affect unwary victims. Once the clues get thicker, the attentive eyes and ears of the government, such as the Federal Bureau of Investigation, collecting all the straws, will have little difficulty in coming up with a report that cannot be ignored. Faced with its presence but not its full contents, the object of the report will feel as did Professor Albert S. Coolidge of Harvard University, whose partisan interests were deemed incompatible with his sitting on a committee of the Library of Congress to administer his late mother's benefactions in the interest of chamber music. Wrote Professor Coolidge in a letter to the *Washington Post* (1956):

On February 17 you printed . . . a letter . . . pointing out that the FBI has scrupulously refrained from evaluating, interpreting, or drawing conclusions from the factual information which it was its duty to supply the Librarian of Congress about my past record. It has simply collected with impressive thoroughness every incident which might be open to a derogatory interpretation. I well understand this, and have been at pains not to appear to blame or criticize the FBI.

I also well understand the frustration and despair of the man whose livelihood depends upon securing loyalty clearance, and who cannot command anything like the resources of the FBI in ferreting out facts and incidents tending to establish his loyalty, integrity, and political awareness.

Support of the Internal Security System

But the matter does not end with the individual immediately affected. The entire institutional environment, in due course of time, becomes saturated with the zest for suspicion. If its logic cannot afford to relent, this campaign is bound to demand of every civil servant the full measure of co-operation irrespective of his mental reservations as an individual. That, indeed, was proposed by an eminently respectable special board of inquiry in a report which found a distinguished scientist, Dr. Robert Oppenheimer, a security risk (1954). Said the report:

There remains also an aspect of the security system which perhaps has had insufficient public attention. This is the protection and support of the entire system itself. It must include an understanding and an acceptance of security measures adopted by responsible Government agencies. It must include an active cooperation with all agencies of Government properly and reasonably concerned with the security of our country. It must involve a subordination of personal judgment as to the security status of an individual as against a professional judgment in the light of standards and procedures when they have been clearly established by appropriate process. It must entail a wholehearted commitment in the preservation of the security system and the avoidance of conduct tending to confuse or obstruct.[7]

An obligation of this kind cuts deeply into the web of personal relationships as well as the civil servant's sense of justice. This is true especially when he persuades himself that the security system makes extravagant demands without compensating for these by adequate personal safeguards. He may feel that the idea of a watertight system is based on illusion and that steps toward achieving such tightness are comparable to the bizarre proposition to inflict preventive custody on all citizens in order to keep them from committing offenses.

Thus it may be said that the contemporary drift is toward a definition of requirements of conduct more comprehensive and more restrictive than would have appeared possible only twenty years ago. The fluidity thus introduced into the concept of civil service tenure can bring about serious abuses, with the appraisal of derogatory information so dependent on the good will of superiors. If the blight spreading in the law of civil service is not checked, the prospects of working for the government are bound to become less appealing for all but the least articulate or the most conventional aspirants.

7. *Time,* June 14, 1954, p. 27.

CHAPTER 8

THE INTEGRITY OF SERVICE

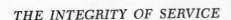

As the arm of political choice, public administration is expected to make that choice fully effective in the discharge of the government's continuing functions. It forfeits public confidence by being indifferent as well as by being inept. But unreserved acceptance of political direction must not lead the career man to turn into a zealous partisan of the government of the day. He cannot commit himself personally to particular policies without compromising the basic purpose of the administrative system as an instrumentality of equal use for any government coming to power lawfully.

As a conglomerate of large-scale organizations, public administration is weighted down by the burdens of institutional isolation, procedural rigmarole, and mental self-sufficiency. Without keeping alive his public spirit, the career man is bound with time to fall victim to the character of his occupational environment. Then his ability will be engaged more and more in the cultivation of bureaucratic ways and in the pursuit of bureaucratic ends. Deprived of the rallying force of a service doctrine, the "university man" may excel only in being "sharp" as he plays the bureaucratic game.

Both in his response to political direction and in his resistance to bureaucratic contagion the career man essentially stands on his own. The fine lines of distinction that must be drawn as he confronts specific issues are not drawn for him either by legislation or by instructions. He must draw them himself. They can be drawn by him only with the guidance of a professional point of view, grounded in an alert sense of public ethics. The ultimate criterion of value for the appraisal of the contribution of the "university man" lies in his grasp of these subtle implications of public service and in his constancy in making them the basis of his actions.

Integrity of service is a matter of central importance in the operation of the merit bureaucracy. It is the controlling factor in the responsiveness of public administration. It is brought to a test in the collision of administrative authority and private interests. It represents a restraining influence in the civil servant's exercise of political rights. These are the topics to be dealt with next.

RESPONSIVE ADMINISTRATION

The Duty of Challenge

Speaking of the British "university man" on the hundredth anniversary of the Trevelyan-Northcote report, Labor's Clement Attlee observed in 1954:

> The first thing a Minister finds on entering office is that he can depend absolutely on the loyalty of his staff and, on leaving office, he will seldom be able to say what the private political views are even of those with whom he has worked very closely. The second thing that he will discover is that the civil servant is prepared to put up every possible objection to his policy, not from a desire to thwart him, but because it is his duty to see that the Minister understands all the difficulties and dangers of the course which he wishes to adopt.[1]

This thumbnail sketch of civil service behavior is highly enlightening in several respects. In the first place, it makes clear that the relationship between the politically responsible minister and the career men who work directly under him is intimate enough to require a bond of personal loyalty. At the same time, although the minister can have full confidence in the loyal backing given him by his top civil servants, and although these must therefore know his mind pretty well, their personal loyalty is so much of an institutional product that it does not furnish him any clues about their political convictions. Second, part of this personal loyalty is expressed in a deliberate probing of the strength of the minister's position, of the policies he feels he should advance, so as to make sure that the minister is clear in his mind about any obstacles in the way, risks encountered, and even soft spots in his reasoning. Loyalty enters the picture because, without drawing the minister's thought to these matters, he would be unable to stand his ground in adverse circumstances, thus falling down on his job as the political chief of the department. Third, and perhaps most extraordinary, the minister can be expected to understand this strange but effective process of making him a stronger leader, without crying out against a "bureaucratic conspiracy" about him.

1. "Civil Servants, Ministers, Parliament and the Public," *Political Quarterly,* XXV (1954), 308. For previous references to the Trevelyan-Northcote report see pp. 54 and 66.

Working Doctrine

This delicate working relationship has been described in very similar and still more specific terms for one of the agencies which in the United States form the staff organization of the President—the Bureau of the Budget. Wrote a top official of the bureau on the level of its political leadership:

The chief tenet in the working doctrine of the professional staff is sensitivity in three different directions. First, for effective work in the Bureau one must be alive to the danger of getting locked up unwittingly in a particular activity. Instead, there must be a tireless search for all points of relevant information. In the conduct of each individual assignment, a product should emerge which combines the best knowledge available at various places, inside and outside the Executive Office of the President, inside and outside the executive branch, and even inside and outside the government. Second, there must be sensitivity toward the factor of time. Even in the timing of action to meet momentary emergencies, one should not sweep aside longer-range considerations. The demands for action must be related to a timetable that connects the past with the future. Third, sensitivity must exist toward the broader frame of reference, the whole political situation. Staff members in the Bureau of the Budget know that political advice comes to the President from many quarters. They know further that the Bureau is not meant nor staffed to amplify such political advice. But they appreciate that it is the Bureau's function to develop as clear a picture as possible of what ought to be done, to be put before those giving political advice.

Hence, in everything that a staff man does in the Budget Bureau he must always keep in mind the larger context in which the Budget Director as well as the President would have to act. The technical recommendations of the Budget Bureau are intended to stand on their objective merit. But that is not enough. For they will not amount to much if they are not carefully fitted into the basic political frame of reference in which the Presidency operates.[2]

It is obvious that the civil service can be expected to function in this way only when it is in possession of an unfaltering feeling for the peculiar responsibility it bears. That responsibility must combine a commitment to speak up, to challenge the basis or the utility of a proposed decision, with a commitment to make the most of the decision once it has been adopted. Exercise of such responsibility requires a willingness to look in two directions—toward what ought to be done, in the light of one's best knowledge, and toward the overriding value of legitimate political choice, as the unifying force

2. Robert E. Merriam, "The Bureau of the Budget as Part of the President's Staff Organization," *Annals of the American Academy of Political and Social Science*, CCCVII (1956), 22.

behind the decision reached. The merit system, the concept of a permanent administrative establishment linked with the dynamics of changing majorities under popular rule, stands and falls with the vitality of this idea of responsibility.

Self-indoctrination

Such personal conduct can be sustained in practice only when it is embodied in a clearly understood theory. A responsiveness so delicately poised does not evolve in individuals as a matter of natural growth. Conscious cultivation is therefore a necessity, and it can be effectively undertaken only out of the spirit of the group. The maturity of a civil service and hence its ultimate efficiency depend primarily on the degree to which the individual civil servant is guided by an appreciation of the basic rules that must govern his conduct. That is the foundation of his integrity.

He must be willing to throw himself wholeheartedly into the struggle for the right decision. But he must also be prepared to support without flinching the final outcome, although he may happen to regard the decision as thoroughly wrong. He must deny himself the right to turn aside, nursing his grudges. At the same time he must not relax his alertness for opportunities of achieving a reconsideration of the issue if he is convinced that he has a better solution to propose.

In all this he needs to pay careful attention to the thinking of the political leadership of the department. The ideal condition was aptly described by General Guderian, the German army's master of armored warfare, when he said of his chief of staff, picked by him personally in preparation for smashing the French defenses at Sedan in May, 1940, that he "understood me by looking at me." Yet, like the military staff officer, the civil servant must be satisfied with knowing the influence of his work on the general record of accomplishment, without doing anything to make that influence noticeable from the outside. He must stay in the background, shrouded by a "passion for anonymity," in the phrase of the late Dr. Thomas H. Jones. Jones himself was a "man never seen"—an academic economist who in 1916 was drawn by Lloyd George into the budding cabinet secretariat and stayed there until 1931 as an intimate adviser and penman extraordinary to a succession of prime ministers coming to office as leaders of different political parties, including Ramsay MacDonald, Labor's first prime minister. In the United States the anonymity of the staff man's contribution has found an eloquent sponsor in Louis Brownlow, one of the inspired architects of effective administrative management in the federal government.[3]

Key to Continuity

When the bureaucracy fashions itself into an instrumentality for the accomplishment of public purposes rather than its own, it becomes fit for a role that transcends time as well as circumstance. It then is capable of maintaining the operating continuity of government as well as making effective the political determinations of the powers of the day. That is why in the turbulent history of continental Europe during the twentieth century the ephemeral nature of constitutional ways has formed a contrast to the perpetuity of administrative ways.

Historically, this is not a new thing. Administrative institutions so firmly rooted in tradition and so much in command of a practical working approach as to furnish support to the political will of any regime have often been able to survive military conquest as well as more peaceful but no less far-reaching transfers of authority. Diocletian's administrative reforms endured well into the Christian empire. The Byzantine system of administration lived on after the fall of Constantinople and was intentionally preserved by the Turks. After the Manchu invasion (1644) the inherited forms of Chinese governmental practice, including the civil service examination system, were left intact under the new dynasty. Again, many features of the administrative system of the East India Company have been carried over into the government of twentieth-century India.

Administrative responsiveness does not function solely as an acceptance of the directing authority of the government of the day. It must also meet the need for looking ahead, for performing scouting services for the government, for anticipating issues and difficulties as they would affect its course of policy. In addition, attention must be given to the requirements of effective public management. These are not primarily related to the government's policy choices but have to do with assuring the government of effective operating support in the administrative system. There are many matters that cannot be attended to satisfactorily by the political leadership but need to be taken care of nevertheless—the achievement of co-ordination, the preservation of continuity in administration, and the recog-

3. Louis Brownlow served as chairman of the President's Committee on Administrative Management, which in its report (1937) gave a strong impetus to the evolution of strengthened administrative machinery, especially for the use of the Chief Executive.

nition of principle, of longer-range concerns. As has been said of the British higher civil servant: "To his defenders he is a man whose adherence to principle and striving for continuity contrasts favorably with the opportunism natural among politicians."[4]

The Impact of Organized Interests

As the pilot familiar with the administrative reefs, the career man behind the political leadership of the department is confronted with the clash of immediate demands, dramatized in the campaigns waged by political parties and interest groups. Envisaging opportunities for interlacing different interests so as to gain a foundation for departmental programs requires insight as well as ingenuity, a tough mind as well as a high sense of public purpose. As the American philosopher Ralph Barton Perry has observed, "Interests are integrated by reflection." But reflection must be guided by an awareness of controlling values. Without this link no basis exists for either personal or institutional integrity. That idea is well expressed by Perry when he declares that "morality organizes interests." It is one of the unfortunate aspects of modern government that the moral orientation in the decision-making process has been left thoroughly underdeveloped.

In the clash between the voice of politically guided action and the voice of principle, the dynamic force of tangible advantage is all on the side of action, whereas principle seeks to halt that force by denial. This is a most uneven match. If those speaking for principle differ among themselves about what it entails, if there is even doubt among them as to whether the case for principle should be pressed face to face with what may amount to an order in the name of political direction, the battle is lost before it has started. In such matters, therefore, it becomes decisive whether the career man, as a result of his preparation or as part of the national background, regards it as his business to bolster the voice of principle and, if so, whether the comprehension of points of principle runs sufficiently broad and strong in the professional consciousness of the civil service to give the case of principle a fighting chance.

In turn, the reaction to be expected of the political leadership is of great importance. It is one thing for the politically responsible official to look upon discussions of this kind as arrogant interference with the exercise of his responsibilities, as attempts at putting a roadblock in his path. It is quite another thing if there is on the

4. R. K. Kelsall, *Higher Civil Servants in Britain from 1870 to the Present Day* (London: Routledge & Kegan Paul, 1955), p. 191.

political level equal respect for principle and even common agreement about what matters are settled by principle, or ought to be so settled. In these respects the relationships between the political level and the administrative level have come closer to a mutual understanding in England than they have in most other countries, largely because the minister and his principal civil servants, by and large, have been rather close in general background.

As a rule, the career man cannot personally follow his recommendation to the point of final decision. He often catches up with it only when the ink is dry under it. But he will usually have an accurate idea of the external influences likely to struggle for the last word. One cannot have lived within a department very long without getting a fairly exact picture of the topography of interests grouped about it and cutting through it. Indeed, the strength of a particular departmental component is often directly proportionate to that of the external interest groupings with which it is allied. Organized interest groups have long found it profitable to watch closely the department that touches upon their main concerns. On the other hand, the presence of such interests may give administrative officials an opening wedge with the legislature in the pursuit of their institutional or personal aspirations. A good inkling of how this works was conveyed in the United States shortly after World War II in the following testimony of the director of the Veterans Employment Service before the Committee on Appropriations of the House of Representatives:

These veterans organizations keep constant watch over everything I do and they are quick to criticize anything within my organization and that has always been their practice. That was so before I came down here, and the employment committee of the American Legion is always wanting to know what you are doing, how you are doing it, and why you are doing it.

The veterans organizations all along have insisted that we should have a restoration of the field assistants, but that is up to this committee. They ride me constantly about such things. I just happen to be a good focal point where they can concentrate.[5]

Range of Group Action

Interest groups, as the career man knows, do not merely watch. They propose, urge, press, object, veto, and even punish. They may wield part of the appointive power in the department when the department head is personally dependent on their support. They may succeed in cowing him if he tries to follow his own line or that of

5. *Hearings before the Subcommittee of the House Committee on Appropriations on the Supplemental Federal Security Agency Appropriation Bill for 1949* (80th Cong., 2d sess.), pp. 644, 657.

the government at large. Where there is no party program to provide a firm formula for the degree of recognition to be given particular organized interests in relation to all others, they may become the direct source of departmental policy. A rather extreme case of punitive action came to light in the United States some years ago in a legislative proposal that would have moved out of the way two federal officials who had stood up to hostile pressures in defense of public policy. Their department head protested this action before a congressional committee as follows:

The declared fight against these two men stems from their support of the existing . . . law and the public power policy of the Congress. The implications of this feature of the bill are clear: Unless a Federal officer disregards a clear mandate from the Congress and administers the law in accordance with the dictates of those who would, if they could, have it amended or rescinded, he risks being legislated out of office. Yet, if he were to follow such dictates, rather than the congressional mandate, he would be in personal jeopardy for violation of his oath of office to uphold the law of the land. I can think of no situation more patently unfair to public officials or more patently dangerous to the public interest.

Moreover, I consider this limitation to be the rankest sort of intrusion upon the prerogatives of executive management, the effect of which is to impugn my judgment as to the ability and qualifications of the officials serving under me and to seriously limit my discretion in the selection of such officials. There is nothing in the record to support this limitation other than the vendetta inspired by a group which, having failed to change the law, now seeks to change the management.[6]

In struggles of this kind the career man is usually caught in the middle. But he has reason to be as wary of professed friends as of sworn enemies. He will know from experience that in a battle over public policy he cannot expect much help from sympathetic interests as soon as stronger counterpressures come to the fore. That is true especially when the sympathetic interests are dependent upon the general good will of the public in their own operations and can therefore ill afford to be forthright in public disputes. Time and again when the going gets tough, civic organizations as well as economic interest groups leave an administrative agency to struggle for itself in the defense or execution of decisions urged by them.

Administrative Neutrality

Responsiveness to political direction is not intended to make the bureaucracy a partisan fighter for politically defined policy. Of course, insofar as government functions as the co-ordinator of inter-

6. *Hearings before the Subcommittee of the Senate Committee on Appropriations on H.R. 6705, Making Appropriations for the Department of the Interior for the Fiscal Year 1949* (80th Cong., 2d sess.), p. 13.

ests in accordance with its program, it is bound to favor certain interests and to show itself indifferent or hostile toward others. That is a matter of the political course and properly within the responsibility of the government in power. When the drawing of distinctions between interests is based on the government's policy, the career man has an obligation to deal with particular interests in harmony with that policy. Under ordinary circumstances—that is, short of an assault upon the constitution and similar exceptional kinds of political action—it is not for the civil servant to substitute his sense of the common good for the position of the government. He should seek opportunities for expressing his views, as part of the adviser's responsibility, but the final word must be that of the politically responsible official. A parallel is furnished in the German civil service act of 1953 with respect to orders of questionable legality. When an order is considered illegal by the civil servant called upon to act, he may carry his doubts to his superior and one step above. But when the order is confirmed, upon request in writing, responsibility shifts from the point of action to the point of confirmation.

For itself, however, the bureaucracy is not entitled to acknowledge or even to cultivate friends and foes among the organized interests. If it did, it could not be impartial. It must seek to advance the general interest and to guard its neutrality toward the special interests. Administrative neutrality in this sense is a militant creed. It supplies an antidote to a class orientation of the civil service. It provides a ground on which to raise a challenge to political favoritism whatever its forms. It keeps the voice of the common good audible in the administrative system. Administrative neutrality therefore does not mean to hide from issues that must be met, to stand aloof while the battle is on, or to have no position to recommend. It is an abuse of the concept of neutrality when it is invoked by the civil servant as a convenient way out of any personal involvement in public decisions or as a justification for hanging tightly to the coattails of those bearing political responsibility.

LEGAL REDRESS OF ADMINISTRATIVE WRONGS

Liability for Damage

When a truck of the Bureau of Irrigation has caused damage by negligence of the driver to private persons or property, can the party who sustains the damage recover from the presumably ever solvent government, or is he reduced to suing the driver, perhaps a temporary employee of the Bureau of Irrigation who was instantly fired? Assumption of liability by the government is obviously the fairest principle for the innocent private victim who suffers damage accidentally while the administrative system is busy with hundreds of thousands of errands which can lead to such accidents.

With the earlier growth of the "administrative state" in continental Europe, the countries there—especially France and Germany—came to recognize the principle of government liability long before it was accepted more universally. In England pressure for abandoning the ancient dogma that "the king can do no wrong"—or that he may not be sued "in the king's court"—won out for the bulk of government activities only in 1947, with the passage of the Crown Proceedings Act. In the United States, comparable legislation dealing with private claims arising from federal torts was incorporated in the Legislative Reorganization Act of 1946. The principle of government liability being now widely acknowledged, all that needs to be done is to give it sufficiently inclusive statutory formulation to assure the affected party of proper and easy recovery for the damage incurred.

The Aggrieved Individual

But administrative agencies touch the individual more often intentionally than by accident. This is the case when they bring their authority to bear upon him to make him do or to restrain him from doing certain things. When acting within its proper bounds, administrative authority, as a rule, can demand compliance with its orders as the lawfully acting arm of government. There remains, however, the question of whether the particular administrative order is actually within the bounds of law and whether the order conforms to the procedural requirements laid down by law. When so challenged, the administrative agency must do more than affirm its authority. To inspire public confidence, review should be separate and independent.

In considering the kind of review to be provided for, we should not overlook the two forms in which we encounter the aggrieved citizen. There are the organized interests—agriculture, business, and labor; steel, oil, and shipping; the railways, motor transport, and the airlines; the doctors, the lawyers, and the teachers; the grazers, the hunters, and the campers. But the aggrieved citizen appears also as the single individual. He may be in need of some official action—a certificate, a license, or a permit. Or he may be caught in the wheels of the administrative process: his house may have been closed as uninhabitable; the government may seek to acquire his property for public purposes against his will; or a quarantine may be slapped upon him. In its group role the public speaks as a powerful chorus, making a show of its influence with those in power or of the votes at its disposal. In its individual role the public talks with the timid whisper of a man standing alone before the departmental colossus. The needs of the public in its individual aspects and in its group aspects must find equal recognition in an adequate legal framework.

Differences in Administrative Law

To provide remedies is the task of law. Such aspects as individual rights, not to be swept aside or punched full of holes by administrative authority, and the fundamental requirement of administration according to law itself are usually dealt with by constitutional law. But the more specific elaboration of basic principles is left to a supplementary body of law known as administrative law.

In the era of administrative action, administrative law has come to mean quite different things. It has been denounced as a crippling interference with the legal system, withdrawing administrative power from judicial control and allowing such power to accuse, to try, and to judge the harried individual all at once. It has been praised for its resourcefulness in keeping government agencies responsible by injecting canons of fairness into the administrative process without impairing the effective exercise of lawful authority for the common good. Long debates have been carried on over whether legal review of administrative action, on suit brought by the individual affected, is in better hands with the regular courts or with a specialized yet independent judiciary, a system of administrative courts. The first alternative represents the traditional arrangement in Britain and in the United States, with certain exceptions. The second alternative, again with exceptions, prevails in France, Germany, and most countries of continental Europe, in Latin America, and in other parts of the world as well.

The Anglo-American Approach

In the Anglo-American legal system two key concepts have been given great significance. The first is that of notice: to let the public or particular groups know in advance of rules to be issued. The second is the concept of public hearing: to allow those affected by administrative actions to register their objections and to propose a solution more satisfactory to them. In addition, legal redress against administrative orders has been provided by the courts on such grounds as violation of other requirements of "due process of law." Notice and hearing are effective devices for making an administrative agency share its plans for regulatory action with the outside world. On the other hand, a system of notice and hearing tends to favor the organized interests strong enough to be represented competently. By bringing together the organized interests around the conference table, the administrative agency has been taught to accept these interests as partners in the making of rules by which they will be regulated.

By comparison, the single individual standing on his own has been the stepchild of administrative law in the Anglo-American legal order. A voice too feeble to be heard in the tumultuous pursuit of group interests, he clamors for recognition of wants and needs which to him are often of vital import—whether his barber's license was rightfully revoked, whether the taxi-stand fee raised from him can be increased freely, or whether the dogwood tree at the corner of his lot must be cut down to increase visibility at the intersection. Unable to carry on costly litigation, he is doubly fearful of legal combat with an administrative agency that can afford to carry the matter to the last appeal and often thinks it must unless ordered to stop earlier.

Moreover, the ordinary judiciary is far removed from the administrative scene. At one extreme have been courts unwilling to probe the factual foundation of administrative decisions. This in many instances has amounted to a refusal to provide real review—on the theory that the judge should not attempt to substitute his judgment for that of the administrative official. At the other extreme have been courts more than willing to superimpose their uninformed preferences upon administrative decisions—on the theory that administrative power needs close judicial watching. The resulting string of court decisions has left the administrative process tattered and torn without any suggestion of better alternatives for serving the general interest. In this unsteady growth a workmanlike approach was slow to crystallize.

The Continental European Approach

What are the principal features of the system of administrative law that has evolved in Continental Europe? Its strong points can be stated briefly. It provides a basis for technically informed assessment of administrative legality. It is alive to the need for showing administrative agencies how to accomplish lawful purposes by lawful means with full regard for the rights of individuals. And it is a low-cost examination of administrative decisions.

Viewed as one system, Continental administrative law shows certain general characteristics. In the first place, despite the victories

which the codification movement has won on the European continent, the body of legal rules which govern the exercise of administrative power has crystallized in the same way as did the common
law. It originated and developed as judge-made law, free to be in-
ventive and experimental. Second, the legal principles of administrative law have continued to expand their protective function in the
interest of the citizen. Third, through a sufficient number of lower
courts integrated under a high court, such as the Council of State in
France in its judicial sections, it has maintained close contact with
the origins of administrative action and the interest of the ordinary
citizen in ready access to justice, at once inexpensive and unencum-
bered by undue formality. And, finally, it has expressed itself
through the voice of a specialized judiciary drawn largely from the
ranks of the higher civil service. Upon assuming their roles, the
administrative judges gain full judicial independence.

Guidelines for Lawful Administration

American terminology identifies administrative law primarily with
the growth and the exercise of quasi-legislative and quasi-judicial
powers by administrative agencies, with the making of rules and the
deciding of disputes. The Continental concept of administrative law
brings into focus the whole web of relationships between governmental agencies and the individual, whatever form these relationships happen to take. Administrative rule-making and adjudicatory
decisions are important, but so is everything done in the day-by-day
conduct of activities as they affect the individual.

Looking at the whole impact of public authority, Continental
administrative courts have formulated substantive guidelines for the
exercise of such authority irrespective of its particular forms. For
example, special attention has been given to the development of
criteria to determine the distinction between lawful and unlawful
exercise of discretion. The administrative courts did not allow free
discretion to be free from legal restraint. They did not permit the
discretionary act to reach beyond the special purpose which the
statute envisaged in conferring discretionary power. Benevolence
of motive does not help the administrative agency in this matter.
The legality of the discretionary act is dependent on proper motivation. The proper motive is identical with that motive which the
statute itself intends to serve. If there be ground for doubt, to be
ascertained by the administrative court, the doubt would indicate
the illegality of the administrative act. Hence an administrative
agency having discretion to act or not to act in meeting, say, public

health hazards, is not entitled to adopt a policy never so to act. More important, when discretion is granted an administrative agency for meeting public health hazards, that discretion may not be exercised to make the citizen do what the agency deems desirable on grounds unrelated to public health hazards. In such disputes the administrative court, familiar with administrative ways, would proceed to sift the agency's motives on the basis of the agency's files as well as of pertinent testimony.

Search for Solutions

In the United States agitation in favor of statutory limitations to be imposed upon governmental agencies culminated in 1946 with the adoption of the Administrative Procedure Act. But it cannot be said that the interest of the ordinary citizen is greatly advanced by such legislation. The weak position of the single individual was brought to light again in 1954 in the "battle of Crichel Down" in England, which has stirred up public demands for strengthening the citizen face to face with an overbearing department by establishment of specialized judicial machinery on the Continental model. The Crichel Down affair developed from the inability of the Ministry of Agriculture to bring itself to relinquish a tract of land to its former owner, despite the fact that there was no concrete plan for making use of it in the foreseeable future. In the end the individual affected regained his property after the matter snowballed so far as to force the minister to resign in political repentance for the stubbornness of his ranking civil servants. But to watch the bureaucratic dragon withdraw its claws upon being challenged was an experience without cheer in this instance, for the individual happened to be a man of means and political connections.

The victory of the common man could be based only on carefully designed legal remedies and a willingness within the bureaucracy to come to the assistance of each individual victim of official inertia, callousness, or lawlessness. It is to the credit of the career man in continental Europe that he has generally been sophisticated enough to give a hand in perfecting the instruments of legal redress against administrative action.

POLITICAL ACTIVITIES OF CIVIL SERVANTS

Growth of Political Freedom of Action

The organic relationship in which the bureaucracy is placed toward the state encourages the conclusion that civil servants should not be heard or seen in politics beyond the institutional role they play as part of their official duty. The opposite, at first glance, seems incongruous. An analogy might be the picture of the hand campaigning against the head. On grounds of theory, therefore, much can be said in favor of a civil service that is neutralized in the contest of interests. For if the bureaucracy becomes conspicuously associated with particular causes, the effects could destroy public confidence in the civil servant's impartiality.

Yet the idea of restraint imposed upon civil servants in the exercise of political rights has been justified quite differently in different national settings. In the first place, the need for a kind of political sterilization of the civil servant has been based on the theory that otherwise "politics," viewed as an evil force, would ruin administration as a force of merit. Political parties, thus seen as driven by greed for spoils and lacking in public spirit, would make governmental agencies their servile creatures, controlling recruitment and forcing the individual civil servant to do their bidding. The outcome would be a dual type of corruption: the parties would pillage with greater impunity, and the administrative system would be surrendered to the spoilsman at the price of efficiency and integrity. This, by and large, has been the approach toward political activities of civil servants in the United States, astonishing though it may seem in a country that prizes democratic ways.

A second view has proceeded from the premise that the civil service is a public instrumentality devoted to public purposes. Hence the bureaucracy would depart from its high mission by stooping to allow its members a partisan role in the group competition for political control. The public service was to be guided strictly by the idea of political neutrality, although it was meant to stand behind the existing political system. Broadly speaking, this was the theory traditional in the German civil service, especially during the empire.

A third concept is grounded on the idea that civil servants ought to exercise the political rights common to all other citizens, save only for such restraints as can be justified in specific terms on the basis of the public obligations of the career man. From such an angle, there is almost a legal presumption in favor of the civil servant's right to engage in lawful political activities, except for forms of participation which would be likely to compromise the impartiality of the bureaucracy. This concept has come to the fore most clearly in the British development of recent years.

The spread of democratic government during the twentieth century and the enlargement of group participation in politics have generally worked in the direction of permitting the civil servant greater freedom of political action. We noticed this tendency in look-ing at the development of civil service unionism (pp. 105 ff.). But while as a matter of law or executive regulation the field of political activity for the civil servant has been widened with time, a much sharper penalty is attached today to his support of any cause that has a smell of radicalism or subversion about it (see pp. 127 ff.).

Conflicting Attitudes in France

A particularly striking example of contradictory forces is shown in France, where the struggle between the authoritarian tradition and the democratic tradition has created special problems in the conduct of public administration. During the Third Republic, France official-ly held to the proposition that the civil service should be politically neutral, but theory and practice seemed to run on different tracks. In the early period when republicanism itself was still something in need of affirmation in the bureaucracy, it was not unusual for cabi-nets to press upon the civil servant the demand that he support the "right" candidate at election time. Only around the turn of the cen-tury did the wind begin to blow the other way. Slowly it became customary for government spokesmen to preach political reserve. An example is the language of a circular which the minister of the inte-rior addressed in 1920 to all prefects in the field:

Without departing from the traditions of defending republican princi-ples and showing common courtesy which your position requires you to maintain in your area, you will take care to refrain from any manifestations or moves which might be construed as incompatible with your status as representative of the Government; above all, abstain from expressing a preference, either publicly or privately, for any of the candidates. . . . You are requested to communicate these instructions to your subordinates.

This reversal was not simply the consequence of a better apprecia-tion of administrative non-partisanship as a foundation of efficiency. In addition, the government found itself in the role of the sorcerer's apprentice unable to marshal the ghosts which he himself had called forth. For in the meantime the partisan use of the government's directing power, together with other factors, had stimulated an aggressive civil service unionism eager to follow the course of its own self-interest. This brought to the foreground the civil servant's claim to full "civic rights."

According to the point of view of the rank and file, administrative discipline should not go beyond breaches of official conduct. Out-side the office the civil servant was to be a full-fledged citizen, not accountable to any administrative authority for public expression of his political ideas or for participation in the activities of political parties. This position, however, was never adopted by the govern-ment. In the Napoleonic tradition the *fonctionnaire* had no such pri-vate capacity. Emphasis on this point differed in the change of gov-ernments, but it did not evaporate during the twentieth century.

As the gulf between these conflicting concepts widened, discipli-nary policy tended to become inconsistent and unpredictable. The government usually maneuvered between insisting upon the precept of administrative neutrality and yielding to the realities of the pres-sure tactics of the civil service unions, most of which were affiliated with the giant Confédération Générale du Travail. No cabinet was strong enough to resolve the basic contradictions through legisla-tion. Each political coalition in power temporized in its own way. In his incisive study of the French civil service during the Third Re-public, Walter R. Sharp summed up the result as follows:

Broadly speaking, the distinction between what is proper and what is improper behavior, whether official or unofficial in character, is confused. There is no adequate delimitation of offenses. Civic and political activity outside working hours has been only partially reconciled with the demands of efficiency and neutrality while on duty. In some respects, French civil servants enjoy the extreme of liberty; in others they often find themselves the victims of petty official persecution.

Freedom and Political Extremism: Germany

In Germany, not surprisingly, the development of civic rights of civil servants since the advent of the Weimar Republic has revolved around the principles of democratic consistency. The Constitutional Convention of 1919 was agreed in its overwhelming majority on the necessity of preventing party competition from dividing the loyalty of the bureaucracy. The constitution proclaimed that "civil servants are servants of the entire people, not of a party." The soundness of this formula was borne out in later years, during which the republic made considerable headway in instilling a democratic spirit in its administrative system, especially among the younger generation of career men. But these gains were partly jeopardized by another con-stitutional provision that "guaranteed" all civil servants "freedom of political opinion and freedom of association" without a single quali-fying phrase. Under the monarchy, association with a political party that attacked the existing form of government had been regarded as a disciplinary offense. Determined to break with the past, the Wei-mar Constitution left no room for discrimination. At the same time its lofty sense of democratic principle caused it to tolerate two polit-ical parties eager to feast on its corpse—the National Socialist (Nazi) and the Communist parties. Thus the constitution gave itself an air of indifference toward the ideological orientation of its civil servants.

To be sure, when acting in his private capacity, the civil servant was not permitted to disregard entirely his official status. In any conflict between rights and duties the latter had to be considered first. As Gerhard Anschütz, one of the foremost students of the Weimar Constitution, pointed out:

> In the exercise of his civil and civic rights . . . the civil servant, even outside the office, must impose upon himself that degree of moderation which derives from his position as an organ of the public at large. This consideration . . . supports the conclusion . . . that the personal freedom of the civil servant, especially the freedom of speech, of the press, of assembly, and of association, is subject not only to such limitations as apply to all citizens but also to those special restraints which result from the duties of his office and of his profession. As was the case under the earlier law, the liberties of the civil servant are restricted by those duties, not *vice versa*.

But drawing such lines in practical terms proved next to impossible in an electorate divided into those who gave support to the republican order and those who were attracted to unconstitutional utopias. The more answers were attempted, the more questions could be raised. An illustration is the comment of an authority on German civil service law, Adolf Arndt (1931):

> As a citizen, the civil servant enjoys the same rights as do others, but in their exercise he is under special obligations. His task to represent the state as an organ of the state carries with it the duty to conduct himself in a manner worthy of his office in his civic participation in political affairs. . . . The civil servant may . . . approve of unconstitutional ends and means . . . [but he must] express his political conviction . . . with temperateness and circumspection, and carefully avoid in the form of its expression any tactlessness, acrimony, or provocation.

It is easy to see the dilemma that eventually arose from the sweeping grant of "civic rights" as in the closing years of the republic the Nazi party began to gain mass support. No one could question that the constitution had intentionally broadened the civil servant's political freedom, especially his freedom personally to stand on the side of the opposition. But did that freedom include membership in the Nazi party? This question was never conclusively resolved. Thus the principle of civil service neutrality was honored in Germany in every field except that of political affiliation and party activity. Indeed, the constitution expressly gave the civil servant the right not only to campaign for a seat in parliament but also to hold it while at the same time keeping his official position. Today, under the civil service act of 1953, he must relinquish his position upon becoming a member of the legislature.

The American Example of Detailed Rules

The French example showed the undesirable consequences of leaving the question of political activities of civil servants to the struggle between the disciplinary authority of individual departments and the collective pressures of the rank and file, without benefit of statutory guidelines. The German illustration demonstrates that reliance on generally respected canons of political neutrality fails to work when the constitution itself gives the civil servant full freedom to participate in the battle between the political parties, especially when not all of them accept the constitutional system. The traditional approach in the United States is radically different from both the French and the German. It enforces a withdrawal of the bureaucracy from "politics," blocking a partisan invasion of the administrative system and simultaneously protecting the individual civil servant against political exploitation by the party in power.

The American approach has been one of specific elaboration of what is prohibited and, by inference, of what is allowed—an approach followed in the federal government by the promulgation of general civil service rules. In 1939, as a reaction to partisan impositions upon a civil service that had grown rapidly under the New Deal, many of these rules were embodied in federal legislation known as the Hatch Act, which was amended in 1940 to bring under its provisions state and local officials paid from federal funds. The Hatch Act expressly bars any active participation of civil servants in "political management" or in "political campaigns." The sharpness of its teeth is shown in the fact that violations of its provisions lead automatically to dismissal, no milder penalty being authorized, in contrast with the civil service rules.

The United States Civil Service Commission is responsible for enforcing these statutory and administrative prohibitions. Prohibited political activities include: serving on any political committee; soliciting or handling political contributions; selling political party dinner tickets; addressing a political club; initiating or circulating political petitions, as contrasted with signing them; becoming a candidate for nomination or election to an office—federal, state, county, or municipal—that is to be filled in an election in which party candidates are involved, or soliciting others to become candidates for nomination or election to such an office; taking any active part in a political meeting or rally except as a spectator; transporting or helping to get out the voters on registration or election day; publishing any letter or article, signed or unsigned, in favor of or against any political party or candidate; and distributing campaign literature or material. Permitted political activities include: exercising the right to vote; expressing political opinions, unless that is done in connection with active participation in a political campaign; making voluntary contributions to a political organization, provided such contribution is not made in a federal building or to another government employee; displaying political pictures at home; and displaying a political sticker on a private automobile, without making a partisan showing while on duty.

As a general principle, the prohibitions of the Hatch Act and of the civil service rules apply to the civil servant's participation in political activities in the sphere of local government as well as on the federal or state levels. Long before enactment of the Hatch Act, however, employees living in certain municipalities near the District of Columbia were permitted to hold local office in those municipalities. Under the amendments to the Hatch Act passed in 1940, the Civil Service Commission was authorized to extend the privilege of active participation in local government to federal employees residing, first, in any municipalities or other political subdivisions of Maryland and Virginia in the immediate vicinity of the District of Columbia or, second, in municipalities where the majority of voters are employed by the federal government. But there must not be any smudges of party activity. Federal officers and employees who are candidates for local elective office must run as independent candidates and must conduct their campaigns in a purely non-partisan manner.

The reservation against party action is explicit also in another provision of the Hatch Act, which, as a further exception, permits federal employees to take an active part in the conduct of non-partisan campaigns or in the electoral determination of "any question which is not specifically identified with any national or state political party," including questions relating to constitutional amendments, referendums, and approval of municipal ordinances.

Britain's Differentiated Solution

In comparison with the inflexible rules of the Hatch Act, the approach taken in Great Britain has been much less heavy-handed. There the evolution of the political rights of civil servants has moved, step by step, toward rather liberal and differentiated solutions. The dominant consideration was the preservation of non-partisan administration, of the basic neutrality of the civil service in the political arena, in contrast to a preoccupation with "clean politics" and excesses of patronage, as in the United States.

The traditional concept added up to an injunction to "take no overt part in public political affairs," including serving on election committees or supporting or opposing any particular candidate or party by public speaking or writing. Although these principles were applied in practice without narrow-mindedness, political self-restraint was backed by strong traditional attitudes on the part of both the public and the civil service.

The logic of this position, however, seemed more clear cut with respect to activities of the government as the sovereign guardian of law and order, including the exercise of regulatory functions, than with respect to activities of the government as a producer. Again, the logic seemed more compelling in regard to those positions bearing substantial responsibility than in regard to public employees down the line. On such grounds various groups within the civil service have urged with increasing insistence greater freedom of political activity. Questions were raised especially about the treatment of parliamentary candidacies. Why, it was asked, should parliamentary careers be open to officers in the army and navy but closed to civil servants? Why should parliamentary activity be on a different level as compared with the holding of elective offices in local government, since 1909 simply a matter of departmental approval? How could the impartiality of public administration actually be adversely affected if office messengers or arsenal employees did get into political campaigns?

In this general perspective the MacDonnell Commission in 1914 proposed in its report to exclude certain groups of subordinate and industrial-type employees from the ban on political activity applicable to other civil servants. The Treasury committee chaired by Lord Blanesburgh in 1925 presented its recommendations along the same lines. It suggested that specified categories of industrial employees be permitted to become candidates for Parliament as well as to engage in other political activities without sacrificing their status in the government service. Moreover, there was considerable support in the committee for the idea that the lower groups in the non-industrial service be granted the same freedom. Both reports, however, were agreed that the impartiality of administration required restriction in the conduct of political activities for the main body of the career establishment on which the integrity and reputation of the entire civil service rested. As the Blanesburgh Committee put it after thorough analysis of all pros and cons: "The constantly extending disposition of Parliament to entrust the exercise of quasi-judicial duties to executive departments . . . as well as the sharper alignment of political parties in these days, unite to make the high reputation for political impartiality hitherto enjoyed by the public service a more valuable guarantee for its continuance, and we can have no assurance that the existing ethic of the Service would long survive that confidence if it were once lost."

Yet this was not the end. The matter was found in need of further study after World War II. The Masterman Committee of 1949 was guided by the same fundamental principle of assuring non-partisan administration but attempted a modified approach. It favored freedom of political action by civil servants insofar as such freedom was consistent with the "maintenance of political impartiality in the Civil Service and of confidence in that impartiality as an essential part of the structure of Government in this country." This was in accordance with the lines of actual development. Up to 1949 relaxation had been effected formally for some 200,000 industrial employees in such agencies as the Admiralty; these were government employees working in what was regarded as predominantly industrial establishments. An additional 60,000 industrial employees of the Ministry of Supply were treated as exempt from the prohibition on parliamentary candidacies.

But about 140,000 other industrial employees, together with the non-industrial civil servants, remained under the prohibition of membership in the House of Commons except upon resignation from the civil service. As to other political activities, industrial employees were under no general restriction. Even a considerable number of non-industrial civil servants was allowed to participate in certain political activities. On this point the governing pronouncement by the Treasury laid down the rule that "civil servants are expected to maintain at all times a reserve in political matters and not put themselves forward prominently on one side or another."

But the handling of particular cases remained within the discretion of the individual departments. Not surprisingly, the Post Office Department, with its large operating force, was least restrictive. It permitted its employees, except the highest grades, to take part in such political activities as canvassing voters on behalf of a particular party at election time. Still greater leeway was practiced generally with respect to the participation of civil servants in the affairs of local government, including membership in local councils—approval being usually as automatic as in the identical situation in Switzerland. Here, again, the Post Office Department led. It left its employees entirely free in their civic choices.

Where To Draw the Line

With so many separate steps toward a liberalized treatment of the political rights of civil servants, the Masterman Committee was pressed for a restatement of general principles. The service unions urged upon the committee a uniform formula, applicable to the entire civil service, which would substitute for explicit general restraints embodied in existing rules the "discretion and good sense" of the individual government employee. Although the Masterman Committee did not go so far, it felt that the industrial groups should be treated alike in sharing the concessions made previously to part of them. More important, the committee recommended that a line be drawn across the non-industrial civil service, leaving almost equally free from express restraints those "below the line"—that is, the bulk of the labor and industrial-type grades sufficiently removed from the actual conduct of administration, especially a large body of employees of the Post Office Department. On the other hand, in the administrative area proper, including receptionists and stenographers, the traditional prohibitions were to remain in effect.

The government was ready to accept the report of the committee with few qualifications. But considerable criticism came from organized civil servants, who felt that the report did not go far enough. This led to the appointment of a special committee of the Whitley Council, which proposed to amplify the Masterman Committee scheme by the establishment of an "intermediate class" between those above and below "the line." To quote the report:

> Civil servants of the intermediate class would be eligible for *permission* to engage in all national political activities except Parliamentary candidature.
>
> The granting of permission would depend on the acceptance of a code of *discretion,* putting certain limitations on the extent to which, and the manner in which, the civil servant could express views on Governmental policy and national political issues generally.[7]

The special committee estimated that under such an arrangement about 62 per cent of all civil servants would be completely free in their political activities, while another 22 per cent would be free, subject to the code of discretion, to take part in all political activities except becoming a candidate for parliament. Some 16 per cent would not be free to take part in national political activities but would be given permission, whenever possible, to take part in local government. This is the division now in effect.

7. Cmd. 8783 (1953), p. 9.

Perhaps the lesson of the British evolution can be summarized by saying that, when the political mores keep partisan action out of the conduct of public administration, general withdrawal of the civil servant from political activities is proportionately less necessary to assure or bolster administrative neutrality. But the liberalizing trend, outside the United States, does not always wait for such conditions. Thus France in 1946 gave the civil servant the right to campaign for himself and for others on official leave with pay. Moreover, while a member of the national legislature he could remain in the service. He would not cease to benefit from promotion, and he would financially be so placed as if he had stayed on duty in his department. Perhaps we need to add that in many countries the political parties have long come to appreciate the advantages of having civil servants among their legislative representation. The career man's technical knowledge and his capacity for getting work properly planned and competently done are assets in the performance of parliamentary as well as administrative functions.

CHAPTER 9

CONCEPTS OF SERVICE

For the role of the civil servant in modern government it is of fundamental importance whom he is asked to regard as his master. Is it
his superior, his division, his department? Each would make him an
institutional loyalist for whom the larger context, the ultimate purpose of public service, is a thing distant, vague, and unreal. Should
he find his master in the public, the nation, the common good? Each
of these, in the last analysis, manifests itself in his individual consciousness or even his conscience; and it is hard to argue that in such
matters he should consider himself endowed with keener sensitivity
than his superior.

Finally, is it perhaps the government that must be recognized as
the master? There is no doubt that the government has directing
authority over the bureaucracy under totalitarian as well as democratic rule. Under democratic rule, however, *the* government stands
in the shadow of *government*. Expressed differently, although committed to loyal service to the government of the day, the civil servant
is expected to place still higher his loyalty to lawful government as
such, in its essential continuity, government after government. This
is a distinction both basic and delicate and one beset with many
practical problems. We need to look at it more closely, contrasting
the concept of service to the state with the concept of service to the
regime, or the particular government in power. That is the purpose
of this chapter.

THE CIVIL SERVANT AS SERVANT OF THE STATE

Equating Public Interest with Government Aims

The impressive historical pedigree of the idea of the civil servant
as servant of the state has given it great dignity. In Brandenburg-
Prussia the early manifestations of this idea came forth in the shift

154

from a patrimonial absolutism toward a more broadly oriented political leadership, supplied in the statecraft of "enlightened monarchy." The dynasty itself turned into an agency devoted to serving the state.

Behind it was a seductively simple equation—that the public interest was necessarily identical with the aims pursued by the king, aided by his ranking civil servants. Hegel in his elaboration of political ethics made this equation subject to examination and to that extent subject to challenge on the basis of the existing circumstances. But his general judgment of monarchy and the civil service, read in the larger context, left the impression that in point of fact he saw hardly any good reason for such challenge. Moreover, he strongly hinted that it was best to undertake any review of the equation of the public interest with the goals of the regime, not before the eyes of the citizenry, but within the bosom of the state. Nor was this all a matter of the point of departure. Savigny, for example, despite his leadership of the "historical school" and the distance that thus separated him from Hegel, contributed to a similar conclusion. His view that in the secular realm all things right, good, and true had a political base—for him, the "spirit of the people"—made it easy to imagine that the ship of state, except for unusually careless navigation, could be held readily on the course of the public interest.

The State as the Spirit of the Nation

Notwithstanding obvious differences, the parallel in the evolution of the British career service should not be overlooked. The accent placed by Burke upon tradition as the harvest of the nation's political inventiveness disclosed the same search for an unchangeable unity which to Savigny was anchored in the spirit of the people. The next wave came in the middle of the nineteenth century with the advance of the English Neo-Hegelians, especially Thomas Hill Green, who saw the state as the product of the will of the citizens centered upon the general interest. Thus the common commitment to accomplish public purposes, not the presence of force or power, was the foundation of government. From another side, John Stuart Mill undertook to erect bridges from the individuality of the single human being to an inclusive social collectivity that spent its benefits upon all and thereby enhanced the individual's personal satisfactions.

These ideas provided much of the ideological context in which the British career service was built piece by piece. Both in legal connection and in institutional design the new civil service was hinged to the crown. But it was a crown that had divested itself of any controlling personal interest in the conduct of government. The crown was well on the way to becoming the symbolic expression of the essential unity of the British Empire. The tie proved so strong that in our day the Empire could be transformed without break into the Commonwealth.

Homogeneity of Value System

The idea of service to the state gave a firm moral basis to the unconditional subordination of the merit bureaucracy under the political leadership furnished at the helm of the state. More important, however, is the fact that the modern civil service was formed in an era which could visualize the state as the natural embodiment of the common good. This is why the Prussian bureaucracy, for instance, repeatedly operated as the equivalent of a party of reform, especially in the first half of the eighteenth century and again in the middle of the nineteenth, when the liberal tide was running high. As a reform party, the civil service provided an important means of intellectual representation to the middle class, on which the monarchy had leaned in the making of the modern state to overcome the opposition of privileged groups, especially the nobility.

In England, during the second half of the nineteenth century, the requirements of the general interest seemed no less self-evident to an upper class that was highly homogeneous in both its value system and its perspectives. The dominant position of this upper class gave public policy an equally unified political character. The elimination of political patronage, though free from the mass effects of the American "spoils system," was first pressed as a requirement of Britain's imperial interests. Thus reform of the civil service became the great administrative achievement of the Victorian epoch.

Loyalty to King and Loyalty to Crown

The task of serving the king of Prussia was made much easier when the civil servant could feel personally pledged to the monarch by his duty of fidelity. But the tensions running through the king's official family can hardly be ignored as soon as we try to imagine how often the men of an era of "enlightenment" had occasion to grit their teeth under a strong-minded ruler such as Frederick William I, whose statesmanship was matched by his rough and ready ways. In his day inspired recognition of the needs of effective political and administrative organization and despotic fury lived under the same roof.

In England, on the other hand, the reformed civil service, more than a century later, found itself implanted in the parliamentary system of government. Service for the crown was therefore not conceived as a personalized relationship to the monarch. The cabinet, as the effective government, was subject to change in party control. Under these circumstances, the creative accomplishment of fashioning a merit bureaucracy loyal to both crown and Parliament seems even greater. As British opinion is prone to emphasize, this development represents the decisive step in the historic evolution of the modern civil service. It is true that the political rivalry channeled in the two-party system remained mitigated, well into the twentieth century, by the basic kinship of the tone-setting elements in the social structure. But our day has shown that the spirit of wholehearted performance does not vanish among the higher service in England under Labor cabinets.

Differing Images of the State

It is obvious, however, that the meaning of being a servant of the state must be derived from the specific implications the concept of the state carries with it. Depending on the circumstances that have affected the nature of their growth, different nations have come to attach different meanings to the concept of the state. In Germany, during her long pilgrimage into national unity, the concept of the state obtained a meaning focused predominantly on the values of a common order and on the formal authority sustaining it. In this sense the state reached an almost tropical flowering, compared with other countries. "Father State," as Thomas Mann wistfully called it, was expected to take his large responsibilities very seriously, to perform them meticulously, and to keep himself wrapped up in sober and forbidding dignity. All this gave even the lowest organs of the state a frequently unearned decorum, but at the same time it had the effect of furnishing public life an unalterable standard of devotion to the public interest as the ultimate yardstick of civic as well as official behavior.

By comparison, both the British and the American developments assigned less value to the ordering hand of governmental authority. In England the concept of the state was turned not so much toward the inside as toward the outside, toward the enlargement and the preservation of the British stake throughout the empire and the world. The role of government at home was decisively limited by the idea of liberty and the parliamentary-representative counterweight to the executive branch. In the United States the concept of the state never came truly into its own. In its feebler version it remained oriented toward society, and the best that could be said of government was that it performed a reinforcing function for society. The public interest was a rapidly changing thing, manifesting itself principally in the seismographic recordings of public opinion and the results of popular elections. In each of these three examples the concept of the state influenced the civil service in a different way.

Disintegration of the State as Unifying Symbol

No less important, however, is the fact that in our day we can observe in all three countries an increasing disintegration of the general view, once rather stable, about what promotes the public well-being and what does not. This is perhaps merely another way of saying that today the general view is formed in the interplay of forces much more diversified in interest and much larger in membership than the groups that participated in this process only a half-century ago. In addition, the dissolution of the idea of the general welfare must be traced, above all, to the impact of the problems of the fully developed industrial state. One of the largest of these problems arises from the collision of two almost equally strong motivations that divide society—the drive toward social policy, on the one hand, and the drive toward private enterprise, on the other. In the resulting battles over what the position of government ought to be in these matters, the concept of the general interest has not proved to be a particularly useful common denominator. Moreover, in the aftermath of World War II a new source of strain made itself felt in the almost unbearable tensions of an international character. These tensions have had an intensifying effect, in many respects, upon the inherited conflicts of domestic politics.

Small wonder that the present-day statesman is a harassed and therefore impatient director of public business. Inevitably, he is placed on the defensive in the frustrating deadlocks caused by obstinate circumstances. When division runs so deep in public life, the civil service is constantly in danger of becoming—or being mistaken for—the political handmaiden of those in power. To what extent is it possible under such conditions to say rightfully, except in a purely formal sense, that the merit bureaucracy is actually engaged in serving the *state*? How far is it still true that the state itself is a sufficiently inclusive and generally recognized value category?

As a unifying concept, the modern state appears to be in slow retreat, except in its travesty under totalitarian auspices. The symbolism of the state no longer renews itself in the continuity of a basic political orientation that provides public opinion with a rallying point, with a sense of principle. In the interaction of successive governments, democratically formed but backed too often by quite different majorities, the state seems to turn into a two-faced monster. Is it surprising that the civil servant, like the citizen, begins to doubt his eyes? The duty of obedience puts his competence at the disposal of the government of the day whenever it has got into the saddle by constitutional means. That is the government he is bound by his oath to serve faithfully. But if, as technical counselor to the government in power and as executor of its policies, the career man thinks primarily of the state in the sense of a longer-range embodiment of the public interest, as the common interest of all, he can hardly expect to enjoy popularity with the powers that be.

In pure theory we might say that political decisions, after all, are not entered upon the ledgers of the civil servant's responsibility. The program of the government must meet the ultimate test in the electoral process, not in the actions of the bureaucracy. This is a satisfactory answer as far as it goes, but it hardly fits those many recurrent situations where either the government as a whole or individual ministers on their own, however principle-minded they may be, must perform sharp turns on short notice. These necessarily require for satisfactory execution the adroit and loyal support of the career man—even if he feels his hair stand on end.

The "Career Man's Mind"

It would be wrong to summarize all this in the conclusion that the idea of the civil servant as servant of the state has today become an illusion. It is in the nature of the merit bureaucracy to function as a projection of the rational approach in political life. In this approach subject-matter knowledge, experience in supplying it, and professional competence in acting upon it all play their part. Their combination, in the day-in, day-out operations of the administrative system, explains the existence of a distinctive quality known as the "career man's mind."

The "career man's mind" represents a reasonably predictable disposition, a way of looking at things, a tendency to give attention to the broader continuities in departmental activities, beyond the passing political urgencies of the hour. Unconsciously as well as consciously, the "career man's mind" is intermingled with his role as supplier of an expert answer to particular problems. The memoir literature of our century reports many instances in which the civil servant's contribution to important political decisions has expressed the character of the state as the reflection of the common good. No doubt the idea of service to the state gives the merit bureaucracy a vitally important general orientation, with a basic standard of self-restraint and a directional needle pointing toward the general welfare. But if the political system is overstrained by sharply contradictory pressures upon it, the state is reduced to a many-headed thing that rarely knows its mind. It therefore would be wholly unrealistic to turn our eyes entirely from the countercurrents that challenge the elementary unity of the state, especially when it is obvious that the civil service is helplessly exposed to them.

The Bureaucracy between Millstones

The dilemma of the career man lies here in the paradox of being both in and out of politics. On the one hand, he is placed, whether he likes it or not, in the cloud of dust swirled up in the conflict of party aims and economic interests. On the other hand, because he is not personally burdened with political responsibility and therefore has no device for clearing his general ledger, he cannot hope for reinforcement by the electorate. Whether he conducts himself truly as servant of the state when defending before his political superiors a particular position on grounds of principle or whether in doing so he makes himself guilty of "lack of co-operation" or even concealed sabotage, he has no recourse to the general public.

If the civil servant is told that in a serious conflict he is entitled, after all, to request his discharge, such advice will hardly seem to him like a desirable solution. To qualify for entrance into his profession, he had to give evidence of a special preparation, usually not tied in specifically with other occupational pursuits. To that he has added a stock of experience which, again, is not easily made useful outside the official environment. Thus it is not easy for him to shift into another way of making his living. He is actually threatened with the loss of the money value of his whole career. Even his pension rights are jeopardized. Should he have to leave public service and seek a comparable position in private enterprise when he is past his youthful years, he can rarely count on an adequate pension. If he knows in his heart that he has dedicated himself to public service, resignation appears doubly impossible. Thus the career man, in a certain sense, is actually chained to his office.

Effects upon Civil Service Behavior

These considerations have a formative effect upon civil service behavior. They explain why the rebel is rare in the administrative world. By the same token, they make it improbable that the career man will show himself in his official activities as an enthusiastic and untiring fighter for the common interest as he sees it. Even though it makes a large difference whether or not he is likely to raise issues in these terms with his political masters, he will usually do so "tactfully" and be prepared for a noiseless retreat.

It should be added that during the drawn-out public debates over the desirable scope of governmental functions, the seesaw of more or less has never come to an end. As a result, the trimming-down and even the abolition of agencies and corresponding reductions of staff have gained considerable practical significance in the occupational outlook of civil servants. The effects of such uncertainties are proportionately larger upon a profession in which the middle-class psychology has particularly strong roots. Thus other things besides the fact that administrative battles are fought with paper explain why civil service offers so little occasion for a heroic life.

More recently, the cold war has given impetus to a reconsideration and a spinning-out of the compatibility requirements for the career service. This has not taken either the same forms or the same sweep everywhere, but the consequences add up to a significant tightening of older rules. The common core of the new prescription is perhaps fairly assessed by saying that today in case of doubt the civil servant must be prepared to furnish proof that he is free from extremist sympathies as well as from traits or habits which could be exploited by espionage agents of foreign powers. The introduction of novel judgment factors as subjective elements which affect the career man's occupational chances takes a toll in self-assurance. Conversely, too, when getting along depends as much on discretionary evaluation higher up as it does in the civil service, promotion cannot be hoped for without a demonstration of considerable adaptability to the point of view and even the hemming and hawing of the superior.

None of this concerns the docile sheep, but it does concern the butting goat. In the office setting unorthodox or otherwise uncomfortable views make no one popular. When it is commonly appreciated that such views invite political suspicions, it becomes the rule of caution to stick to the company of sheep. But the ensuing weakening of the intellectual energy and the moral courage of the career service can hardly be dismissed as unimportant.

The Bureaucracy as Stabilizing Force

With all that, what is left of the concept of civil service as service to the state is by no means negligible. In the change of political leadership according to the voters' choice, the merit bureaucracy, as a constant element, provides a stabilizing influence. It represents not only the continuing aspects of the administrative process, crystallized in long experience, but also an unbroken general line in the evolution of governmental programs, marked by series of cherished precedents. True enough, by political choice the line may be bent or entirely abandoned. Even then, however, it is probable because of the advisory role of the career service that the changed or new line will be settled upon by the political leadership in knowledge of the circumstances which brought about the old line.

In this fashion the merit bureaucracy operates like a brake; it favors a coherent evolution and discourages excessive swings of the pendulum. Relatively speaking, the permanent machinery of public administration thus provides a pull toward the center, toward the things that may be expected to stay the same. But the influence exercised by the civil service is an uncertain influence in the sense that unwelcome advice can always be rejected. Under sharp pressure from above, the influence cannot become effective. Ordinarily, however, the career man's participation in the formulation of detailed plans for giving effect to a new governmental program supplies many opportunities for casting proposed measures in the mold of a broad concept of the public interest.

How far that actually occurs depends, in no small measure, on the political vision of those who represent the incoming government, provided they give themselves time for it. To a still larger extent, however, it depends on whether or not the career service, in the balance of the circumstances, can still recognize behind the particular government the state itself in the larger sense. As an orienting influence upon the civil servant, the idea of service to the state has undiminished value. On the other hand, we can hardly say today without reservation, as a matter of institutional fact, that the civil servant is actually permitted to function truly as the servant of the state.

THE CIVIL SERVANT AS SERVANT OF THE REGIME

Tool of the Powers To Be?

If the civil servant cannot comfort himself with the belief that he officiates as the servant of the state, does that leave him no choice but to put up with being looked upon as the servant of the regime, of the government of the day? If a "servant of the regime" is meant to become its unreserved protagonist, this question must be answered in the negative for various reasons.

It is true that a capacity for placing the aims of the political regime above personal conviction, and hence a capacity for operating as a willing support of any lawful government, has been a key factor in the historical growth of the career service. Indeed, the legal removal of the merit bureaucracy from the political battleground is understandable only as the measure of the civil servant's success in serving each government on equal terms. This is a test asked of him only in recent times. The relative frequency of change in the government, compared with the stability of government in the age of absolutism, is the direct consequence of the development of the modern constitutional state on democratic foundations. Moreover, it is well to remember that the relative insulation of the civil service from the contest of political parties, as a matter of principle, is found in the main only in the countries of Western civilization.

But the larger part of the globe is under different rules in this regard. In most countries it is a self-evident maxim that all officials must identify themselves completely with those in power—or wield enough power themselves to stand their own ground. That applies not only to the totalitarian state and to the totalitarian demimonde which imitates that state. It also applies to nearly all those political systems that are authoritarian or dictatorial without showing the tight mass organization and the comprehensive structure of power typical of totalitarianism.

It makes little difference whether these systems consciously oppose the constitutional state or, on the contrary, struggle toward its threshold in search of a better scheme of things. In both instances the immunity of the civil servant from partisan impositions may be recognized in the letter of the law, in response to the Western example. Practically speaking, however, the legal side of the matter amounts to little. If we count by countries, the civil servant who fawns before the regime in power is the predominant type. If we count by professionally trained civil servants, the result more nearly approximates a balance between unmistakably regime-minded bureaucracies and career systems governed in fact by the idea of nonpartisanship.

The Totalitarian Prescription

For the democratic states of the West the servant of the regime as a type prevalent in other parts of the world is of subordinate interest, especially from a practical point of view. That applies, above all, to the administrative system of the totalitarian state, with its monopolistic structure of power. Nevertheless, a few general remarks may be in order. It is characteristic of the totalitarian state to cultivate strenuously the idea that it represents the result of a pact with eternity, that it is the last word in political engineering. It is equally characteristic of the totalitarian state, if oddly contradictory, that it feels sure of its totality only on the basis of the compulsory coordination achieved by the one-party system. Granting these two things, it appears quite logical to infer that the government employee must acknowledge but one political will and one source of power—that is, the established regime. Like the citizen, the functionary cannot be permitted to seek shelter behind mental reservations in the realm of politics.

Viewed superficially, this may seem at first a tempting simplification of the problems of the career man in the political context. As it was said so suitably in Hitler's Germany, the civil servant enters the honorable calling of "political soldier," and the men who exercise political command rub their hands in sardonic elation as the columns of public administration stomp along in drill formation. Ironically, however, the servant of the regime is constantly in danger of being caught up in the political rear guard. Nowhere is the bureaucracy as frequently and furiously charged with stupidity, cumbersomeness, and alienation from the people as in the Soviet Union. Nowhere is the government employee as often used as a political lightning rod as in the totalitarian state. Nowhere is he as insecure in his legal status and his social standing. If the disciplinary power crashes down upon him, he will bear the marks forever.

This is so even when the public servant can hopefully allude to his membership in *the* party as he tumbles into hot water. Such protective cover is of little avail when he is burdened with the sins of the "apparatus." His guilt is one of association, for he must accept responsibility for the defects of the "apparatus" as a necessary consequence of being part of it, in whatever capacity. Moreover, the administrative underling in the totalitarian state is by no means automatically worthy of so exclusive a distinction as party membership. The bureaucracy at large is therefore a relatively low-ranking cadre and hence a very convenient scapegoat. The only exception, generally speaking, is the political agent who is shoved into key spots in the administrative system to serve primarily as a watchdog. For this reason, he necessarily occupies a special position. Usually he is able to save his skin by offering the skins of others.

It should not be assumed, however, that the totalitarian state can afford to throw the merit principle away. Rather, merit has acquired a larger meaning. Merit in the usual sense, as a basic standard of government recruitment, is balanced by evidence of wholehearted deference to the approved ideology. It should be remembered that Lenin during the years of his exile in Switzerland unrelentingly battled the left-wing idealists on the proposition that it would be indispensable for a successful revolution to have at its disposal a sufficient supply of specialists trained in the techniques of political overthrow. If that is necessary for bringing off the revolution, it is certainly no less necessary after the seizure of power. Despite the continued attraction which the image of the common man personally attending to official functions has for romantic souls, Lenin had enough administrative sense to realize that the use of amateurs in the conduct of public affairs is distinctly limited in modern government by practical considerations.

Transitional Strains

We have talked thus far about service to the regime principally under totalitarian auspices. But does not the servant of the regime exist also in democratic systems of government? To some degree the beginnings of such specific identification with the political regime were present in the special legislation "for the protection of the republic" which was passed in a period of exceptional stress and strain under the German constitution of 1919. This legislation, in its application to the career service, was intended as a sharp restraint upon those suspect of antirepublican sentiments. We must add that in the early years after World War I, which brought to an end the German Empire, opinion about the intrinsic merits of the new republican order was widely divided, especially in the middle class. Besides, the abrupt break between the monarchical system and the novel parliamentary-democratic arrangements brought with it extraordinary problems for a civil service raised under the old system and taken over by the new. Certain elements of the German bureaucracy gave the appearance of failing to show themselves equal to these problems. But it is to be admitted that the appropriate solution for anomalous situations like this one is a matter of considerable difference of opinion.

There was even a good deal of uncertainty about what civil servants ought to do upon the rise to power of Hitler and his cohorts in 1933. Playing for time and alternating grandiose pronouncements about the great traditions of the civil service with legal changes designed to break its back, the new government pressured the career man into a gradual, if incomplete, surrender to the regime. Nevertheless, it had the effect of a bombshell when the Constitutional Court in 1954 insisted in an obiter dictum that the transformation of the civil service into an establishment of the regime had been so thorough as to carry with it a legal termination of the civil servant's status with the collapse of the Third Reich at the end of World War II.

Decline of the American Spoils System

Europeans are prone to point to the American development during the Jacksonian period and its administrative practices as the classical example of a bureaucracy pledged to the regime. In the rebellion of the newly settled West against the consolidated capitalistic power position of the East, the democratic idea conquered the political defenses of a quasi-oligarchical social order. The strategy of this thrust made it logical for Andrew Jackson to proclaim the principle that in the people's state the ordinary citizen was entirely good enough for the administration of public offices, much better, in fact, than a biased, self-interested officialdom. Despite the flowering of the patronage principle, however, the old-style merit rule of President Washington lived on in the chief clerks of the federal departments as a matter of practical necessity.

Since the passage of the civil service act of 1883, the spoils system has retreated. In the sphere of federal administration party patronage has shrunk to so small a volume that Americans today are inclined to wonder whether or not that is good for the nation's political health. But the development should not be taken as a symptom of increasing public virtue. Rather, it is the consequence of a sounder appreciation of the operating demands that the economic and social order of our day makes on the machinery of public administration.

Moreover, during the twentieth century it has become increasingly clear that the President cannot afford to be casual in filling those posts which are burdened with political responsibility. He must think first of gaining able and widely esteemed partners for the direction of the federal departments. The politician has lost more and more ground as a serious candidate for this kind of task. A parallel tendency has simultaneously come to the fore in the balancing of different shadings of partisanship on the level of the cabinet. Thus the President and his principal advisers like to make use, in the exercise of the nominating power, of this or that public figure affiliated with the other party, especially when the particular individual is reasonably free from conspicuous ties to his own party or from other conflicting obligations. These choices are further supplemented by those presidential nominating decisions in which the President is held by legislation to pay special attention to party affiliation, especially in order to preserve the bipartisan composition of many of the so-called independent regulatory commissions and boards, such as the Interstate Commerce Commission, the Securities and Exchange Commission, and the National Labor Relations Board.

The political control group in the executive branch, or what is called the official family of the President, shows therefore not a few of the colors of the spectrum, ranging from sharply accentuated identification with the President's party to a middle-of-the-road type of bipartisanship and even to a conscious indifference toward the acknowledged position of either party. This mixture is explained primarily by the shadow-like character of the two major parties in their capacity as competitive organs of national representation. The internal cohesion of both parties in their national structure is weak, and the elected representative, regardless of party label, is usually more concerned with retaining the support of the dominant interests in his local constituency than with acting on the planks of the national program of his party. As a result, the contrast between the two parties becomes a very superficial thing in many respects.

Effects of Political Change in the Presidency

All these factors combine to produce a larger result—namely, that normally no striking changes in the political course come about when one party is replaced by the other in the control of the presidency. There are exceptions to this rule of experience; for example, sharper turns are very likely or even necessary under the impact upon the public of dramatic events, such as the economic breakdown in the early thirties. No occurrences of such magnitude preceded the electoral victory of the Republicans over the Democrats in the presidential campaign in 1952, and hence the promised "change" could hardly be expected to reach deeply. It may therefore seem strange that the thought of a new political leadership generated considerable disquiet within the federal civil service. But the explanation is not too difficult to find.

In the first place, the change at the helm of the presidency brought to an end twenty years of uninterrupted Democratic rule in the executive branch. During this period, in battling the "great depression," the federal government had taken on many new functions. The newly created agencies, frequently erected as temporary emergency establishments, were manned in many instances by hastily recruited provisional employees. These could be expected in their majority to be sympathetic toward the New Deal and its works. To critical eyes, they presented the appearance of a swarm of faithful Democrats. When in due course temporary agencies acquired the aura of permanency, their personnel in time was taken over into the regular civil service. To that extent the merit bureaucracy took on more of a party hue than seemed the case before, at least in the political agitation of the Republicans, who therefore could be assumed to feel that fewer Democrats and more Republicans in the civil service would help to restore its responsiveness to the incoming government. Moreover, from the same political point of view the civil service was under a cloud as the concrete expression of the proliferation of governmental functions—a main target of the Republican party. Finally, there was also the matter of the costs of government. The Eisenhower administration had publicly avowed its determination to bring the federal budget into balance again, presumably by sharp reduction of public expenditures. A considerable decrease in positions was therefore in the cards. Abolition of positions had the added attraction of being the most convenient method of getting rid of unwanted subordinates.

These factors combined to produce an "oppressive atmosphere"[1] in the federal civil service, a considerable nervous burden on many. Since then, however, quite a few things have changed. Employment figures for the executive branch did go down, but such shrinkage had occurred repeatedly in the postwar period and was forecast once more because of the subsiding Korean emergency. It is altogether true that in some federal departments civil servants were pushed about quite a bit. On the other side of the ledger, however, one must note that President Eisenhower interposed effective resistance to the pressure coming from office-hunters in the Republican party. Nor can the fact be ignored that the incoming agency heads, by and large, showed due appreciation of the benefits to be derived from the skill, experience, and subject-matter knowledge available in the career service.

As one striking example, although the Bureau of the Budget in the Executive Office of the President exercises its planning and control functions in the President's name, the newly appointed director of this bureau decided against any changes in its internal structure of authority, especially in the direction of the individual staff groups through which the bureau operates as a non-political career establishment. Every civil servant remained at his familiar place. Almost without interruption, the Bureau of the Budget continued its advisory role in the formulation of the legislative program of the President, in close co-operation with his immediate staff in the White

1. Herman M. Somers, "The Federal Bureaucracy and the Change of Administration," *American Political Science Review*, XLVIII (1954), 151.

House office. The administrative-technical concerns and the political concerns were blended here without much fuss or bother. It is no exaggeration to say that developments such as this mark a new chapter of the history of American public administration.

The American Version of the Career Man

Is the country moving toward the European prototype of the merit bureaucracy, with its firmly established institutional traditions and the prestige attached to civil service? An answer in the affirmative would require substantial qualification. In a political system that leans historically on the concept of society, in a system that withholds all laurel from the state and substitutes for it the pragmatically operating manifestations of control called government, the public service, too, has more of a common man's character than an official solemnity. This is demonstrated, for instance, in the eminently sensible way in which official titles are ignored in the personal relationships of civil servants, although the exuberance of the American classification practice leaves few without some kind of official designation. It is further shown in the custom to refer to one's position, even when it attests high rank, simply as a "job." The same relaxed attitude comes to the fore when the superior is addressed by his first name, even if he is older. Above all, there is an almost complete lack of a distinctive common social outlook that runs through the civil service, especially the upper groups, which are not organized into a consolidated higher career.

All this does not mean, however, that the merit bureaucracy is endowed with a greater sensitivity toward political leadership than is true of its European counterpart. Self-restraint in allowing personal views to interfere with the course steered by those in control is a common feature of the ideology of civil service. But it is natural that deference to public policy is not so consciously cultivated in an administrative system that denies itself the insignia of authority and borrows its ways from the ordinary man as in a career service that looks upon itself strictly as an instrumentality of the state. The American civil servant is first an individual, with all his likes and dislikes, and only second a conscious part of the operating government. Hence he is not particularly well conditioned to neutralize his personal preference or partisanship in the face of set goals of policy. Even so, however, the record leaves little doubt that he can be trusted, collectively speaking, to do his work for each government lawfully in power—as indeed he must so that the aspirations of representative democracy be converted with assurance into practical results.

Importance of Alternation in Government

Without the civil servant's sense of duty the merit bureaucracy would be incapable of reacting predictably to direction from the top. But this point has both administrative and political implications. Politically, predictable reaction to direction is the means of putting into effect the requirement of constitutionalism that the machinery for making and carrying out decisions must be available for each lawful government in unimpaired and usable condition. The administrative contribution toward this end, however, has an important counterpart in the constitutional sense of the government in power. It too must fully recognize this requirement. Otherwise the merit bureaucracy could be corrupted by its own virtues—subordination of one's personal opinion, impartial and faithful attention to the needs of each successive government, and unadulterated expert counsel in giving effect to political programs irrespective of whether these tend toward the left or toward the right. These virtues beckon the career man continuously toward the portals of blind service to the regime.

That is true in exact proportion to the gradual decline suffered by the countervailing idea of service to the state in the administrative systems of our time. As a matter of fact, the thing that guards the civil servant against making himself over body and soul to the established regime—as in the totalitarian state and other political systems that govern from above—is essentially the regime's replaceability. Alternation in the control of the government, in terms of fact as well as in terms of political principle, is the source of salvation. The logic and the probability of change in control erect insurpassable barriers to a planned transition toward service to the regime. When such barriers are lacking because alternation in the control of the government is no longer within the reach of anybody's imagination, the political pressure upon the civil service becomes overwhelming. In this kind of situation no career service has proved able to meet strong pressure successfully.

THE UNCERTAIN FUTURE OF THE CAREER MAN

The Lines of Control

This review of two fundamentally different concepts of service does not suggest that the career man is described accurately as a member of a ruling body with independent power drives beyond hope of control. Yet much is being made of this contention. What is the explanation?

First of all, the merit bureaucracy of our day is a mirror of the modern state, with its tremendous range of tasks, its large-scale administrative structure, and its highly developed functional specialization. Under popular rule the administrative system operates under various types of arrangements designed to serve the purpose of control, both from within and from the outside. Examples abound in the specific elaboration of superior-subordinate relationships, the channels of appeal within each agency, the directing power of electoral decisions, and legal redress before courts of law or administrative tribunals. But control over authority should not be conceived as traveling along a single telephone wire. On the contrary, all control operates in a level-to-level sequence, or from one level to the next. And the number of levels, depending on both the circumstances and the way of counting, may come to a surprising total.

From the voter to his government and finally through the five, six, or seven levels within the individual department, control must stretch across great institutional distances. On each level it collides with the inertia of set ways. Indeed, the wear and tear to which control is exposed is greatly increased by the weight it throws about. Running through the organizational theory of private enterprise is an emphasis upon ready achievement of results. By contrast, the organizational theory of government puts all action under strong safeguards to keep authority in bounds and subject to precise accountability. Hence in importance control is on a par with action, if not of a higher stature, quite at variance to what happens to it as control struggles onward from level to level.

Defensive Instincts and Rule of Law

Understandably, the public comes to assume that those who hide so skilfully in the maze of levels may well exploit their virtual immunity from control by fashioning escapes from the restraints imposed upon them. That assumption appears most plausible in relation to the least transparent part of the machinery of government, the executive branch, which, unlike the legislature and the courts, does not allow the citizen to watch any part of its proceedings. So it is easy to imagine that the dark world of administrative anonymity is populated with faceless but incredibly clever paper-shufflers who conspire diabolically to choke off the constitutional liberties of the people.

But civil servants, habituated to advising and doing things as told, have little inclination to take over the business of governing or to undermine the constitutional system. The specialist feels more at ease when he can submit proposals to a political leadership willing to take responsibility for the decision than when this responsibility is being pressed upon himself. Moreover, the reams of rules that serve to achieve a full accounting for every action in the sphere of public administration condition the civil servant to a veneration of the letter of the law and even of the comma of the regulation. Going by the book, after all, is the principal means of self-protection.

Typically, therefore, the civil servant clings to his instructions and stalls without them. But behind his behavior we must recognize also consciously cultivated professional doctrine. This is usually strongest in the higher career service, when it is possessed with a sharp sense of obligation and a deep-seated respect for the legal limits of administrative authority. The principle of legality as an ever present check on the exercise of authority thus can become second nature to the bureaucracy, as it has long been in Germany.

Apart from extraordinary conditions, the career service tends to work as an influence adding strength to constitutionalism. A responsibly operating administrative system is a large reinforcement of the whole concept of constitutional procedure. That is why in Germany at the beginning of the past century the legally regulated, technically efficient machinery of public administration was looked upon as a kind of applied constitution in contrast to the idea of the formal constitution—operating as an effective partial substitute for a formal constitution.

Mice and Elephant

When civil servants feel the ruthlessly applied political whip, they begin to behave like scurrying mice. In more normal times, on the other hand, the bureaucracy, notwithstanding the support the constitutional order has from it, often gives itself the appearance of a sleepy elephant. He is pulled by the tail to get him going, but that does not concern him. One makes a great noise under his very ears, and still it takes a long time before he starts moving. The public therefore feels entitled to conclude that the elephant is intolerably stubborn. But in the metaphor of the stubborn elephant we encounter merely some of the negative consequences of the habits of bureaucratic life.

The routines of day-by-day business come to be thought of as unchangeable aspects of the laws of nature. Departures from the "way it is done" make necessary a special effort to learn the new way, which the bureaucratic mind is anxious to avoid. In addition, the cult of specialization leads the expert to suppose that no one understands things as well as he does. For this reason there is really no need at all, he thinks, to turn an ear toward suggestions or protests coming from outside. Nor does it make sense to bother one's self over the end product of administrative action. The end product as such is outside anyone's specific jurisdiction—and responsibility, in the bureaucratic setting, never extends beyond the grooves of one's own jurisdiction. Specialization, moreover, has given the civil servant a priceless opportunity for building up an occupational language of his own, mostly unintelligible to ordinary mortals. It is a language likely to endure even under such onslaughts as Sir Ernest Gowers' *The Complete Plain Words* (1954), a revolutionary publication if only for the fact that it was commissioned by the British Treasury and turned out by Her Majesty's Stationery Office. To put it generally, the bureaucratic view insists that one must show understanding and patience in dealing with the public, but one must not take particularly seriously the know-it-better attitude shown by those on the outside who look in the window.

Control and Sensitivity

Control over the civil service—and, in the same way, control within the administrative system—is therefore in no way comparable to a central switchboard operation. Nor does it function automatically as soon as the hand touches the button. The level-to-level relationships would make that impossible. Even the occasional explosion high above comes down merely as a sudden thunderstorm, as an occurrence that simply happens. Afterward, everybody sits about wet and sad for a while, until everything is nicely dried again.

It follows that effective control presupposes a large measure of alertness and sensitivity in the bureaucracy. These qualities operate in quite the same way in which a fine horse instantly obeys the slightest signals of the skilled rider. That is the explanation why the casually assembled manpower of a patronage system reacts to control inadequately if at all. Capacity for full response and willingness to respond must not be taken for granted. On the contrary, both require painstaking and planned development and conservation. Both must have deep roots in the "career man's mind." This mentality, in turn, needs a hospitable climate not only in the general tenor of civil service law but also, and more importantly, in the characteristics of a nation's political life. The horse cannot perform to perfection by itself; it must have a skilful rider.

Trying Times

If the future of the merit bureaucracy appears far from rosy from the vantage point of today, this has to do primarily with the nature of our times. There are few indications that sufficient attention will be given to the problem of how government could make best use of the career service and what might be done to develop guidelines to this end. It must be admitted that a solution requires statesmanlike perspectives and a determination to persist. These are unusual qualities today, and few will try their hand at a task that in the nature of things cannot be accomplished quickly and in one fell swoop. The common variety of governmental programs bubble up from the political fermentation of public life. Behind them is the pressure for action which the voters or influential interests give priority. The fundamental requirements of the political system and its effective working are too big as well as too far away from the arena in which the ordinary run of interests is lined up for battle. That explains why these more important requirements are pushed from the national agenda. They have no natural spokesman, nor do they affect the interest of all citizens so plainly that they set off popular crusades.

In the middle period of our century the constitutional state finds itself engulfed by domestic and international conflicts, actual and potential, in the face of which it must prove itself anew. The relationship between the free-enterprise economy and the exercise of governmental authority, the general direction to be pursued by public policy, the ideological struggle at home as well as abroad, the reciprocal effects of the capacity for national self-assertion and the capacity for preserving the democratic way of life, the bond to be reinforced between civic responsibility and political leadership—in all these matters the constitutional state faces exacting tests of its institutional resources.

If the constitutional state is to meet these tests, it will have to rely in part on its ideological reserves, in part on the political maturity of its electorate, and in part on the quality of national stewardship. In addition, however, the basic effectiveness of the constitutional state is linked today in constantly increasing scope with both the productivity and the integrity of the administrative system—and perhaps these two are essentially the same. It is in this vast realm that modern government performs the host of activities which in their detail hardly meet the eye but which extend in a thousand ways throughout the economic and social order. Reduced productivity in public administration brings about a vast if incalculable loss for society at large as well as for the political order. The effect is that of a per capita tax which never yields revenue. Because the tax is not formally levied, everybody appears to be willing to pay it.

CHAPTER 10

PERSPECTIVES

At the end of an introductory treatment of bureaucracy as condensed as this, it would hardly make sense to attempt a listing of conclusions. For the most part, the conclusions are woven into the discussion and have been presented in its course. Too much of the discussion would have to be repeated for a meaningful restatement of the conclusions. But we should perhaps not miss the occasion for taking another look at the subject from a distance, for asking some larger questions about it, and for venturing at least tentative answers.

First we may ask whether technological developments will significantly modify in the predictable future the structure and working of the administrative system of modern government. Will the advent of machines with "brains" reduce manpower to the pulling of switches and thus usher in the demise of large-scale organization as we know it? Will a machine-controlled rationality, operating without constant direction, supersede day-by-day supervisory authority? Next we need to consider what is the relative success of the merit bureaucracy as a means of accomplishing sound choices in the conduct of public affairs. Is the citizen being choked by merciless "processes"? Are decisions truly *made,* or do they mostly "happen"? And, finally, we should give some thought to the possibility of coming to a more satisfactory interlocking of political responsibility and administrative responsibility, to a better definition of the proper role of each, and to a clearer understanding on the political level of what use to make and not to make of the administrative machinery.

EFFECTS OF TECHNOLOGICAL EVOLUTION

Progress of Automation

Continuing advances in applied research, especially the recent development of electronics, have stimulated popular speculation about a push-button world. In that world, it is assumed, much of the mental as well as nearly all of the physical labor could be left to obedient robots. This is the vision conveyed in Orozco's painting in the library of Dartmouth College, which shows a hulking worker reading a book, perhaps Shakespeare or even T. S. Eliot, while the gleaming control room is filled with the hum of gigantic engines that need only occasional attention.

Utopia, however, is not likely to come upon us like lightning. As a matter of fact, the progress of automation has been quite gradual and relatively inconspicuous. It can be traced far into the past and offers little promise of changing Western man's environment abruptly. The abacus, for example, has been in use for a long time; and, although representing an innovation no less startling than today's computing monsters, it has not wrought telling social change. Similarly, one finds no evidence of revolutionary transformations where automation in its modern characteristics has been introduced into office work, as in the insurance business. Displacement of labor has not been dramatic. The structure and the basic operating processes of the enterprise have barely changed. The biggest gain has been in speed and accuracy of performance.

In appraising the foreseeable impact of automation in our time, it is probably more important that large-scale organization has been built up to its contemporary order of magnitude without basic change in administrative technology. While the past half-century witnessed a striking growth in the size of organizations both public and private, the administrative devices relied upon for direction, co-ordination, and control have hardly changed at all. Except for modern frills, they would look like old stuff to a Roman governor. Thus the dimensions of large-scale organization have been permitted to outrun the optimum of efficiency that these traditional devices can be expected to contribute. One of the most important effects of automation may be to redress the balance, to give large-scale organization an operating technology that would enable it to function with greater ease and versatility.

For one thing, automation is likely to furnish a strong incentive to cut down the welter of routine controls. The scientific principle embodied in machine operations, the impersonal objectivity of a tech-

nical process that neither gets rattled nor falls asleep, the predictability with which it grinds out predetermined results at a clip—
these factors leave little reason for watching every turn of the
wheels. Few things would do so much to diminish the bureaucratic
cumbersomeness of large-scale organization as reduction of internal
controls to a limited number of key points. The proliferation of
internal controls has flourished in public administration. It is particularly marked in administrative systems that have suffered from an
excess of legislative superintendence and from a deficiency of professional spirit. In such systems automation may prove itself a liber-
ating force by leading to a disposal of many of the reviews piled
upon reviews.

But automation will also give impetus to fresh ideas about the
engineering aspects of administering governmental functions. For
example, it is no doubt only a matter of time before customer contacts between the government and the public will be confined to
"application houses." All requests from individual citizens, to be
made on standard cards ready for punching, will go to the nearest
"application house," which will serve as the joint receiving point for
all governmental agencies. Action upon such requests will be noted
in the form of a small metal disk containing everything that needs
to be said in a single line of jumbled code letters and figures, together with the serial number of the applicant. Personal appearances
at the "application house" will be discouraged in the name of economy and efficiency; but there will be psychologists on duty at all
times. "Processing" of each request in the agency having jurisdiction
will be greatly accelerated by the absence of agitated or confused
applicants wandering about the halls, and the textbooks on public
administration will deal with "public relations" simply by running
an index entry, "*see* Application house."

"Operation Scatterbrains"

New approaches to administrative technology are also bound to
come to the fore as nations persist in preparing themselves for the
disaster of a thermonuclear or similarly devastating attack. Here we
must start with the premise that the concept of the capital city was
totally obsolete even before the end of World War II. To be sure,
halfway measures will have some appeal while public opinion gropes
for a comprehension of the peril. Short of ignoring the threat as beyond effective defense, however, desperately little choice remains. It
is reasonable to suppose that eventually only one formula will prove
practicable—complete dispersal of government as a normal, peace-

time method of operation. This would mean not only that the directing and planning elements of the executive branch would be scattered throughout the country (hence "Operation Scatterbrains") but also that the regional and local centers of field administration would be disbanded. Way off the highway, for instance, a hiker emerging from the forest will come upon a fence with the sign, "Visa Division, Department of State."

Under such circumstances many adjustments will be necessary in the familiar forms of carrying on administrative work. Ordinarily, it will no longer be possible to use the lunch period for a relaxed discussion of current business with one's opposite in another agency or even in another division of one's own department, for their locations may be a thousand miles away. A conference that actually brings the participants together in one room will be an unusual occurrence except for those stationed at the same location. With division chiefs at many different places, there will be no chance for them to drop in on the department head for a few minutes to set him right on this or that or to get his "line" on something for which guidance is needed in a hurry. But refinements in communications will compensate for much of the loss of physical proximity. Group discussions, for instance, will be carried on over vast distances by means of desk sets that not only will carry the voice but also will show the face of each speaker. One of the pleasant things about this type of conference will be the participants' chance to yawn freely out of range of the screen.

But even "Operation Scatterbrains" will leave intact the basic elements of administrative organization and procedure as these are known at present. The level-by-level structure of authority will remain, although many intermediate controls may have been cleared away as unproductive and burdensome. The number of needed specializations will be substantially larger, and each will be narrower and thus more self-contained than today. Lining up these specializations in the accomplishment of broader purposes will require, on a scale even larger than the present scale, a trained capacity for planning, direction, and co-ordination. That entails seeing the parts in relation to the whole, achieving the necessary degree of unity of operations, and sustaining an alert sense of responsibility. These essential qualities will continue to be in great demand in the administrative system. So will the kind of mind that not only can comprehend the working rhythm of vast and intricate machinery but also can recognize the axiomatic subservience of its output to the public interest.

On balance, then, we may expect an uninterrupted and wide-spread influence of technological developments upon public administration. The effects are bound to result in numerous changes over the entire range of operating processes. Thus they will modify in many particulars the institutional environment. But it appears unlikely that the outcome will be a new administrative world that would baffle the practitioner of our day. He may take delight at the wealth of novel gadgets and the surprising ways of doing the same old things. But, as he looks about and sniffs the air, he will happily conclude that bureaucrats are still bureaucrats.

PROBLEMS OF DECISION-MAKING

Functionary or Common Man?

To an important extent administration attains its ends by the making of decisions. As spheres of decision-making, administrative systems operate differently depending on various controlling factors. We come to grips with these factors when we ask: What images prevail within the individual administrative system about its own role? What working doctrine governs its actions? What kinds of men tend to emerge in its top cadre? In a certain way each of these factors may be seen as a consequence of the others. In some respects, however, each factor has an independent impact. Fundamentally, the combination of factors can be reduced to two alternatives that manifest themselves in the predominant characteristics of the particular administrative system. On the one hand, the administrative system may serve as a self-reliant source of technical competence. On the other hand, it may function as a response to impulses that play upon it from the outside.

Viewed from a different angle, in the first instance the bureaucracy regards itself as a separate body. It derives its identity from being unified for the performance of functions that are peculiarly in its charge. This gives the civil servant the distinctive marking of the functionary. In the second instance the bureaucracy looks upon itself as identified with the people. It expects its cue from the people or from those acting on its behalf, content to be a transformer of popular drives into governmental operations. This casts the civil servant as the common man's brother and thus as the common man himself.

As functionary the civil servant has come to life in the prototype of the guardian bureaucracy—dutiful, dedicated, and deferential to authority but also acting like the common man's self-assured mentor mounted on a pedestal above him. In the prototype of the caste bureaucracy the functionary consciously isolated himself from the people, allying his own interests with the interests of the few and placing both above the interest of the many. At the same time a narrow-minded authoritarianism sapped the spirit of service and filled the void with a ritualistic devotion to set ways and empty formalities. At the opposite pole the common man's version of civil service came to flower in the patronage bureaucracy of the spoils system. By throwing out the functionary altogether, this prototype promised to make public administration the domain of the ordinary citizen and thus the people's agency. In actual fact, however, the citizen first had to qualify as a partisan; and he was bound to lose out in competition with those who made their living as partisans. As a result, the patronage bureaucracy as an institution of popular rule had all the ills and little of the dignity of administration by amateurs. Indeed, office-holding appealed to the office-holder mainly for what he could get out of it for himself, for his political friends, or for those who were willing to show their appreciation of favors received.

None of these three prototypes as such commends itself for public administration in our day, in a setting dominated by democratic choices, middle-class values, and technical competence. Having rejected these prototypes, however, we are still faced with the necessity of a basic choice. The choice is between the civil servant as functionary and the civil servant as common man. Is he to withdraw into a fraternal order with its own point of view, standing apart from the general public to that extent but developing from his sense of mission the stamina of fearless advice coupled with the self-discipline of faithful service to each lawful government in power? Or is he to think and act like everybody else, being part of the multitude, offering his counsel when there is an opportunity for doing so, but not letting his better insight get in the way of what is asked of him? Even when the choice is not presented quite in these terms, it nevertheless raises a real issue. Do we want a bureaucracy that has the courage of its integrity, capable of displaying administrative statesmanship but likely to talk back to us on occasion? Or do we want a bureaucracy with its "ear to the ground," rarely making much of a fuss over anything but so relaxed in its professional attitudes that we can walk straight through it?

The Purpose of Democratic Administration

It has become popular to talk about "democratic administration" without always making clear exactly the intended meaning of the phrase. Obviously, under auspices of democratic government the administrative system must simultaneously reflect a consistent democratic orientation and answer to those exercising political control. Moreover, if only for reasons of good management, each public employee should have assurance of fair treatment and proper recognition of his rights. It is no less important that the individual participant's contribution to the group process of administration be made the object of frequent acknowledgment and thus be removed from the cold shadow of hierarchy. But democratic administration, above all, is to be a source of strength for democracy. To give strength, it must have strength to give. It does not give strength if its voice is that of the echo, if its attitude is that of an errand boy who mistakes public whims for manifestations of the general interest.

This does not mean that a politically unmanageable bureaucracy is preferable to one too limp to manage itself. They are equally undesirable. But a civil service is not likely to develop its full potentialities in public spirit and technical competence unless the facts of its existence allow it to think of itself as the color guard of the common good. To this end it must have an identity of its own, built upon the consciousness of its public function, a function worth performing in exact proportion to the benefits accruing ultimately to the people. Expressed differently, the civil servant should be a functionary first; he is not free to emulate the common man when that impairs his role as functionary.

The Administrative End Product

But ideal and travesty live close together. When stressing the link between the civil servant and his public function, when speaking of him as a functionary in this sense, we would not like him to turn into a stuffed shirt, a haughty formalist, or a petty tyrant. On the contrary, we want him to be profoundly concerned with what the common man thinks as well as with what the common man needs. Function provides great temptations to become self-contained, to retire into an ivory tower, and to resent intrusions from the outside. In meeting these temptations, nothing is more helpful to the functionary than to see himself through the eyes of the common man. In this respect it makes quite a difference whether or not the top cadre in the administrative system, by the nature of its composition, finds it difficult to use the eyes of the common man. There should never be a shortage of higher civil servants whose own social background connects them with the outlook and the worries of the common man.

Ironically, where the civil servant shuns the insignia of the functionary, where he self-consciously plays the part of the common man, public administration is far from breathing a distinctive popular vitality. On the contrary, a civil service consciously accepting the primacy of public opinion is prone to attach correspondingly greater value to precedent and procedure as anchors in the winds of pressure. The written rule becomes more important as a railing to which to hold when the waves of public sentiment sweep freely across the deck. To put it differently, when the civil servant can trust his resources in knowledge and experience to give him something to stand upon as particular administrative issues arise, when his counsel carries weight with his political superiors, when he will not be accustomed to a reversal of his department's position as soon as a storm is building up—in these circumstances he will have a freer attitude toward prescriptions imbedded in fixed routines. Then he will more often act on the "rule of reason," assuming personal responsibility for his action. Lacking such assurance, he will hold on to the letter of the manual for dear life. As a result, an administrative system dominated by the idea that it should live close to the people may provide a particularly hospitable climate for the flowering of "bureaucracy."

But, even when there are no special incentives in this direction, large-scale organization and "red tape" are intimately connected. It would be difficult in a large-scale organization to point to a single decision of some consequence that is reached without being part of a specified operating method, pinned down by checks and balances, reviews and concurrences, supporting files and staff papers. Indeed, it might not be too much of an exaggeration to sum up the progress of modern management, and especially of public administration, as an elaboration of the methodology of decision-making. Time was when the making of decisions was the lonely task of the man in authority. Today's decision-making is a group process, enveloped in procedure and yet frequently eluding responsibility. Authority can be outflanked by personal or group influence, internal as well as external, despite the fact that such influence may simply be the product of sundry interests that happen to converge at one point. Much of what has been written in recent years about the "executive function" in the context of the large-scale organization centers upon the need for coming to decisions safely. Much of the institutional development has been along the same path, ranging from the creation of special management staffs to the establishment of committee machinery. But the plural character of group action has retained a good deal of its irrationalities.

In the operating experience of the administrative system these irrationalities burst forth at various points—in the struggles over jurisdiction, in the intransigence of specialization, in the contest for position. They flare up also in the relationship between the career man and his political superiors. They come alive further in the relations between the department and the larger world surrounding it —the legislature, the political parties, the interest groups, and the general public (which acts mostly in the form of special publics). In each general area the frequency and the intensity of unproductive clashes are minimized when conflicting positions can be adjudged by reference to a commonly accepted standard. In the clash of division heads, for instance, that standard may be established departmental policy. In the argument between the career man and his political chief, the standard may be found in governmental practice of long standing. In the collision of the department with the outside world, the most important standard would be the government's program; and, if that program has its foundation in the platform on which the governing party or parties triumphed at the polls, the program is likely to be respected as a valid standard by the parties, the interest groups, and the citizenry alike. To the same extent that such a broader coherence is superimposed upon the group process, the shredding effect of self-centered motivations will be kept in bounds. When this broader coherence is feeble, the productivity of the group process as a source of decisions is likely to be low.

The Problem of the Right Decision

No doubt the modern bureaucracy, in the organization of its technical competence, possesses a tested methodology of decision-making. In addition, this methodology is rather well adapted to the making of decisions on the political level of action, provided sufficient strength and unity exist on that level to permit a satisfactory linking of administrative responsibility and political responsibility. But the emphasis placed on the *manner* of reaching decisions—above all, on the procedural approach—has its obvious limitations. To be sure, to rely on a soundly conceived and well-understood way of coming to decisions in itself contributes to the likelihood of reasonable results. But the procedural safeguards are too easily and too often converted into criteria for the evaluation of the decision reached. It is one thing to say that the decision was made in meticulous conformance with applicable procedure. It is quite another thing to say that it was the right decision.

Who could say that it was or was not? Who could claim to be the authentic source for such an answer? In an age preoccupied with relativity, it is hardly surprising that nobody seems eager to press this claim. It is least surprising that the career man eschews an answer. He may venture to express the judgment of the "expert," with due caution, but he would decline to enter the realm of "political judgment."

At first glance this may appear to settle the matter. Yet the conclusion does not satisfy. For it is clear that it inflicts defeat upon the rationality of public administration itself. That rationality requires a deep concern with whether decisions are right or wrong—before they are released upon the public. In this screening operation the career man's appraisal is a critically important factor. His is the analytical responsibility in any event. How can a proposed decision get by unless, on the judgment of those having technical competence, it is a suitable response to an understood need? For that matter, the response should be the best response conceivable, in terms of both what the law authorizes and what the need calls for. This entails also an evaluation of alternatives. Obviously, there can be no assurance about what would be the best response if no informed and imaginative search is undertaken to measure out the range of feasible choices. Nor must we overlook the point that in marshaling the sharp force of authority it is a rule of reason, if it were not a rule of law, to select the mildest means that meets the purpose.

In all these matters the initial responsibility for judgment lies with the civil servant, as one well equipped to judge; and in the absence of an overruling political judgment his judgment is final in fact. He cannot be expected to do this sifting of considerations if he is meant to go by rote, especially if his political superiors insist that he simply carry out their orders precisely as they are given. But the situation is different when the sifting hand of the career man is welcomed, when the public has reasonable confidence in his judgment, and when it is widely recognized that for good performance the engines of administration must be lubricated with the oil of discretion. Under such circumstances it would be preposterous if the civil servant confined himself to periodically checking the links in the chain of decision-making. Beyond such concern with procedure, he should exert himself to make sure that each proposed decision is the right decision. Nor should he stop when he comes to the boundaries drawn around the rationality of day-by-day utilitarian choices—when he has assured himself of the means-and-ends relationships of administrative purposes, the attainment of economy and efficiency, the calculus of benefits. The right decision must meet a higher test. It must accord with the general interest, the constitutional spirit, and the moral principle. Nothing short of this will do.

But does not such a view of the career man's responsibility collide with his functional role as an agent of those exercising political control? Indeed, is there anyone entitled to speak with final authority on the general interest, the constitutional spirit, and the moral principle? These questions must be answered. Let us admit that there are many critically important matters on which nobody is entitled to speak with final authority. Can they therefore be ignored? They must be coped with, and every honest attempt in this direction adds to dealing with them as adequately as their nature permits. To be sure, as this contest for better solutions goes on in the conduct of governmental functions, the administrative judgment is obliged to yield ultimately to the political judgment when there is a difference between the two. Moreover, the political judgment must furnish policy guidance for the operation of the administrative judgment, to insure the primacy of political responsibility. Again, however, the alternatives are clear. It is one thing for the career man to fall on his face whenever his advice is received coldly by his political superiors. It is quite another thing when he is meant to play his part in a virile contest for a decision that draws strength from being supported by the administrative judgment as well as by the political judgment.

Decision-making in the administrative system is most likely to turn out an acceptable end product when the bureaucracy is a responsible partner of the political leadership. This provides at the same time the most satisfactory setting for the career man to function as the monitor of good administration. Perhaps the greatest contribution that can be made by the higher civil service is to keep its eyes on the things that roll off the administrative assembly line. How well do the "finished goods" serve the needs of the general public? How closely do they fit the legitimate interest of the individual citizen as applicant? No more effective antidote to "bureaucracy" can be hoped for than that which the critical mind of the career man itself is able to supply. But his mind needs to be alerted to the urgency of this task. His thinking needs to be lifted above the daily drag. And his loyalty needs to be focused upon the record of the political system rather than the record of his department.

HOW TO USE THE BUREAUCRACY

The Political Aspect

To speak of decision-making in the administrative system as a partnership of the bureaucracy and the political leadership makes sense only on the assumption that each sees the other in these terms and acts accordingly. As a practical matter, however, the assumption is a considerable distance away from the facts, more so in some countries than in others. One way of making the distance conspicuous is to compare the mass of formally adopted working rules that govern legislative action and administrative action, respectively, with the paucity of equally specific rules that center upon the operating relationships between both elements. This is not to say that there ought to be more rules on the subject. Rather, there ought to be a fuller understanding, on both the political level and the administrative level, about how to get the largest returns from the desirable interlocking of responsible direction and responsive operation.

Those in political control should recognize that they are depriving themselves of the advantages of effective machinery for giving application to their policies when they fail to create the conditions for resourceful public administration. As a minimum, this would entail a measure of self-restraint by the political leadership in the manner in which it pursues its aims, especially in the use it makes of the administrative system. Moreover, it is distinctly a responsibility of those in political control to take the initiative in defining, in sufficiently precise terms, the working relationships between the political level and the administrative level.

The Administrative Aspect

But it is clear that significant advances in the functional efficiency of the "administrative state" cannot be expected without corresponding changes in the working style of the administrative system. In this respect perhaps the most important thing is the acceptance within the higher civil service of a reorientation toward its role. The men of the top cadre must shift their attention from watching "processes" to measuring their impact, from "getting things done" to giving each citizen his due, from the technology of administration to its effect upon the general public, from utility to ethics. Not what is being said but what is being done will decide whether the "administrative state" will stand out eventually as a benefactor or as a destroyer. It is for the civil servant to realize that much of what can be done must be his doing.

Responsible administration cannot unfold its full strength except within a governmental structure that subordinates technical competence to political control. But this relationship is not likely to have as much substance as it needs to have if its elaboration is left to a few basic principles. In the overdue elaboration of the relationship between technical competence and political control, a large share falls to the bureaucracy, to its working doctrine, to the ideology of service that it may infuse into the administrative system.

SELECTED REFERENCES

The principal purpose of this section is to indicate various types of material pertinent to a fuller study of the subject of this book, especially more recently published materials. The references have been selected primarily for use by American readers. Except for a sample of notably important works, no attempt is made to provide an orientation in the literature published in languages other than English. The references here listed do not include periodical articles, reviews, and similar contributions, although in certain instances these are as important as the books cited. Most of the books themselves, however, refer to periodical literature. Special attention may be called to the listed bibliographies, for they have done much to open up the field of comparative administration.

BIBLIOGRAPHIES

CALDWELL, LYNTON K. *Comparative Public Administration: An Outline of Topics and Readings.* Albany, N.Y.: Graduate Program in Public Administration, 1953.

MERTON, ROBERT K., *et al.* (eds.). *Reader in Bureaucracy.* Glencoe, Ill.: Free Press, 1952. Contains a bibliography especially strong along theoretical and analytical lines.

RIGGS, FRED W. "Notes on Literature Available for the Study of Comparative Public Administration," *American Political Science Review,* XLVIII (June, 1954), 515–37.

WEIDLUND, JANE, *et al. Comparative Public Administration: A Selective Annotated Bibliography.* Ann Arbor, Mich.: Institute of Public Administration, University of Michigan, 1957.

DESCRIPTIVE AND ANALYTICAL STUDIES

ALLEN, C. K. *Bureaucracy Triumphant.* London: Oxford University Press, 1931.

AMERICAN ASSEMBLY. *The Federal Government Service: Its Character, Prestige, and Problems.* New York: Columbia University, Graduate School of Business, 1954.

APPLEBY, PAUL H. *Big Democracy.* New York: Alfred A. Knopf, 1945.

BARKER, ERNEST. *The Development of Public Services in Western Europe, 1660–1930.* London: Oxford University Press, 1944.

BECK, JAMES M. *Our Wonderland of Bureaucracy*. New York: Macmillan Co., 1932.

BENDIX, REINHARD. *Higher Civil Servants in American Society: A Study of the Social Origins, the Careers, and the Power-Positions of Higher Federal Administrators*. Boulder, Colo.: University of Colorado Press, 1949.

BERGER, MORROE. *Bureaucracy and Society in Modern Egypt: A Study of the Higher Civil Service*. Princeton, N.J.: Princeton University Press, 1957.

BIENSTOCK, GREGORY, et al. *Management in Russian Industry and Agriculture*. London: Oxford University Press, 1944.

BLAND, F. A. (ed.). *Government in Australia: Selected Readings*. 2d ed. Sydney: Pettifer, 1944.

BLAU, PETER M. *The Dynamics of Bureaucracy: A Study of Interpersonal Relations in Two Government Agencies*. Chicago: University of Chicago Press, 1955.

BONTECOU, ELEANOR. *The Federal Loyalty-Security Program*. Ithaca, N.Y.: Cornell University Press, 1953.

BRECHT, ARNOLD, and GLASER, COMSTOCK. *The Art and Technique of Administration in German Ministries*. Cambridge, Mass.: Harvard University Press, 1940.

BROWN, R. DOUGLAS. *The Battle of Crichel Down*. London: Bodley Head, 1955.

BURNHAM, JAMES. *The Managerial Revolution*. New York: John Day Co., 1941.

CAHEN-SALVADOR, JEAN. *La Représentation des intérêts et les services publics*. Paris: Sirey, 1935.

CHANG, CHUNG-LI. *The Chinese Gentry: Studies on Their Role in Nineteenth-Century Chinese Society*. Seattle: University of Washington Press, 1955.

CHARLESWORTH, JAMES C. (ed.). "Bureaucracy and Democratic Government," *Annals of the American Academy of Political and Social Science*, No. 292 (March, 1954).

COLE, TAYLOR. *The Canadian Bureaucracy: A Study of Canadian Civil Servants and Other Public Employees, 1939–1947*. Durham, N.C.: Duke University Press, 1949.

CRAIG, JOHN A. *History of Red Tape*. London: Macdonald & Evans, 1955.

CRIDER, JOHN H. *The Bureaucrat*. Philadelphia: J. B. Lippincott Co., 1944.

CRITCHLEY, THOMAS A. *The Civil Service Today*. Toronto: Longmans Green & Co., 1951.

DAHL, ROBERT A., and LINDBLOM, CHARLES E. *Politics, Economics, and Welfare*. New York: Harper & Bros., 1953.

DALE, HAROLD E. *The Higher Civil Service of Great Britain*. London: Oxford University Press, 1941.

DIMOCK, MARSHALL E., and HYDE, HOWARD K. *Bureaucracy and Trusteeship in Large Corporations*. Washington, D.C.: Government Printing Office, 1940.

DORWART, REINHOLD A. *The Administrative Reforms of Frederick William I of Prussia.* Cambridge, Mass.: Harvard University Press, 1953.

DUNNILL, FRANK. *The Civil Service: Some Human Aspects.* London: Allen & Unwin, 1956.

FAINSOD, MERLE. *How Russia Is Ruled.* Cambridge, Mass.: Harvard University Press, 1953.

FINER, HERMAN. *Road to Reaction.* Boston: Little, Brown & Co., 1945.

———. *The British Civil Service.* Rev. ed. London: Fabian Society, 1937.

FINER, S. E. *The Life and Times of Sir Edwin Chadwick.* London: Methuen, 1952.

FRANCIS, ROY G., and STONE, ROBERT C. *Service and Procedure in Bureaucracy: A Case Study.* Minneapolis: University of Minnesota Press, 1956.

FREEMAN, J. LEIPER. *The Political Process: Executive Bureau-Legislative Committee Relations.* Garden City, N.Y.: Doubleday & Co., 1955.

FRIEDRICH, CARL J. *Constitutional Government and Democracy.* Rev. ed. Boston: Ginn & Co., 1950.

FRIEDRICH, CARL J., and COLE, TAYLOR. *Responsible Bureaucracy: A Study of the Swiss Civil Service.* Cambridge, Mass.: Harvard University Press, 1952.

GLADDEN, E. N. *Civil Service Staff Relationships.* London: Hodge, 1943.

———. *The Civil Service: Its Problems and Future.* London: Staples Press, 1945.

GRANICK, DAVID. *Management of the Industrial Firm in the USSR: A Study in Soviet Economic Planning.* New York: Columbia University Press, 1954.

GREAVES, H. R. G. *The Civil Service in the Changing State.* London: Harrap, 1947.

GRÉGOIRE, ROGER. *La Fonction publique.* Paris: Librairie Armand Colin, 1954.

HAYEK, FRIEDRICH A. *The Road to Serfdom.* Chicago: University of Chicago Press, 1944.

HERRING, E. PENDLETON. *Public Administration and the Public Interest.* New York: McGraw-Hill Book Co., 1936.

HYNEMAN, CHARLES S. *Bureaucracy in a Democracy.* New York: Harper & Bros., 1950.

JÖHR, WALTER A., and SINGER, HANS W. *The Role of the Economist as Official Adviser.* Translated from German. London: Allen & Unwin, 1955.

JURAN, J. M. *Bureaucracy: A Challenge to Better Management.* New York: Harper & Bros., 1944.

KELSALL, R. K. *Higher Civil Servants in Britain from 1870 to the Present Day.* London: Routledge & Kegan Paul, 1955.

KINGSLEY, J. DONALD. *Representative Bureaucracy: An Interpretation of the British Civil Service.* Yellow Springs, Ohio: Antioch Press, 1944.

KISCH, H. M. *A Young Victorian in India: Letters.* Edited by ETHEL A. WALEY COHEN. London: Cape, 1957.

KRACKE, E. A., JR. *Civil Service in Early Sung China, 960–1067.* Cambridge, Mass.: Harvard University Press, 1953.

LASKI, H. J. *The Limitations of the Expert.* (Fabian Tract No. 235.) London: Fabian Society, 1931.

LASSWELL, HAROLD D. *Psychopathology and Politics.* Chicago: University of Chicago Press, 1930.

LEIGHTON, ALEXANDER. *The Governing of Men.* Princeton, N.J.: Princeton University Press, 1945.

LIPSET, SEYMOUR M. *Agrarian Socialism.* Berkeley: University of California Press, 1950.

MACMAHON, ARTHUR W., and MILLETT, JOHN D. *Federal Administrators: A Biographical Approach to the Problem of Departmental Management.* New York: Columbia University Press, 1939.

MANNHEIM, KARL. *Freedom, Power, and Democratic Planning.* New York: Oxford University Press, 1950.

MATTINGLY, HAROLD. *The Imperial Civil Service of Rome.* Cambridge: Cambridge University Press, 1910.

MAYO, ELTON. *The Social Problems of an Industrial Civilization.* Boston: Harvard University, Graduate School of Business Administration, 1945.

MERTON, ROBERT K., *et al.* (eds.). *Reader in Bureaucracy.* Glencoe, Ill.: Free Press, 1952.

MILLER, BARNETTE. *The Palace School of Muhammad the Conqueror.* Cambridge, Mass.: Harvard University Press, 1941.

MILLER, EDWARD. *The Abbey and Bishopric of Ely: The Social History of an Ecclesiastical Estate from the Tenth Century to the Early Fourteenth Century.* New York: Cambridge University Press, 1951.

MILLS, C. WRIGHT. *White Collar: The American Middle Classes.* New York: Oxford University Press, 1951.

MISES, LUDWIG VON. *Bureaucracy.* New Haven, Conn.: Yale University Press, 1944.

MONCK, BOSWORTH. *How the Civil Service Works.* London: Phoenix, 1952.

MOORE, BARRINGTON, JR. *Terror and Progress, USSR: Some Sources of Change and Stability in the Soviet Dictatorship.* Cambridge, Mass.: Harvard University Press, 1954.

MORRISON, HERBERT. *Government and Parliament: A Survey from the Inside.* New York: Oxford University Press, 1954.

MOSCA, GAETANO. *The Ruling Class.* New York: McGraw-Hill Book Co., 1939.

NIGHTINGALE, R. T. *The Personnel of the British Foreign Office and Diplomatic Service, 1851–1921.* (Fabian Tract No. 232.) London: Fabian Society, 1930.

NILES, MARY C. *Middle Management.* Rev. ed. New York: Harper & Bros., 1949.

RENNER, KARL. *Demokratie und Bureaukratie.* Vienna: Universum, 1946.

ROBSON, WILLIAM A. (ed.). *The British Civil Servant*. London: Allen & Unwin, 1937.

———. *The Civil Service in Britain and France*. New York: Macmillan Co., 1956.

ROTOURS, ROBERT DES. *Traité des examens*. Translated from *The New History of the T'ang Dynasty*. Paris: Librairie E. Leroux, 1932.

———. *Traité des fonctionnaires et traité de l'armée*. Translated from *The New History of the T'ang Dynasty*. 2 vols. Leyden: Brill, 1947.

SEABURY, PAUL. *The Wilhelmstrasse*. Berkeley: University of California Press, 1954.

SELZNICK, PHILIP. *TVA and the Grass Roots: A Study in the Sociology of Formal Organization*. Berkeley: University of California Press, 1949.

SHARP, WALTER R. *The French Civil Service: Bureaucracy in Transition*. New York: Macmillan Co., 1931.

SIFFIN, WILLIAM J. (ed.). *Toward the Comparative Study of Public Administration*. Bloomington, Ind.: Department of Government, Indiana University, 1957.

SPERO, STERLING. *Government as Employer*. New York: Remsen, 1948.

STEIN, LORENZ. *Die Verwaltungslehre*, Part I: *Die Lehre von der Vollziehenden Gewalt: Ihr Recht und ihr Organismus*. Stuttgart: Cotta, 1865.

SULLIVAN, LAWRENCE. *The Dead Hand of Bureaucracy*. Indianapolis: Bobbs-Merrill Co., 1940.

TIXIER, G. *La Formation des cadres supérieurs de l'état en Grande-Bretagne et en France*. Paris: Librairie Générale de Droit et de Jurisprudence, 1948.

VEBLEN, THORSTEIN. *The Engineers and the Price System*. New York: Viking Press, 1933.

WALDO, DWIGHT. *The Administrative State: A Study of the Political Theory of American Public Administration*. New York: Ronald Press Co., 1948.

WEBER, MAX. "Bürokratie," in *Wirtschaft und Gesellschaft*. ("Grundriss der Sozialökonomik," Vol. III.) 3d ed. Tübingen: Mohr, 1947.

———. *Essays in Sociology*. Edited by H. H. GERTH and C. WRIGHT MILLS. New York: Oxford University Press, 1946.

———. *The Theory of Social and Economic Organization*. Edited by A. M. HENDERSON and TALCOTT PARSONS. New York: Oxford University Press, 1947.

WHITE, LEONARD D. (ed.). *The Civil Service in the Modern State: A Collection of Documents*. Chicago: University of Chicago Press, 1930.

———. *The Federalists: A Study in Administrative History* [1789–1801]. New York: Macmillan Co., 1948.

———. *The Jeffersonians: A Study in Administrative History, 1801–1829*. New York: Macmillan Co., 1951.

———. *The Jacksonians: A Study in Administrative History, 1829–1861*. New York: Macmillan Co., 1954.

———. *The Prestige Value of Public Employment.* Chicago: University of Chicago Press, 1929.

———. *Further Contributions to the Prestige Value of Public Employment.* Chicago: University of Chicago Press, 1932.

———. *Whitley Councils in the British Civil Service.* Chicago: University of Chicago Press, 1933.

WHITE, LEONARD D., *et al. Civil Service Abroad: Great Britain, Canada, France, and Germany.* New York: McGraw-Hill Book Co., 1935.

WHYTE, WILLIAM H. *The Organization Man.* New York: Simon & Schuster, 1956.

WILHELM, THEODOR. *Die Idee des Berufsbeamtentums.* Tübingen: Mohr, 1933.

WILSON, H. H., and GLICKMAN, HARVEY. *The Problem of Internal Security in Great Britain.* Garden City, N.Y.: Doubleday & Co., 1954.

WOODRUFF, PHILIPP. *The Men Who Ruled India: The Guardians.* London: Cape, 1954.

FICTION AND SATIRE

FRANK, PAT. *An Affair of State.* Philadelphia: J. B. Lippincott Co., 1945.

GOGOL, NIKOLAI. *The Government Inspector.* Trans. D. J. CAMPBELL. London: Sylvan Press, 1947.

HAWLEY, CAMERON. *Executive Suite.* Boston: Houghton Mifflin Co., 1952.

POTTER, STEPHAN. *One-Upmanship.* New York: Henry Holt & Co., 1952.

SNOW, CHARLES P. *Homecoming.* New York: Charles Scribner's Sons, 1956.

TOLSTOY, LEO N. *War and Peace.* Trans. L. and A. MAUDE. New York: Simon & Schuster, 1942.